About the Author

By the age of sixteen, John Woodgate (1934–2018) was training as a journalist with the *Daily Mail* in Fleet Street until his two years of National Service took him away to Cyprus where he worked as decoder for the Royal Corps of Signals. It was in 1959 that he embarked on a career as a police officer that would shape the rest of his life. Following his first rural beat in the small Essex village of Moreton, he went on to become the longest-serving sergeant at Ingatestone, retiring as acting-inspector after thirty years of service.

Anecdotes of a Village Bobby

John Woodgate

Anecdotes of a Village Bobby

Olympia Publishers
London

www.olympiapublishers.com
OLYMPIA PAPERBACK EDITION

Copyright © John Woodgate 2024

The right of John Woodgate to be identified as author of this work has been asserted in accordance with sections 77 and 78 of the Copyright, Designs and Patents Act 1988.

All Rights Reserved

No reproduction, copy or transmission of this publication may be made without written permission.
No paragraph of this publication may be reproduced, copied or transmitted save with the written permission of the publisher, or in accordance with the provisions of the Copyright Act 1956 (as amended).

Any person who commits any unauthorised act in relation to this publication may be liable to criminal prosecution and civil claims for damage.

A CIP catalogue record for this title is available from the British Library.

ISBN: 978-1-80074-961-0

This is a work of non-fiction.
This is a collection of actual events the author experienced during his career.

First Published in 2024

Olympia Publishers
Tallis House
2 Tallis Street
London
EC4Y 0AB

Printed in Great Britain

Dedication

This book is dedicated to my grandchildren.

Acknowledgements

With thanks to my devoted wife Joan who supported me throughout my career and raised our four wonderful children.

ROMFORD 1960

Introduction

The police has always been, for some unaccountable reason, one of those institutions in which sons follow fathers, grandfathers and even great-grandfathers. We as a family came close to claiming such a distinction when I followed my father into the police and David followed me. However, David's introduction to the police cadets was due entirely to pressure from me (borne out of regard for his future) rather than inclination from him, and when I consider that at his age I was subjected to no such pressure, it is a joy for me to see how he went on to find adventure, excitement and sound achievement elsewhere.

I suppose it could be said that my decision to join the police in the first place was the result of distinct pre-war memories of seeing my father in the uniform of the Folkestone Borough Police, and a few years after the war, in the British Transport Police. The truth is that I never gave my future much thought at all until I was fifteen and on the point of leaving school to venture out into the cold, wide world.

Living in London as we then were, I remember enquiring what qualifications were needed to get into the Thames River Police, then as now an arm of the Metropolitan Police. Little realising that the romantic notion of cruising up and down one of our great waterways became reality for only a very few, and only then after the required number of years pounding the beat and then producing the required marine documents and certificates. I surprise myself even now with my own naivety for I was convinced that I had only to apply for the job, to have a uniform issued and be ushered straightaway onto a gleaming blue motor launch! Needless to say, on learning what was required I had no great aspirations for walking the still-bombed-out streets of London's East End for x number of years, so let the matter drop. Thus it remained for the next ten years during which time I had met Joan (1951), married her (1955), moved to Southend and by 1959 was the proud father of three children (Diane arrived after I joined the police).

I would like to stress, as the title implies, that this is nothing more than an anecdotal review of thirty years in the Essex Police. It is neither an autobiography nor a history of the police, simply an accumulation of amusing and sometimes sad incidents which occurred during that time. This I do, not for myself or my children, for they shared so much of it with me, but for my grandchildren in the hope that I can offer them, should they evince such interest in the first place, something I was never to experience at their age. Something a little more tangible than the indistinct memories I have of my own grandparents. My mother's father had died when I was just four and I remember nothing of him.

My father's father, James, as I cast my mind back to the mid-late 1940s, was a simple carter who drove a beautiful chestnut mare called Kitty all over London, pulling a heavy cart laden with goods of every description. When short of work, and this was often, carters would queue up at Cheapside, in the City, and negotiate loads and prices with whoever wanted goods delivered. This was really the last vestige of the old Victorian hiring fairs. I would sometimes travel with him, sitting up front on the hard wooden bench-seat with a blanket or tarpaulin around me in bad weather, or simply lying about on the bales or barrels when it was fine.

This, and the memory of him sitting at home in a big wooden

chair puffing away on one of his collection of pipes, is the sum total of my knowledge of him. It was only much later that I came to regret not having known him better. Unfortunately, at this time, the late 1940s, when I was still in my teens, he was in his seventies and in my eyes already ancient! Born in 1871, in the unforgiving surroundings of a Victorian workhouse in Princes Road, Lambeth, he was the illegitimate son of Lucy Jane Woodgate (yes, your great-great-great-grandmother!), then a thirty-seven-year-old servant, no slip of a girl, working in Kennington. Was it fear or shame that moved her to refuse all details of the father's identity when it came to registering James' birth? It has come down through the family, in whispers only and with what accuracy I do not know, that it was her employer, a man named Turner, who was responsible. Thus in an age when servants were given very little thought, who were cynically used and then turned out onto the streets, one can only feel compassion for a woman driven to bearing her child in that most dreaded of all institutions, the parish workhouse. Thus it was that she gave her own name to her baby and why it is that we still bear it to this day.

What tales he could have told of his early life, for Lucy died just three years after his birth and we have no idea who brought him up. London in the 1870s was, for the working classes at any rate, a hard place in which to live. Relentless poverty, hunger and hard work was the order of the day for so many. Did he suffer this or something better? He never spoke of it. There is for me one sad little memory that remains of him sitting in his chair, puffing his favourite Meerschaum pipe, his mind miles away, but murmuring repeatedly, "Poor Lucy, poor Lucy." In my ignorance, I assumed he could only be referring to my Aunt Lucy, his eldest daughter, who lived just a few doors from us in Clapham, and I wondered what was wrong with her. It was only much later I learned that he was referring not to her but his own mother. He never explained himself but whatever it was, even after seventy years, was still too painful to talk about. Alas, though, all is now gone and can never be retrieved, for the shades that closed over him in 1953 did so with such finality as to leave little or nothing of his passing. On hearing of his death, I was serving with the army in Cyprus so could not even attend his funeral.

In the early 1930s, before I was born, my parents had moved away from the close-knit community in which both their families had grown up in Walworth, south-east London; my mother's family from Pitman Street, and my father's just around the corner on Warrior Road. They chose Folkestone where my father's aunts, Aunt Alice and her sister Rose, lived. They owned a laundry business and were comfortably off. My father there joined the Folkestone Borough Constabulary. If there were any return visits to Walworth over the next ten years, then they were very few and far between for I cannot remember any being made until just before the war ended. Then, quite suddenly, there came a number of visits when I witnessed the awful devastation of the bombing and the dreaded 'Doodlebugs' and Rockets (V1's and V2's) which Hitler was sending over on a daily basis. This dates those visits to 1944–45. Our stay in Folkestone was fairly short-lived, six or seven years perhaps, for by 1940 the Germans had overrun France and were threatening to invade England. With Folkestone so close to Dover, it would obviously have been in the front-line of any invasion and children in such danger spots were being evacuated further inland in their thousands; a fact my mother had firmly set her face against for parents were not allowed to accompany their children. The post-war tragedy of this policy was the heartbreak of so many families being split up and moved, never to see each other again. My parents would have none of it and managed through a relative to find two-roomed accommodation in Sandy, Bedfordshire, about fifty miles north of London, comprising a front sitting-room and an upstairs bedroom. Sparse but quite comfortable. By then my father had left the police and moved into lodgings in Coventry where he worked for the Standard Motor Co., then manufacturing aero-engines for the war. I well remember visiting him there with my mother and younger brother within a day or so of the infamous Coventry blitz, and of walking around the now totally destroyed medieval cathedral which even then was still smouldering. Amidst the ruins, and no doubt as a gesture of defiance, a makeshift altar had been erected from those ancient stones and a crude cross placed upon it from charred, still-warm bits of timber. I remember gazing at it uncomprehendingly.

Having been a soldier during the 1920s, my father was recalled to the Dorset Regiment and posted off to India. Thus, far from seeing anything of my grandparents and other relatives in London during the war, I saw little or nothing of him either until he returned in 1946. By then I was twelve and my brother ten when this almost complete stranger walked back into our lives.

I left school in July 1949, at the age of fifteen, with prizes for English. On my last day, the headmaster actually handed me a letter of introduction to the editor of the *Daily Mail*! I remember handing it over on my arrival at Northcliffe House in Fleet Street where I quickly learned that whatever starry-eyed notions I may have had towards a journalistic career were to be speedily dashed. Everyone but everyone starts at the bottom on a newspaper, and I would be no exception (this was borne out a little later when I encountered an ordinary-looking, brown-overalled, grease-covered 'print-worker' beavering away in the machine shop). He was, I later learned, the eighteen-year-old son of the associated newspaper's chairman, Lord Rothermere, and grandson of the founder Lord Northcliffe! He too was having to learn the business from the bottom.

Like so many before me, I started as a messenger in the tape room, the totally absorbing news-gathering centre of the paper. Six months later, I was sent off to the circulation department where, at the age of eighteen, I had to leave for my two years' national service in the army. I returned in 1954 and became engaged to Joan, whom I had met in Fleet Street. We married a year later and moved near to her parents in Southend. I continued to commute to London for another year or so but the endless, dreary journeys finally proved too much, and despite being offered a generous bribe of another pound a week on top of the seven or eight I was already earning, I bade farewell to eight bustling and exciting years with the newspaper. By then I was within sight of my police career.

Chapter One

I joined the Essex County Constabulary for three reasons: firstly, I was quite simply out of work; secondly, the dormant feelings about police work re-surfaced, and along with it the knowledge that it offered security as well as a career; and, thirdly, because I was an inch too short, at 5'11", to join the local Southend Borough Police.

It all started on 17 June 1959, for that was when I, along with a dozen or more other candidates, attended Chelmsford Magistrates' Court to be attested. The ceremony was brief but something which I believe remains in everyone's memory – not least I suppose because most of us had never stepped foot inside a court in our lives. Each applicant was required to mount the steps into the witness box and there, with the testament held high in the right hand, read the oath from a printed card. I cannot now remember the precise wording, for it was pretty lengthy, but it included 'truly and faithfully serving our sovereign lady, the queen', safe-guarding her subjects' lives and property, preserving the peace and public order, and all 'without fear or favour, malice or ill-will…' The chairman of the bench then made a short speech of welcome, telling us what fine young men we were, how proud they were of their county force and what onerous responsibilities we were undertaking. The clothing parade, where everything is thrown at you with only little regard as to whether it fitted or not. I was lucky in being of standard size and having everything fit fairly well, but there were one or two odd-shaped recruits who paraded around to the great amusement of the rest with trousers, tunics or helmets of outrageous proportions.

All this equipment had to be taken home to be cleaned and pressed. It was only then that I realised that the only items which were actually new were the blue shirts which came with two collars requiring collar studs, their pristine fronts displayed through polythene wrappers. Each of the two tunic jackets bore the unmistakeable imprint of its previous owner's numerals on the shoulders, the trousers showed every sign of wear and tear, and even my cape had someone else's number inside it! Waste not, want not in those days.

It was only a matter of days after returning home laden down with all this that I decided to don the complete uniform and show myself off to my parents in London who, we had decided as a surprise gesture, should be kept completely in the dark until my appointment had been confirmed.

I wasn't daft enough at this early stage, while still waiting to go off to police college, to actually venture out of doors in uniform. Instead, be-decked in all but helmet and concealed under my civilian raincoat, I sallied forth. Could I have been mistaken for anything else, as I walked towards the railway station wearing black trousers, black boots, blue shirt, black tie and the unmistakeable gleam of a silver tunic button showing above the front of my raincoat? Suddenly, my reverie was interrupted by a squeal of brakes and the sound of breaking glass. A car had stopped at a pedestrian crossing and been rammed from behind by another. Only yards away from where I stood, the two drivers were surveying the damage. It occurred to me that it only needed a glance from one of them for me to be called over to deal with the accident – and I hadn't the faintest idea how to go about it! Swiftly, and like a thief in the night, I turned up my collar and hurried from the scene, expecting at any moment to hear a call for me to return.

I completed the trip without further mishap and walked into our house at Clapham. The look on the faces of my parents as I took off my raincoat was something I shall never forget. My father was so proud, he insisted on taking me down to Aunt Lucy's (his sister just down the road) to show me off. I was then just twenty-five years old.

I will not go into detail of the thirteen weeks we spent at the beautiful stately home of Eynsham Hall, near Witney in Oxfordshire, except to say that it was a period of intense and unremitting mental toil as we strived to master what was for us all a totally alien subject – law. Thrown in for good measure were 'practicals' in which our instructors played the part of the 'bad guys' in every conceivable situation, seeking to convince us how easy it was to deal with any problem so long as you were possessed of fifty per cent common sense and fifty per cent legal knowledge (throughout the rest of my service, I found these ratios altered to ninety-five per cent common sense and five per cent law).

A full-dress parade was held every morning for which our boots were always 'bulled' army-fashion, and our uniforms pressed the night before into razor-like creases. For five minutes or more before marching onto the parade ground, we brushed each other down to remove every single speck on our uniforms. Like basic training in the army, I was to find that this very high standard of smartness was not maintained on division.

Amidst all this pressure though was a great sense of fun. I remember one such 'practical' where we came upon a 'road accident' which had occurred in the main driveway of the hall.

One of the instructors' cars was slewed across the road and

the 'driver' was bemoaning the fact that he had just struck and killed a sheep. There, lying on its back in the roadway, was the gymnasium's vaulting horse, its four wooden legs pointing to the sky in a state of advanced rigor-mortis. We fell about laughing and the whole exercise on how to deal with the most common of all our duties degenerated into complete farce.

Our studies were lightened somewhat by physical training of an equally intensive nature, with five- and ten-mile runs, swimming (in which many of us gained our bronze medal for life-saving), and sports in general. I was in the tug-of-war team and regularly met local village teams on an 'away' or 'home' match basis. Not least were sessions in the gym on self-defence. This was taken particularly seriously by our instructors, and if nothing else imbued in us all a self-confidence which in retrospect I found extremely valuable in situations where an air of supreme confidence was all that was needed to diffuse an ugly-looking confrontation.

The end of each of the three months saw the passing-out parade and dance of the preceding course. We, of course, attended two of these before our own turn came. It had become traditional for each course to leave its own particular mark for those that followed, nothing serious, just a token that they had survived without too much brain damage. The first dance we attended resulted in a pair of girls' knickers being found the following morning hoisted to the top of the flagpole, their acquisition being not too difficult considering the number of local girls that attended these evenings. That was pretty tame stuff compared with the following course's contribution. Standing on the first floor landing was a huge brass gong which was used thrice daily to summon us to the dining rooms. Its ornate oaken frame proved no match for the pranksters who succeeded in spiriting it away, its absence remaining unnoticed until the duty officer went to sound it for breakfast. In the meantime, I had retired to bed which happened to be on the first-floor landing within yards of the gong. As I got into bed, I discovered the frame partially hidden underneath. Realising what I would be in for if it were found there, I crept out and hid it in the nearest bathroom. A search mounted the following morning found both items intact and nothing more was said.

For our own ceremony the following month, we decided to do something a little more spectacular. A certain PC on our course owned a bubble-car which were then very popular.

Around midnight, with the dance coming to an end, four of us crept out into the car-park and taking a corner each lifted the machine bodily and carried it back to the hall. There we were joined by two more conspirators and between us we managed to carry it into the entrance hall and then up the wide staircase to the first floor. There we gently lowered it to the floor beside the gong. The raised eyebrows of senior brass the following morning was something to behold!

Towards the end of the course, we were each asked our preference as to where we wished to be posted. This again was reminiscent of the army, for there I was asked a similar question and opted for Kenya or Tanganyika (why, I'll never know, but I suppose it sounded romantic, and to someone brought up in London there was a certain ring about Africa). I got Cyprus and Egypt instead, which wasn't a bad posting at all. Now, faced with the choice of where to serve, I naturally chose Rochford as the nearest county station to Southend – and the police could never be like the army, could it? Not much! With the powers-that-be knowing full well that my wife and children were living in Southend, I found myself posted to Romford, the opposite end of the county. There, single men's lodgings were found for me in South Street, which although comfortable enough were nothing like home. I was to remain there for something like six months before a police house was found for us at Gallows (or, Plough) Corner. I have often wondered where I might have been sent had I asked for Romford in the first place.

Thus it was that in early September 1959, I reported to the huge, red-brick, rambling old police station in South Street. Built nearly a hundred years before (and demolished in the 1960s) it had lost none of its Victorian charm. Narrow staircases led into a veritable rabbit-warren of an interior, where despite its apparent roominess, it still afforded us 'poor bloody infantry' precious little room. In fact, the parade room, although long and narrow, still boasted only a single contribution to our comfort – a row of hooks for our helmets and capes. There, in this dark, dismal-looking place, I started my police career.

Romford Police Station in South Street. This was my first posting from Eynsham, and I served her from 1959-60. Built in 1875 it was demolished c.1966

I remember very well being thrown in at the deep end, as it were, on a quiet Sunday morning as I was walking South Street. It was about eight o'clock and my patrol was really nothing more than a pleasant stroll through peaceful and still-deserted streets. I looked up to see the area car, surprisingly single-crewed, coming towards me from Golden Lion Corner. It pulled up and the driver wound down his window.

"Ever been to a sudden death, John?" he asked.

Now, that was something I could honestly say in all my two or three weeks' experience that I had not actually dealt with. I replied with a firmness I did not actually feel.

"Well, er–no, not exactly." I remembered our somewhat primitive introduction to the subject at Eynsham where, in the absence of real bodies, we were shown albums of the most gruesome deaths, suicides, murders and post-mortems, all designed, we were cheerfully told, to prepare us for the moment when we would be the first to arrive at the scene. I felt, in my own mind at least, capable of remaining on my feet for a nice clean over-dose, a clinical hanging or a simple 'died in his sleep', all were common enough in this job, I knew. I was not to know that I was about to discover the difference between Eynsham's photographs and reality.

The driver wound up his window and said, "Hop in then, I'll get headquarters to tell the station that you're with me." With that, he put the car into gear and off we went.

Trying to appear as nonchalant as possible, I left it for a minute or two before saying, "Where is it?"

He replied, "Jutsums Lane", then a moment or two later, "railway bridge". It slowly dawned on me that there was every possibility that this would not be a 'clean one'.

"A railway line job?" I asked.

"Right first time," he said. "Now what else would you rather be doing on a lovely morning like this?"

I felt like telling him.

"Ever dealt with one before?" he asked.

I could honestly say that I had not; indeed, the only dead body I had seen in my life was when, at the age of about thirteen, I was required by some macabre family ritual (totally out of keeping with my normally protective parents) to say farewell to a very elderly Aunt Alice as she lay serenely in her coffin in her front parlour. Not only that but I was obliged to place my hand on her ivory cold forehead.

A few minutes later, we pulled into the side of Jutsums Lane.

"Nothing to worry about," said my colleague, as he started the steep climb up the embankment, "it's only a question of picking up the pieces. They won't jump up and bite you, and with any luck we'll be back at the nick in time for breakfast."

I looked at him as we climbed. He was a man in his early or middle forties, with something like twenty or more years' service, a cheerful, bluff and reassuring character. At that moment, I was very glad he was there. By the time we reached the top, I was quite prepared for the sight of bits of body scattered along the railway line, for I'd heard it all before from others who had dealt with such things – it would either be clean with the head neatly severed or extremely messy, there were seldom in-betweens. We stood for a moment looking up and down the line.

"There it is," he said, pointing down the track.

There, sure enough, about a hundred and fifty yards away lay the body of a man face-down and parallel with the track. It was intact! I could see the head still on the body! Then the thought occurred to me, how can a train kill somebody without leaving a mark? We walked up to where it lay.

"Oh my God!" my partner said, and put his boot underneath the body. With a heave he turned it over – and my stomach went with it. There was only the back of the skull left intact, the rest was scattered along the track.

"Well, John," he said, "take a damn good look. Don't worry how you feel. Believe me, just look at it and look at it until it becomes ordinary, then bend down and take a closer look. After that, we'll pick up the pieces!"

I did as he suggested, and he was quite right; the longer I looked, the easier it became to accept, and it was not long before we really were walking along the track picking up the pieces. An undertaker arrived a short while later, summoned by headquarters via our radio, and with little ceremony the body was placed in a plain box and taken away.

One of my earliest embarrassments occurred soon after my arrival at Romford when we learned that the HMI (Her Majesty's Inspector of Constabularies) was due to make a visit. This is rather like a general's visit in the army, when for days beforehand everything is painted and polished and the men paraded in their best uniforms for inspection. We were due to be briefed on all this by our guv'nor, Chief Supt Wombwell, a crotchety type, and all the officers who had been selected for the HMI's parade were to attend the briefing at two p.m. on this particular day. Now, I had just bought a car, a 1932 Austin Ten, from a colleague, Det Tabrett of Harold Hill. He wanted ten pounds for it as he was after an Armstrong Siddeley Sapphire going cheap. That old Austin was a veritable box on wheels, a sit-up-and-beg car, but so dainty and dignified that I immediately christened her 'Sweetie Pie'. I couldn't afford her, of course, that ten pounds wiped me out at the bank. In fact, that was the first time in our married lives that Joan and I actually had ten pounds with no calls on it and I had to tell her I had blown it on a car! She was not amused.

Living at Plough Corner as we did, I decided to drive into Romford for the briefing, but Sweetie Pie had just one little idiosyncrasy – if she didn't start at the first turn of the handle (starting handle that is), she would not start at all.

And that was exactly what she decided to do on this occasion. I had, of course, left it too late, believing the car to be quicker than a bus, so by the time I flagged down the first Romford-bound bus and got to the police station the briefing had already started. As I entered, I saw at the top of the hall the Chief Super, flanked by other officers of senior rank, and there sitting in rapt and silent attention were about a hundred of my colleagues. There was no way I could creep in unnoticed, and as I sat down at the back I heard the chief's voice stop in mid-sentence.

With a hostile look he demanded in a loud voice, "Who are you?" I stood up.

"PC Woodgate, sir, I'm sorry I'm late."

The super stared hard at me. "You were due here at two o'clock."

I could not think of an intelligent lie so decided to tell the truth.

"I'm afraid my car wouldn't start, sir," I said.

The effect was electric! The chief sat back with a shocked expression on his face. He looked around at his colleagues in silent disbelief before turning back to me.

"Your car wouldn't start? Your CAR, you say?" Another long pause as he continued to stare at me. "Am I hearing things? Constables with cars now? You're obviously being paid too much. Sit down!"

My pay at that time was just over eight pounds a week (a notoriously low wage and at that time subject of a Royal Commission) so I suppose his shock was justified.

While talking about that little car, I recall Roy Tabrett telling me to be careful when closing the passenger door because he had just replaced the glass in the window. He did not expand any further on the subject and I quickly forgot what he had said. That is until about a week or so later when I dropped Joan off at Harold Hill. As she got out, I leaned across and closed the door. There was a crash as the entire window shattered and fell back into the car. It was only then that I realised that each piece was a jagged shard and not, as one would expect, a pile of Triplex fragments. I tackled Roy about this and he told me that he had broken the same window a little while back and not able to afford a new one, so had replaced it with ordinary glass! No wonder it shattered. I think he helped me out with the cost of a replacement though.

A short while later, a number of us Probationary Constables were due to attend a fortnight's probational course at headquarters in Chelmsford. Normally, we would have travelled by train or bus but as a car-owner, I offered a couple of my mates a lift each morning and evening. We were due on parade at nine o'clock on this particular Monday morning but, of course, that was not to be. Halfway up the hill running into Brentwood (no Brentwood by-pass then), the car gave a lurch and I knew I had a puncture! Jumping out, we hauled the spare from the rack over the rear bumper, only to discover we had no jack or wheel brace.

In desperation, and thankfully in uniform, we ran across the road to an undertaker's and persuaded them to supply us from one of their fleet of shiny limousines. They seemed to see the funny side of it and before long we were mobile again. Now, knowing that even at a top speed of 55 mph, which was about Sweetie Pie's limit, we were going to be late, I decided to ignore headquarters' car park and drive instead directly to the training school – then part of the old headquarters building. At a speed borne of desperation, we rounded the block to the parade-ground in front of the training school only to find everyone lined up being inspected. Unprepared for this, for I was convinced we had missed the parade altogether, I hit the brakes, skidded on loose gravel and came to a stop in a cloud of dust. The senior instructor stopped in mid-stride and turned to stare at three very dishevelled constables tumbling out of an ancient car.

In a voice which must have reached the chief constable's office, he yelled. "What the bloody hell do you think this is, Brands Hatch? Get fell in!"

Police Headquaters

Romford had long before earned for itself the title of 'best training ground in the county' for police recruits. For the young policemen, Friday and Saturday nights certainly sorted the wheat from the chaff, but in those days arrests for fighting were not the be-all-and-end-all of the job. Many a cuffing was given and received without the ritual of a walk to the station. There were three well-known warring families in the town, the Ports, the Bartholomews and the Lazaruses. They feuded constantly and never ever complained to the police.

One night at around midnight, I was walking up the side of an old coaching inn in the Market Place when I saw in the darkness of the yard a huddled shape lying on the ground. Despite its battered face, I recognised the owner; one of the three 'families'. He had been thoroughly worked over and although still conscious had sustained quite nasty head injuries.

I leaned over him. "Well, what happened to you then?" I asked.

"Nothing much," he mumbled through split lips. "I walked into a door, that's all." I looked him over.

"A door equipped with an iron bar by the look of it," I said. "Are you going to tell me who did it?"

He looked up at me and said, "Don't worry, it'll get sorted, just get me out of here."

I went to a local phone box and called for an ambulance. A short while later, I helped to put him aboard and then took a walk back to the nick. The sergeant looked at me suspiciously as I walked in, for leaving your beat without permission was a capital offence.' I told him what had happened, and on learning who was involved he simply shrugged his shoulders. He knew that whatever had happened, it would 'get sorted'.

When one works exclusive foot patrols, eight hours a day every day of the week, the chance of getting off your feet was always welcome. One such opportunity presented itself when allocated the duty of observer on the area car. At the start of each shift, we would crane our necks over the sergeant's shoulders as he wrote down in the duty roster each man's designation, Al beat,

B3 beat, E2 beat, front office (quite a perk), and then area car. If those two magic words were written against your name, you knew you were guaranteed four hours in a comfortable motor, plus the prospect of being sent off to deal with a much greater variety of jobs than was normal on a foot beat – that was the difference between having a radio and not having a radio. For on foot, they could only contact you once an hour. In those days, Romford division boasted two plain black Morris Oxfords as area cars, call-signs Romeo 5 for the town, and Romeo 7 for the rural area – Harold Hill, Plough Corner, Collier Row, Havering, Hornchurch and Emerson Park. Between these places was a lot of countryside, and I loved cruising along unfamiliar country roads. The driver, of course, wore a peaked cap but not the observer. The reason was that as this was not your normal duty there was no need for such extravagance. Instead, the observer wore his helmet – and yes, the roof of a Morris Oxford was high enough to accommodate an officer with his helmet on! Going over bumps though was sometimes a bit uncomfortable so we cradled our helmets in our laps ready to put it on as soon as we stepped foot outside. Nowadays, car crews seem to walk around without their caps as a matter of course, but in those days it was yet another of the capital offences.

One of my favourite drivers was Jack Draper, a wonderful man with a tremendous sense of humour. A first-class driver with an uncanny nose for criminals; you knew as soon as you were allocated Jack that your four-hour stint on the area car would not be without incident. I remember one quiet Sunday afternoon, we were sitting at Gallows Corner watching an unbroken stream of traffic entering and leaving the roundabout. It all looked the same to me, just hundreds upon hundreds of cars returning to London after a day out at Southend.

Suddenly, Jack started the engine and we surged forward. I sat up with a jerk looking quickly about for whatever it was that had taken his interest.

"That black Wolesley," he said, pointing along the A127.

I looked, it seemed all right to me, just two ordinary-looking men in the front, nothing about the car to get excited about.

"What's wrong with it?" I asked, as Jack weaved expertly through the traffic in pursuit. His eyes were glued on the car ahead as he started to overtake.

"Look at the boot," he muttered.

I looked. It seemed all right to me.

"What's wrong with it?" I asked. By then he had overtaken the Wolseley and cut in front.

"Blind," he said, and I reached up to tug the cord running along over our heads to the POLICE STOP blind in the rear window. I gave it a pull. The next few moments taught me an invaluable lesson for it cost us two prisoners. I kept the blind up for about five seconds to give the driver behind plenty of time to see it and stop. By the same token, it also obscured our rear window.

"Let it go, for Christ's sake, I can't see a thing!" Jack yelled. I let go and felt him braking hard. Too late! The Wolesley had stopped in the middle of the road, both doors were wide open and two figures were already haring off across the nearby fields – all that in a matter of seconds! I was just about to set off after them when Jack held me back.

"It's no good," he said. "Let 'em go."

He bent down and opened the boot of the Wolesley. It was full of sacks of scaffolding clips, subsequently of course found to have been stolen along with the car!

I felt awful about losing that pair, and apologised for hanging onto the blind, but Jack dismissed it as just one of those things.

"But how did you know to go for that particular motor?" I asked.

Jack grinned. "Didn't you notice the boot?" he asked. "It was a couple of inches lower than it should have been." *In all that traffic...!*

That was the way he worked and that was why it was always such a pleasure going out with him. He never did make it to sergeant because he could never pass his exams, but he was the most natural copper I ever knew. A year or two later, I was more than pleased to read on force orders that he had been given the chief constable's commendation (the most coveted of all) for 'persistent good work in the field of crime'. He deserved it.

I remember another incident with Jack which typified his sense of humour. I was on 'first half nights' with him, that is ten p.m. until two a.m. and we were returning to the station for our refreshment break.

"Sign off, John," he said, and as I leaned forward fumbling in the darkness for the mic I felt him reaching across to help me.

I pressed the mic's transmit button and announced, "VG from Romeo 7, off watch at base for refreshments. Romeo 7 over.".

I glanced across at Jack and saw him grinning. That broadcast had sounded a bit odd to me but I couldn't put my finger on it.

I said, "Come on, what have you done now?"

He started to laugh and pointed to the radio set. In leaning over, he had flicked the tannoy switch to 'broadcast' and my words had blared out of our loud-speaker for everyone in central Romford to hear! It's a funny thing with tannoys, when you are speaking through them you hear only your own voice, not the reproduction.

I remember with great clarity one little incident which was to remain with me for many years. I was making a point at Golden Lion Corner (junction of South Street, London Road and North Street) on a really wet and nasty day. The rain had been bucketing down ever since I had left the nick, and although I disliked the unwieldly things my leggings had certainly come into their own. Although my leather gloves were soaked through and my hands cold and uncomfortable. There was some small relief, although not much, in having my raincoat collar turned up around my ears. Fortunately, the Golden Lion Inn was a Tudor building with a typical first-floor overhang. At least standing under that kept the worst of the elements at bay. As I stood surveying the few similarly soaked wretches daft enough to be out in such weather, my sergeant, Bill Bould, turned up.

"All right, Sarge," I said in time-honoured tradition, indicating that everything was 'all right' on my beat.

He looked me up and down and said, "What have you got your coat collar turned up for?"

I looked up at the teeming rain and then at his collar. It was down.

"To stop the rain running down my neck, Sarge," I replied with as little sarcasm as I could muster.

He drew himself up and said, "You do not go around with your coat collar turned up except in the most inclement weather, and we don't get inclement weather in this country. Turn it down!"

Like a good probationer, I did as I was told, but was so tickled with the Cockney humour of it that it stayed with me. Many years later, as a sergeant at Chelmsford, I met one of my young PC's outside the Shire Hall. It was a miserable day, raining hard at the time and he had his coat collar turned up…

Before leaving the subject of Romford, I must relate, while it is still (after thirty years!) fresh in my memory, one or two anecdotes about some of the more hilarious characters we had then in the Essex Police. One youngster, whose name now completely escapes me, had a peculiar gift of being able to squat down on his haunches like a Russian dancer and run around like that at considerable speed. Whilst on nights, he would wait until the early hours when little traffic was about, and then hide himself in an alleyway or shop-doorway in South Street to wait until a car came along. As the car approached, the PC would squat down in this position and run straight across the road in front of the approaching driver and then disappear up the alleyway opposite. The results were absolutely hilarious. Driver after driver would slam on his brakes and stare with disbelief at what he had seen - a three-feet high policeman in cape (which of course in that position completely obscured his legs) running across the road. A few of them actually called at the police station to report it but the officer on duty would of course pooh-pooh the very thought and accuse the motorist of being drunk! To this day, there must still be a good many mature and respectable men who believe in three-feet-high policemen – for they've seen them!

This very same totally mad copper had yet another trick up his sleeve, once again involving poor unwitting motorists in the early hours. As a vehicle approached at some distance, he would leap athletically (weren't we all athletic in those days!) onto the top of a pillar-box, the single cylindrical ones that were so common then, sit cross-legged on the top and arrange his cape so that it hung down around the box.

As the motorist passed, he would slow down staring hard at a three-foot high policeman with no legs on top of a pillar-box. Convinced that it was a dummy, he would continue to stare and then to his horror realise that the dummy was staring back with a totally deadpan expression, his head turning as he passed!

Another character, who even now makes me cringe whenever I think of him, was Sergeant Eric Fretton. He was totally mad. One night, I was told to do what I could to clear out a number of tramps and dossers who had taken to sleeping in a row of derelict Victorian terraced houses in North Street. Before I had a chance to do anything about it though, I was met at my point (after midnight) by Eric Fretton. At the end of the regulation ten-minute wait, he said, "Right, come on, mate, let's clear those dossers out."

We walked up North Street to where the row of houses stood. "Wait here," he said, "we're not going to chance breaking a leg on those old staircases." With that he walked into the tiny front gardens and returned with an armful of half-bricks. Piling them in the middle of the road, he picked up the first and threw it with great accuracy through the first bedroom window. "Come out, you lazy buggers!" he yelled, and proceeded to aim more bricks through more windows.

The result was electrifying. Within a minute or two, figures were flying out of the houses in all directions.

Viewing the scene with great satisfaction, he brushed the brick-dust off his hands and said, "That saved us a bit of time, didn't it?"

I was still a probationer then full of 'doing the right thing', but as not a single complaint was ever made I assumed the dossers thought they had enough to hide without risking a visit to the nick. It is only now with everyone being made aware of his "rights" that so many seem to complain at the drop of a hat.

One more quick tale of Eric Fretton. The story did the rounds, and knowing him I quite believe it to be true, that one day he arrested a youngster who (foolish youth) gave him some trouble.

Eric duly locked him up in a cell and a short while later

returned with a wrapped parcel under his arm. Opening up the cell he walked in and said, "So, you are going to complain to the court about me, are you? Well, let's give you something to complain about." With that, he took out of the wrapping paper a large kipper and proceeded to beat the bloke all around the cell with it.

Only when the fish was in tatters did he stop and say, "Right, let's see if they believe that!"

True to his word, the fool-hardy prisoner did complain in graphic detail and wondered why the magistrates nearly laughed themselves silly. Believe it or not, Eric Fretton actually finished up as Commander (Chief Superintendent) in the Metropolitan Police!

Chapter Two

My first year in Romford had taught me much; enough it seemed for my sergeant to call me into his office one day to ask whether I fancied the idea of going out onto sub-division, that is a smaller station away from the main hub of activity with substantially less guv'nors breathing down your neck and where you were left more to your own devices. Yes, I said, I was quite ready for that, thank you kindly. Where was he thinking of sending me?

"Harold Hill," he said, "Get a bike out of the shed and take a ride up there. Introduce yourself to the sergeant. You start next Monday."

A place like that, I knew, meant fewer men on shifts and a more free and easy atmosphere. I knew too that with the exception of the main shopping centre, all the beats were cycle patrols which meant no more hoofing it around on foot for eight hours a day. In addition, since we were now living as a family again at Gallows Corner, I had considerably less travelling to get to work.

I went to the shed at the back of the nick and chose the best-looking of several decrepit old cycles that lived there. I checked the tyres and brakes, wiped the dust off the saddle and started off on the two- or three-mile ride to Harold Hill. I knew it as a vast, sprawling housing estate built just after the war to re-house bombed-out Londoners. From Romford, I remembered I had to turn left at Gallows Corner and then take the main Farringdon Avenue onto the estate. Suddenly, I froze.

Where was the nick from there? I had only ever visited it in the area car and had never taken a lot of notice of how to get there. Reassuring myself that I would recognise the place when I got there, I carried on. Not a bit of it! Within a few minutes of arriving at Farringdon Avenue, I looked around and realised that compared with the familiar old streets of Romford this place was completely anonymous! I hadn't a clue where the nick was! Kicking myself, I wondered what I should do. Carry on cycling, I decided, I am bound to find it in the end. I did, and finished up again in Farringdon Avenue!

Inventing excuses for when I returned empty-handed to Romford, I suddenly spied a little post office. Should I or shouldn't I? Knowing that if I did, I would look an absolute fool, I decided I would rather suffer that than face an incredulous sergeant. I went into the shop. Thankfully, there were no customers. I explained to the sub-postmistress that I was from Romford and looking for Harold Hill Police Station, could she help me? The look on her face was memorable, to say the least, and of course I couldn't blame her. Then, doubtless wondering whether it was April Fool's Day, she gave me instructions on how to get there and I retreated with grateful thanks and my tail between my legs. There was a telephone box outside that same post office which was one of a number around Harold Hill used as 'point' locations; that is, once an hour the PC had to present himself there at a set time and wait for ten minutes, either to be visited by his sergeant or inspector, or to receive a message for something which had occurred, or needed dealing with, on his beat. About three o'clock in the morning, a month or two after my ignominious arrival on that corner, I was standing patiently in a steady drizzle when it occurred to me that it was a lot drier in the box than out of it. I opened the door and stepped in. It was so quiet in there. Within a few moments, I felt my eyes closing. *If the phone rings,* I thought, *I'll not be far from it.* Suddenly, I stood up with a jerk, it was still dark and peaceful out there. I checked with my watch and realised that I had been asleep on my feet for about five minutes, something I've never been able to do since.

My memories of Harold Hill, short though my stay there was, are all happy. I found the people in general to be kind and courteous, despite stories to the contrary that they were just Eastenders transplanted into the county. Perhaps my ten years or so living in Clapham taught me more than I realised about Londoners, how they think and how they react, for I found I got on pretty well with them all. A great inspiration was my guv'nor, Chief Inspector Len Fisher, who was in overall charge at 'the Hill'. He was a man then in his middle or late forties, tall, and good-looking. He was certainly a hard man but fair, and neither us nor the locals ever managed to get anything over him. He had been posted to the Hill at the very outset while much of the building was still in progress and had grown up with the estate. When he retired some years later he had richly earned, both from us and the local population, the title 'Father of Harold Hill'.

The Post Office just off Farringdon Avenue, Harold Hill. Scene of my embarrassment when I could not find Harrold Hill Police Station. The telephone box in which I fell asleep is still there (on left).

I well remember one particular Christmas when Romford Division put on a 'do' for all the policemen's children. This was held somewhere in Hornchurch although I cannot remember exactly where. In addition to the usual games, there were turns put on by professional entertainers culminating in a parade of officers all in fancy dress. To my surprise, and I must admit, embarrassment, for I was a very young probationer then who still regarded senior officers with a God-like awe, I saw Len Fisher parading with the rest of them as one of Cinderella's ugly sisters, with all the hideous make-up that that involved! I remember wondering what on earth had possessed the man that he could expose himself to the inevitable howls of laughter and suggestive comments from an audience almost entirely consisting of subordinates. It then slowly dawned on me that it was because he was so self-assured and respected that he could take on such a role, that the evening was for letting our hair down and enjoying ourselves irrespective of rank or position, and that on the morrow we would all once again be back on our beats with the guv'nor.

I do not recall too many incidents worth noting during my stay on the Hill. A couple come to mind though. One of our jobs on night duty was to check every door of every shop, office and factory. (I wonder how often that is done now?) Door handles would be tested and windows checked front and back. Flat roofs, with access, would be climbed and alleyways investigated. Many a time premises were found insecure and the keyholder got out of bed to check his property. I was always told that if the early turn found a burglary in any of these properties, the night man, whose job it had been to check them, would be called out of bed to explain why he had missed it.

It had never happened to me, perhaps because I was still conscientious enough to check everything, or perhaps because I was plain lucky. Lucky that is until I was called upon to explain how a certain greengrocers in Hilldene shops had got burgled without my knowing it. Fortunately, it was decided not to actually get me out of bed after only three hours' sleep, but I was nevertheless instructed to report to the Hill as soon as possible. With more than a little foreboding, I got on my bike and made my way to the nick to be asked by the sergeant how often I had checked the padlock on this shop's roller blind. I answered that I had checked it several times during the night, the last time just before I went off at six a.m.

"Did you actually give the padlock a tug?" he said.

"Well, no, not exactly," I replied. "It was in the closed position so it must have been locked."

The sergeant gave me a hard look. "Well, next time think of old-fashioned chewing gum. That padlock had been forced, the door opened and the padlock closed by an outside accomplice who had filled the lock with chewing gum and closed it again. They were in there doing the shop while you were outside checking it!" I never passed by a padlock after that!

There was another occasion when I was on late turn, again on the Hilldene Avenue beat, when during the early evening a crowd of about thirty or forty youngsters had congregated in the shopping precinct. Now if we allowed this to continue unchecked, trouble invariably flared so we always 'moved them on'. Most times, a few words from the patrolling bobby was enough to break them up into small groups and wander off – that is until they saw you disappear and then they would congregate again. On this occasion, though, having given them the usual verbals to break up and get on their way, they decided to stick fast and see what happened. I told them again, and again they simply defied me. I was beginning to wonder whether it was worthwhile arresting the ringleaders for obstruction when what should hove into sight but the area car. The driver pulled up and asked if I was all right. Yes, I assured him, but the yobbery had decided not to co-operate.

"Well, we can't have that can we?" he said. Then getting out of the police car, he called to the group, "Are you going to move or not?" No reply and no movement. "That's fine by me," he called, then winked at me and got back in his motor. He drove on down the road for about seventy-five yards, swung the car round and mounted the pavement (which was unusually wide). He sat there for a moment with the vehicle pointing directly at the group and gently revving his engine. Still no response. Suddenly, he slipped into gear and drove straight at them! They stared for a second or two, for they did not have much more than that, not believing what was happening. Then as fast as their legs could carry them, they split up and ran. I anticipated all sorts of 'questions in the house' about that one but none ever came.

It was on night duty at Harold Hill that I first met PC John Sutton. In fact, I was given the job of showing him around on his arrival. I cannot remember what service he had in then, but it could not have been more than a year or two. We soon got into the habit of carrying a flask of coffee in our saddle-bags and joining each other in secluded places for a welcome hot drink and chat. Like the majority of us at that time he was ex-army too, but I quickly learned there was something rather special about him. He had transferred from his unit to the SAS and had served for a considerable time in Malaya at the time of the communist 'troubles' in the early 1950s. Then the whole of that country was in danger of going up in flames and the British forces had been given the job of tackling the guerrillas in their own environment – the jungle. There the communists specialised in terrorising the local population, destroying rubber plantations and communications, ambushing army units and waylaying convoys. This campaign turned out to be one of the most unpublicised chapters in British military history despite the fact that we totally routed the communists and returned the country to democratic rule.

One of the most effective British army units was the SAS who entered and lived off the jungle for weeks and months at a time, setting up their own ambushes and gathering intelligence. One such patrol of which John was a member set up a world record (in military terms) for the longest unsupported jungle operation lasting a hundred and twenty-eight days before returning to base.

With typical modesty, or perhaps the Official Secrets Act, he did not enlarge on what they got up to during that time, but I imagine it was pretty hairy. It was some years later whilst on detached beat at Moreton that I got to know a Major John Cooper, a founder-member of the SAS, who remembered John Sutton

well from his own years in Malaya, and who confirmed what he had told me. It was no surprise to see John climb the promotion ladder very quickly finishing up, I believe, as a superintendent by the time he retired from the police in the late 1980s, just a year or two before I retired.

Harrold Hill Police Station, Gooshays Drive. I served here from 1960-61. Station taken over by Metropolitan Police in 1965.

There are times on night duty when the mind plays tricks on you. A combination of darkness, solitude and silence heightens the senses to a pitch where the slightest movement or sound can be magnified, misunderstood or simply jangle the nerves.

About the worst time for this is about three or four o'clock in the morning, the dead hour when the night is well-worn and the dawn still a long way off. It is the hour when the print-workers are at last tucked up in bed and the milkman's rattle begins to disturb the pre-dawn. This, when you are alone on deserted streets, is 'nerve time'.

One morning at about half-past-three, I was standing at the top of Romford Market Place close to what was then Mercury Gardens. As my eyes wandered up the road towards Gidea Park, I caught sight of a black, silent shadow moving across the road. I stared as the figure of a man, hunched up, hands in overcoat pockets, strode purposefully across my line of vision. For a moment, I wondered whether to let him go but curiosity made me set off in pursuit. By the time I reached the spot there was no sign of him.

Flashing my torch now at empty shadows, I turned quickly into a side-road probing the front gardens as I went. I came to another corner, rounded it – and nearly jumped out of my skin! There right in front of me stood the figure of a man, tall, powerfully-built, enveloped in a long black overcoat, and with a face that unnerved me. Pure white, like death, with dark staring eyes and a black shaggy beard which hid most of his features.

He broke the momentary silence. "What's the matter?" he said, staring hard at me.

Under cover of my cape, I had already hooked my thumb into the strap of my truncheon. Then assuming an air of authority, which I certainly did not feel, I flicked my torch over him and demanded, "What are you doing creeping about the streets at this hour? Who are you? Where are you from?"

He suddenly broke into a smile which completely changed his countenance and said, "Is that all? Just a check? Well, I can't tell you what a relief it is to know that I am liable to be checked at this time of the morning!" He went on the explain that he was a chronic asthmatic with a serious sleep problem and on particularly clear, cold nights he would get up and walk around to clear his chest. Nothing more than that. He happily produced identification and I sent him on his way with a relieved, though cheery 'Goodnight'.

Had I passed this man in the cold light of day, I would not have given him a second glance, but at that time of night with heightened senses it took upon itself an eeriness that made the flesh creep. It's funny how a little daylight can change one's whole perspective.

Talking of night-checks, I don't know how many are done these days, I imagine they still are, but I can certainly say that everyone we saw in the wee hours were stopped and spoken to, and if we were not satisfied with their answers, we searched them and their vehicles too for that matter. More often than not, the person checked was a night printer who would reward you with that day's Daily Mail or Mirror with the front page stamped VOUCHER. I tell you what, if you can get hold of a couple of early editions of any newspaper, you can sail through any roadblock!

Most of those we checked were like my man in Romford, quite happy to be stopped and appreciative of the reason why. Some actually enjoyed it and stayed for a natter but now and again, you would run into a bolshie barrack-room lawyer who would demand his rights and not answer any questions or permit any search. It was then that they needed reminding that the area had recently been subject to a spate of burglaries and that their unwillingness to co-operate must inevitably arouse our suspicions, and we could arrest on suspicion. This was in fact an over-simplification of our powers, but we usually had no trouble after that.

In the stopping of cars at night, I was lucky in that I never had any problems. For some, though, there was the occasional driver who would deliberately 'fail to see' a large policeman standing in his path, flashing a powerful torch and with his arm raised. It was then not uncommon for the copper to hurl his truncheon at the recalcitrant driver's windscreen as he passed by. Most times the bang as it hit the screen, or as sometimes happened, shattered it, was enough to stop anyone (and if he continued after that, he quickly found himself the subject of an alert). This unconventional means of stopping vehicles in the early hours had apparently gone on for years and was certainly condoned by the sergeants if not inspectors and above.

All came to an embarrassing end one night though when a driver who had failed to see or had ignored such a signal was treated to the traditional flying missile. It hit the windscreen, bounced off without causing any damage, and then ricocheted into the front window of a nearby shop. The officer watched in horror as the window shattered!

Now how can a truncheon bounce off a windscreen and then go on to smash a window? The odds are stacked against it but it happened in Romford High Street. Not surprisingly, the shopkeeper too was a bit miffed at being got out of bed at three in the morning to board up his window, and I remember quite clearly the written order that 'this practice shall cease forthwith'. Those very words indicated that it had become a 'practice'.

Back to where we started – nerves at night. Later on at Harold Hill, I was on the factories beat in Farringdon Avenue. On nights, it was then my habit to pull my bike into the shadows of a doorway where I could relax with a flask of coffee from my saddlebag, safe in the knowledge that I was invisible but could see everything that passed.

On this particular night, I was leaning back against the door sipping away at my coffee when I picked up the unmistakeable sound of heavy breathing. I paused, looking out into the darkness. Nothing. The breathing continued though and was getting closer.

Lowering my coffee to the ground, I loosened my truncheon. The breathing was close now but with it came the sound of shuffling, slippered feet. *Whoever this is,* I thought, *is in for a nasty surprise.*

A moment later, the breathing and shuffling reached my doorway and I stepped out, torch blazing and truncheon ready. Nothing. Absolutely nothing! But then the breathing and the footsteps had stopped too. I stared about and then down. There, three feet away and blinded by my torch was a very surprised hedgehog staring angrily up at me. I let my breath go and stood looking down at him, relieved that I was not going to get involved in a fight with an intruder in a deserted factory estate. It occurred to me what noisy creatures hedgehogs really were in the silence of the night. No wonder their staple diet is worms, they would frighten off anything else.

Switching off my torch I stepped back, and with a snuffle and a snort Mr Tiggy shuffled on his way no doubt wondering too what peculiar specimens one comes across at three in the morning.

Chapter Three

I had not been at Harold Hill very long, I think less than a year, when I heard that PC Len Cook was retiring from Plough Corner. Why the station, which was built in the early 1920s, was named after the public house next door and not after the commonly accepted Gallows Corner I do not know. Perhaps somebody felt that connecting the police with the grisly gallows which once stood at these crossroads was inappropriate.

The fact that we were already living in the one of the block of four terraced houses which formed Plough Corner (we were at No 8 and the police station No 2) quite probably had something to do with my being posted there from Harold Hill. Bearing in mind that I was still in my first two years of probationary service, it was somewhat unusual to post an officer of such limited experience to a section station which boasted only four constables to a shift, and just two sergeants. There was no inspector. The sergeants, PS Gerry Wilmott and PS Jim Barningham, worked nine a.m. to five p.m. and five p.m. to one a.m. a fortnight, for we were then still working fortnightly shifts. With the PO's working normal earlies, lates and nights, it was obvious that from one a.m. we were left very much on trust so far as supervision was concerned. It was always a point of honour that we did not abuse this freedom even though we were, on paper at any rate, supervised by a Romford Sergeant or Inspector who was supposed to turn up now and again to visit us at our various night points.

Plough Corner Police Station at Gallows Corner, Romford. I served here from 1961-63. The Police Station is on extreme right and our house on the extreme left.

My stay at Plough Corner of just over two years was certainly the happiest of my service so far. Two of my shift-mates were Bert Howard and Gordon Betteridge, who shared very similar personalities, they were both quiet, totally reliable and experienced officers, exuding calm professionalism on the one hand with a dry and ready wit on the other. They both turned out to be ideal colleagues and we remained good friends for many years.

For me, the prospect of working in such a relaxed atmosphere was a novelty I had not experienced before. However, the opportunity for getting into trouble on nights was admittedly not very great for we all had various tasks to perform, what with properties to check and points to make every hour.

Nevertheless, I was quickly initiated into one of the most jealously guarded secrets of the section.

In those days, whether it was a foot or cycle patrol, being found off your beat was a very serious matter. If for any reason you needed to stray over your boundary, it was always best to ask first rather than be caught. This strict rule was waived though twice-a-night at midnight and five a.m. when we were allowed back at the nick for a cup of tea. If a Romford Inspector or Sergeant turned up, then he expected to be invited to share a cup, but at any other time it was a run-and-hide situation.

Now, it so happened that in addition to the other regular tea-stops that we had on our beats, like all-night bakeries, factories etc., there was, in Upper Brentwood Road, a very fine house which boasted a conservatory. There, the lady of the house laid out a tray of tea and biscuits every single night for her visiting bobby, and before going to bed lit a small paraffin lamp which gave adequate light, and in winter a paraffin stove. The tea was always in thermos flasks and the biscuits were often accompanied by cakes and other goodies.

We never knew who she was, nor did we ever meet her, but unfailingly night after night the tea and biscuits would be there to be gratefully consumed. In addition, easy chairs were set out for our comfort. Once a year at Christmas, we would all chip in a couple of shillings and leave a big box of chocolates and a Christmas card signed by us all beside the tray. Unfailingly, the following night we would find a charming letter of thanks addressed to her 'Dear Bobbies'. What a gracious lady.

We were in the habit of meeting there between midnight and five a.m., the only problem being for those who had to travel well off their beats to get there, but we all managed it. The garden of the house was surrounded by a six-foot close-boarded fence with a wicket-gate, and it was an easy matter to slip the latch on the gate, wheel your cycle quietly into the garden and then let oneself in. We were, naturally, extremely careful not to disturb the owners and talked in whispers the whole time. One night, when as luck would have it I was off for some reason or other, Bert Howard and Gordon Betteridge were sitting in the conservatory when they heard the click of the gate-latch and then quiet footsteps approaching up the garden path. Assuming it to be one of the other PC's, they started to pour out another cup of tea. The door opened and in walked Jim Barningham!

As they stared open-mouthed, he smiled and said, "I've always wondered what the attraction was around here." Then on looking about, "They certainly do you well, don't they!" He proceeded to make himself comfortable in one of the chairs, held out his hand and said, "Is that my cup of tea?"

To give him his due, he never mentioned the incident again and never paid another visit. Having followed them, he was now quite happy that their disappearance involved nothing more sinister than a cup of tea, and thereafter we continued our nocturnal visits.

Talking of sergeants following us around reminds me of one incident involving Bert Howard. Close to Plough Corner nick there was, and still is, an industrial estate which had to be thoroughly checked several times a night for there were rich pickings to be had for a determined burglar.

In the early hours of one morning, Bert was doing his usual rounds when he spotted a car parked in a cul-de-sac beside one of the factories. A few yards away were two men. Turning, they saw Bert approaching and both made an immediate dash for the car. Jumping in, they roared off up the service road making straight for him in their effort to escape. The thought passed through Bert's mind that if he were hit by the car, then he was likely to remain there for a considerable time before he was missed and a search organised – no radios in those days! As the car reached him, he jumped sideways into a doorway and then a second later heard the unmistakeable sound of a windscreen smashing. He stepped out to see the car careering off and Jim Barningham (again) standing there with his drawn truncheon. Although he never admitted it, and Bert certainly didn't ask directly, there was no doubt that Jim was doing his usual 'following' job to see that we did ours properly, but then had the presence of mind to use his truncheon on the car's windscreen when he saw Bert in trouble.

The house in Gidea Park, scene of our illicit tea-stop supplied by a lady we never met, and our discovery by Jim Barningham. The conservatory is just visible over the fence. The gate we used is still there thirty years later.

Neither of them were able to get the vehicle's index number so both would-be breakers got away with it. Except, of course, that Bert and Jim's action prevented a certain burglary.

Enough of Jim Barningham. Gerry Wilmott was quite a character too. An ex-Metropolitan copper, he had transferred to the county a few years before and was another memorable sergeant of my early years. I remember one particular day standing at a point near Gallows Corner when Gerry rode up on his bike.

"Come on, John." he said, "We've got a suicide up at Rise Park."

This was quite a nice area a couple of miles along the A127 towards London. I got on my bike and off we went.

For some reason, I had registered the incident as some form of emergency and within a hundred yards was outstripping Gerry.

"Hey! Slow down," he called. "The bloke's dead and rushing there isn't going to bring him back to life!" We found the address and a distraught wife in her middle fifties.

"What happened, love?," we asked.

"In the garage," she relied.

We went out and opened the garage door to find a very dead husband hanging from the rafters. It later transpired that they had enjoyed a cup of tea before she went out to do her shopping. On her return, she could not get in and despite calls there was no sign of her husband. She opened the garage door intending to go through to the back door and literally bumped into his swinging body. On our way back afterwards, we both agreed it was a pretty callous thing for him to do – he could at least have left a note on the front door.

It's a peculiar thing but after a pretty uneventful year or so at Harold Hill, almost humdrum in fact when one considers that it was supposed to have been a rough and tough area, my days at Plough Corner were packed with incident.

I remember the telephone ringing one quiet Sunday afternoon while I was trying to catch up on a few reports, and a somewhat distressed female from Gidea Park reporting that her cat was stuck on her roof. Was there anything we could do? My immediate reaction was to suggest giving it a gentle push but my training dictated otherwise.

"How can a cat get stuck on a roof?" I asked.

"Well," she said, "it climbed out of my dormer window and then slid down the tiles until it hit the gutter. It's out there now and can't climb back."

With a sigh of resignation, I replied that someone would be round to have a look. I reported the facts to Gerry thinking that with his Met. training he would dismiss the affair out of hand or at least suggest the Fire Brigade or RSPCA. Not a bit of it! County training must have rubbed off on him.

"Come on, mate," he said. "Let's get 'round and have a look."

A few minutes later, we both turned up and found the address to be a three-storey building (four if you count the roof). Along with the anxious pussy-lover, we climbed up to the dormer-window and looked out. There, sure enough, down a steep slope of slippery tiles crouched the mewing moggy, unable to climb up and facing a thirty-foot fall if it didn't.

"Hmm," said Gerry. "Not too much of a problem. What do you reckon that is to the gutter, John, six feet?"

Like a lamb to the slaughter I agreed.

"Okay," he said, "you get out of the window and slide down, I'll hold on to your ankles." I looked at him in disbelief.

"And supposing you can't hold me"?" I said. "That's a thirty foot drop down there." Gerry grinned.

"No problem," he said. "Get on out there!"

Feeling much less confident than I looked, I opened the lower window and edged my way out. It looked even higher in the fresh air. I looked back at Gerry. He nodded his head vigorously and took a firm hold of my ankles. Slowly, as I slid down the mossy tiles it occurred to me that they were going to make a hell of a mess of my uniform. The stupid cat simply crouched there looking up at its hero. I reached out a hand. Not far enough. "A bit more," I called. Finally, and with infinite relief, I reached out and grabbed the mewing creature. I felt pressure on my ankles as Gerry hauled while I helped as best I could by holding the cat with one hand and levering myself up with the other. Safely restored to the arms of its owner, we received her thanks with the traditional, "'all in a day's work, ma'am," before dusting ourselves down (me, that is) and getting on our way. Gerry laughed all the way back.

There have got to be better ways of spending a Sunday, I thought.

As I have said, life at Plough Corner was certainly packed with incident, and not all of it painless either. A couple of hundred yards from the nick, along the Southend Road, was Cook's Cars which incorporated an all-night petrol station.

After checking the factories on the adjoining estate, it was my habit to walk along to see how the attendant was. Nowadays, such a person would be much better protected than they were then (early 1960s) for all he had was a small wooden hut on the forecourt. His bosses could not have thought much of his welfare for although he had been robbed a couple of times, they took no steps to improve his lot. He decided therefore to protect himself on nights by bringing with him his huge black Alsatian. I got to know both man and dog quite well and always made a fuss of it when I called. I told the fellow more than once that it was the soppiest Alsatian I had ever met.

On this particular night, it was something like one o'clock in the morning, I made my usual call. We chatted for a few moments before I bent down to make my usual fuss of the dog. As I did so, I felt a sudden and violent bang in the face, no pain, just a bang. I staggered back a pace wondering what the hell had hit me and then suddenly saw blood pouring down my tunic front. "Oh my God!" I heard the man say. "What's happened?"

Holding my hand to my face, I said, "Your bloody dog's gone for me, that's what's happened!" and then finding myself with no handkerchief, I said, ""Give me a cloth, quick!"

The silly berk grabbed the nearest thing to hand – a filthy, oily rag.

"That's no damned good, is it," I said. "Haven't you got anything else?" Finally, he found me something a little cleaner, but not much, and then said. "It looks pretty bad."

By now, I was feeling just a bit queasy but had recovered enough of my wits to say, "Well, ring for an ambulance then, I'm not going to cycle all the way to Harold Wood Hospital like this. And while you're at it, ring Romford Police and tell the night sergeant what has happened and where I am."

A short while later, I was lying on a sort of operating table with a doctor peering intently down at me. My left nostril had been opened up in two halves and my upper lip badly slit.

"That'll need a few stitches," he said. "I'm going to give you some injections to deaden the area, but let me tell you now that the nose is one of the most sensitive parts of your body so you might feel it a bit."

Feel it a bit! The needle felt as if it was red hot. I certainly felt it!

Eventually, he put in upwards of a dozen stitches, every

single one of which I felt, then stood back and said, "Right, that's it, you can go now." I actually had the courtesy to try and thank him but my lips were so swollen and painful that I could only mumble.

As I walked into the waiting area, it was now about two o'clock in the morning, I suddenly felt faint and staggered a bit. Delayed shock, I suppose. I felt a nurse take me by the arm and lay me down on a bed. I looked up and found her to be the blackest woman I had ever seen. She was in her forties, handsomely built and very motherly.

"You lie still a moment," she said soothingly. "I'm going to get you something." I saw her cross to a wall cabinet, open it, and as sure as I live and breathe, she took out half a bottle of brandy! Taking a medicine glass from a shelf she poured a very liberal portion, lifted up my head with her hand and gently poured it down my very grateful throat.

I leaned back on the pillow and tried to thank her but she put her finger to her lips and whispered in a rich West Indian accent, "Not a word, man! This is strictly against the rules but you'll feel better for it." I certainly did, and what an angel she was.

I will never forget her.

Waiting for me in reception was the Romford Sergeant who looked at my blood-soaked tunic and shirt and my stitched up face. "Gawd! You look as if you've been through a mangle," he said. "Come on, I've got the car outside, we'll take you home."

Later, as I crept into bed I gently woke Joan. I had decided it better to warn her what my face looked like while it was still dark rather than wait for her to discover it for herself in the morning.

An unusual and tragic sequel to this tale was that on the following night the same Romford Sergeant called on matey-boy at Cook's Cars, examined his dog licence and then reported him for keeping a dangerous dog! The matter never got to court though for about three weeks later there was a particularly nasty crash on the A127 and both the owner and his dog were killed.

PC Frank Brand, also at Plough Corner, was a brilliant and talented cartoonist. By the time I reported back for duty a week or ten days after this incident (time enough for the stitches to be removed) he presented me with a great cartoon of an elephant ambling along with a richly decorated howdah on its back, this being crammed with armed policemen peering out of the canopy. The caption read, 'Plough Corner Dog Hunt'. I still have that somewhere.

One of my most embarrassing moments, and I had a few, occurred one day as I was dealing with a minor road accident in Main Road, Gidea Park, just south of Gallows Corner. I was in the process of completing the accident book when I glanced up and saw an old Austin Ten saloon tearing down the road towards me ('tearing' being nothing more than a figure of speech for an early 1930s car) hotly pursued by a headquarters traffic car – nothing less than a powerful Wolesley 6/90 capable of about 115 mph. The situation was ludicrous.

As I stared in disbelief, the traffic car skidded to a halt and the driver, who was unaccompanied, shouted across to me, "Get in, quick!"

Telling my two drivers to sort the accident out between themselves, I ran across the road and jumped into that beautiful motor. The driver, PC Derek Arbour, hurriedly explained that he had stopped the Austin on Gallows Corner roundabout and as he was about to speak to the driver he had suddenly accelerated away.

Now a trial of speed between a then thirty-year-old Austin

Ten and a new Wolesley 6/90 was simply no contest at all and I was stupid enough to venture such a remark. Derek looked at me pityingly. "If it's a stolen motor, it's a stolen motor, isn't it? And there are two on board, I can't chase 'em both if they leg it, can I?"

Sheepishly, I explained that although I had seen the motor I hadn't realised there were two in it.

"There they go," he said, and I saw the Austin careering left into Upper Brentwood Road. We followed, gaining on them rapidly. Suddenly, it turned right at much too great a speed into a side-turning. Seconds later, we did the same but under much better control. There it was, come to grief, just fifty yards into the turning and with its bonnet buried in a tree. Steam was pouring from the engine and the two occupants were already running like mad up the road towards a T-junction.

Derek reached the junction, turned right and immediately slammed the brakes on. Without a word, he jumped out and ran. At the very moment I was opening my door, I saw two figures running full pelt towards me, the second figure only about two yards behind the first. I knew I did not have a chance of grabbing the first but there was every chance of getting the second. I ran hard up behind him and decided to play dirty, kicking his leg out from under him. He flew through the air and hit the gravelled roadway with an almighty crash. A second later, I jumped bodily onto him and twisted his arm painfully up his back. My words were very 'hackneyed', "Well, are you coming quietly?" The man turned his head to look at me.

"Let me go, for God's sake, I was trying to help you catch them!" I didn't believe him, of course, until I felt Derek's hand on my shoulder.

"Let him go," he said. "He's not one of them!" I looked up

and saw Derek holding a teenager by the arm.

I looked again at my prisoner. Middle thirties, expensive suit, white shirt and tie. Certainly not a tearaway. It did not need much to tell me that I had made a fool of myself in not looking before I leapt. As I started to apologise to the have-a-go hero, a neighbour came up to tell us that the second youngster had disappeared down a garden path between two houses opposite.

"I'll' get him," I said, and made off. As luck would have it, the second youth had reached a dead-end when he found his path blocked by a locked garden gate. There was nowhere for him to go so he simply turned to face me as I approached. I none-too-gently propelled him back up the path and across to where his mate now sat in the back of the police car.

Once again I apologised to our helper, a Mr Huckle, who had sustained a cut hand, badly grazed knee and a torn suit.

Telling him the least I could do was to get him to hospital, I also asked for his name and address so that I could organise a letter of thanks and reimbursement for his damage. He replied that there were no hard feelings and that he quite understood the spur-of-the-moment mistake. It was only then that I discovered that he was in fact a bank manager!

The upshot of this was that the car turned out to be not stolen at all but the legitimate property of the driver who had only run off because he knew...wait for it...his driving licence had expired! Truly! And his mate had done likewise because, as he said later, he couldn't think what else to do! Can you believe it? A wrecked car, two arrests and a couple of hours in police custody for the sake of an expired licence! The bank manager got his letter of thanks from our chief, plus the cost of a new suit, and somehow or other the press also got to hear about it for within twenty-four hours; my name was featuring in the national as well as local press (the reports of which date the incident to August 1963). Fortunately, there were no repercussions so far as I was concerned, my chief being quoted as saying, "It is so rare for the public to help us that this officer's mistake was understandable," which I thought rather ungracious. For many years afterwards, whenever Derek Arbour and I bumped into one another, his first words were always, "Knocked over any good bank managers lately?"

Chapter Four

At this juncture, I should introduce my family. By now (1963), I was twenty-nine years old, married for eight years and the father of four children. David was born in 1956, Sharon in 1957 and Colin in 1959, all at Southend. David and Sharon were born at home, as was quite common in those days, in Harcourt Avenue, while Colin came into the world via Rochford Hospital just months after I joined the police. Diane was the exception, for by the time she was born in 1962 I had been a policeman for three years and we were living at Gallows Corner. She was introduced to us courtesy of Oldchurch Hospital, Romford, (Joan playing a small part in her arrival too), and far from having the tang of salt in her veins, as the other three have, she is unique in almost being an Eastender – a fact she will not thank me for!

But back to matters anecdotal and embarrassing. One night at about midnight, I was on office duty (we always manned the police office from ten p.m. till one a.m. on nights) when a young, dishevelled girl of about sixteen came in. She explained that she had run away from her home in Kent, somehow made her way to our neck of the woods where she had either picked up or been picked up by three or four boys. She had gone with them to a field close to the nick and had submitted to, encouraged or otherwise allowed one or more of them to have their evil way with her – or her with them. She was not alleging rape but rather that she had in the process lost both her handbag and knickers, was tired and hungry and wanted to go home! By this time,

Gerry's ears had pricked up and he came out of his office. On learning what it was all about he suggested that I accompany her to the field to search for her missing property. Once found, I was to take her to Bob's Transport Café just across the road where she could get something to eat while he telephoned her parents to arrange for her return.

Of course, our route to the field took us straight past Bob's and I was conscious of a number of inquisitive faces peering out at us as we passed. We turned down the lane beside the field and about fifty yards further on she stopped and pointed out a narrow gap in the hedge. This, she said, was where she had emerged. Clambering through in the dark was no mean feat, armed though I was with a torch, and I soon lost my footing and took a tumble into the ditch (fortunately dry) which lay on the other side.

We searched around for some minutes before finally succeeding in finding both handbag and knickers, the latter of which she unashamedly put on again without so much as a glance at me standing nearby. We then made our way back, struggled once again through the hedge and onto the road. A few moments later, we were in Bob's cafe.

Standing at the counter with her as she ordered a take-away, I looked around at the dozen or more truckers crouched over their sausage and mash. They were grinning like Cheshire cats. The girl turned to me and exclaimed, "You should see the state of your raincoat!" and started brushing off an accumulation of dead twigs and grass! The grins of the assembled drivers broadened perceptibly, for without a doubt they had followed our progress both to and from the field. I pushed her hand away roughly and turned to the assembled drivers.

"It's not what you think!" I called, but it was no good, they simply fell about! I was not a happy person as we made our way back to the nick.

Another embarrassing moment involving a young girl occurred one summer's evening when I was again on office duty. The peace was suddenly shattered with the sound of screeching brakes, a door banging and a lot of angry shouting outside in Straight Road. I stood up and looked out. There across the road stood a battered old Ford Dormobile with one of its back doors hanging open, the body of a young girl lying in the roadway, and two men fighting – or at least one having a right go at the other.

I ran out and separated the protagonists before turning my attention to the girl. She was conscious and struggling to get to her feet.

"What the hell's going on then?" I said.

It transpired that there were about six people in the van, the driver and his mate in the front and the other four, which included the girl, in the back. All were of the same family. Apparently, one of the back doors had not been shut properly and as the van entered Straight Road from Gallows Corner at too great a speed, the girl had lurched against the door which had opened. She had promptly disappeared and hit the road. The girl's brother did no more than go round to the front of the van, yank the driver out and proceed to give him a thumping for his carelessness. By then, Gerry Wilmott had joined me and we helped get the girl, who was about seventeen, across to the nick.

We were hardly through the door when her arms and legs suddenly went haywire and I realised I was watching for the first time a person having an epileptic fit. Now, despite all our first aid training at Eynsham, I had no recollection of having been taught anything about fits, and my first reaction was to physically restrain her in case she injured herself. It was not an easy task made worse by her suddenly flinging herself across the office counter. *Ah,* I thought, *now I can hold her down until she recovers,* and quickly hoisting her legs onto the counter I leaned over and put my weight down on her. At that moment, the door opened and thinking it was just one of her family, who were still arguing the matter outside, I said over my shoulder. "Get out!" A rather familiar voice then cut in.

"What on earth is going on here?" I turned 'round and looked into the face of Romford's Inspector. All he could see, of course, was an extremely noisy family outside, a constable almost on top of a struggling girl on the inside, and Gerry Wilmott emerging from his office (where he had been phoning for an ambulance) to reassure him.

"It's all right, sir, everything's under control." But he took a lot of convincing.

Mentioning as I did 'a warm summer's evening' a couple of pages back reminded me of a day when it wasn't so warm, in fact the winter of 1962 when snow lay on the ground a foot deep. With Gerry Wilmott on days, I reported for late turn duty along with Bert Howard and Gordon Betteridge. By two o'clock, I saw that Gerry had put Bert Howard on office duty two p.m. to five p.m., and Gordon on 'reports' in the back room which thus kept them safely tucked up in the warm. Looking to see what I had been allocated, imagining it to be something like station duty which covered everything, a bit of house-work, making the tea, cleaning and tidying etc., for only a madman would go out in those conditions, I read with disbelief 'El Beat', the centre of Gidea Park!

I turned to Gerry. "Are you serious, Skip?" He was!

"What's with a bit of snow?" he said. "Make hourly points at Gidea Park Station" (about a mile and a half from the nick). "Don't take your bike out though, it's too dangerous!"

With that, he turned and stared out of the window at the bleak Arctic landscape which was then Gallows Corner.

I looked at Bert and Gordon but they could only manage to raise their eyebrows and shrug their shoulders in sympathy. Without another word, I put on my leggings, cape, gloves and helmet, and left.

Within a dozen yards, I found the snow coming halfway up my legs with every step and I was having to walk by lifting each foot vertically.

This is ridiculous, what's he trying to prove? I thought.

As I entered Main Road, Gidea Park, from Gallows Corner, a near-empty bus swished by. At least someone else was having to be out in it, I thought. Then the idea struck me. Policemen in those days travelled free on buses, not officially that is, but by unwritten agreement so long as they were in uniform and not taking up a seat. We therefore stood on the open platform with the conductor until we reached our destination.

A few minutes later, another bus came along bound for Romford. I hopped aboard to a welcoming wave from the conductor and there I stood chatting to him all the way to Romford Market Place. There I got off, crossed the road and waited for the next bus which took me to Gidea Park Station where I made my point waiting for a call that never came. Ten minutes later, I was on another bus bound for Hornchurch. By then it was time for a cup of tea at the local bake-house near Gidea Park Station before making my next point.

This went on for four hours with Gerry not visiting or telephoning me once. His surprise was obvious though when I walked into the nick at six o'clock full of the joys of spring, none the worse for wear, and with hardly a trace of snow on me. He never found out why, but I had to tell Bert and Gordon – for one of them was out in it second half while I got office duty!

It is difficult to put one's finger on it precisely but police-work in the late fifties and early sixties seemed, looking back on it, much more light-hearted and care-free than perhaps it is today. Laughter, practical jokes and ridiculous situations were commonplace in spite of the fact that our working restrictions appear to dictate otherwise. Perhaps it was because we were younger and more malleable then, or perhaps because most of us were ex-servicemen, we found the more relaxed discipline of police life easier to cope with.

Certainly, discipline was much stricter than in most other occupations; it had to be, of course, and our equipment was to say the least basic compared with today. Pay, too, bordered on the ridiculous. Swapping services for a moment (military, that is), there was an old adage in Nelson's navy that if you kept a man busy, you kept him happy and improved his efficiency. There was just such an admiral (who founded the Essex Police in 1840) who firmly advocated such a policy – and we found over a hundred years later that it had diluted only slightly in that time!

It is only on looking back that one realises how unnecessary and pettifogging much of that 'discipline' was, like standing to attention (whatever you were doing) when an inspector walked into the room, or commencing every written report with 'I beg to report...', and not forgetting, 'I respectfully request...' There were too the annual house-inspections, ostensibly to check whether you needed any decorations or improvements carried out, but which meant that just prior to the inspection the policeman's wife cleaned and scrubbed for what had in reality become more than just a visit to check the decorations.

Then there were the annual uniform parades, perhaps the biggest farce of all compared with today, when the tailor and his assistants would arrive at divisional headquarters to measure us for new uniforms. The infinite care taken with those measurements was quite reassuring, but most of us who had been through it before knew that in three months' time, we would all be there again for the ritual of the fittings – and it was then that the comedy would start for few of the uniforms bore any relation to the measurements taken!

Then, later in the year, we would undergo what was euphemistically called 'uniform cleaning' where we would bundle up the regulation 'one jacket and two trousers' to be sent away for dry-cleaning. The only snag was that when they were returned some weeks later, we found that the cleaners had sent them back in such huge, misshapen and tightly tied bundles that, once delivered, had to be taken home and re-pressed!

Out on the streets too we had our problems, for in the absence of radios the nearest public phone or obliging passer-by was all we had if we ran into trouble. Yet, funnily enough, this never seemed to breed reticence in any of us, we would still throw ourselves headlong into situations which today would certainly qualify for 'back-up'. One great advantage we had though, so far as Essex was concerned anyway, was a far greater respect for the uniform than exists now. I certainly dealt with incidents then, which today I would never have got away with, and all of it based on that one commodity – fear or respect, whatever you like to call it, of the uniform.

I can illustrate this quite easily by relating just one incident that occurred while I was on nights at Plough Corner. Halfway down Main Road, Gidea Park, was a line of four or five shops set back from the footpath. All were quite modern with a forecourt fronting them and a service entrance behind. One of these was Stanwood's, a double-fronted radio and television store. During the course of this particular night I had, of course, checked both front and back before going in for my break. After that, I had other things to do so I did not get round to checking it in 'second half'. At about half past five, I was cycling back to the nick and had actually passed Stanwood's when I paused, deliberating whether to give it a last check before I went off duty at six. Deciding that it would only take a moment or two, I turned round and cycled down the side of the shops and along the back, glancing at each rear door in turn. Ahead of me, in that service road, I saw a lorry parked up immediately behind Stanwood's. It had not been there earlier, I was certain.

Reaching the back of the store, I stood staring with little immediate comprehension into Stanwood's small delivery yard. The ground was literally carpeted with wood shavings, and as I stared I saw two huge steel doors which had once protected the store from intrusion leaning tidily against the gaping aperture they once covered! Both had been neatly removed by the simple expedient (though enormously laborious and time-consuming) of drilling holes all around the door frame with a hand-operated brace and bit and then literally lifting the entire door and frame away from the wall. An electric drill would surely have awoken the occupants above.

As if in a dream I walked across the yard, rustling through the shavings as I did so, and then into the store itself. I could not believe what I saw – or rather didn't see. It was empty! Cleaned out! Not so much as an electric shaver staring back at me. *God Almighty!* I thought, *I'm well and truly for the high jump this time.* The odd item or two nicked from your beat was one thing, but this was taking the mickey on a massive scale! What the hell do I do? Who do I confess to?

It's got to be the skipper first, then the DI, then the guv'nor.

I walked slowly back into the yard. The lorry was still there, a tarpaulin cover draped over its back. I pulled it to one side and shone my torch into the interior. I couldn't believe what I saw. It was crammed full, from front to back and floor to roof with televisions, radios, vacuum cleaners, you name it, it was there. The loot from Stanwood's – intact! I searched the immediate area as thoroughly as I could but not a soul or sound disturbed the peace and quiet of that morning. I walked back into the store and found a telephone – about the only thing still working – and rang Gerry Wilmott.

"I've got a serious break at Stanwood's, Skipper, cleaned out," I said. I heard him curse. "It's not quite as bad as it sounds though, I've got everything back!" Gerry could be forgiven for thinking that I was having him on!

Minutes later, he arrived on his bike. "My God! They've done a good job here," he said, surveying the empty store. "The CID are on their way and I can see the DI being got out of bed for this, so there'll be no sleep for you for an hour or two as he will certainly want to see you about this."

Now, I took this to mean a rocket at the very least; in fact, I more than half anticipated being put on a charge for neglect of duty for allowing it to happen in the first place.

A little while later, the DI turned up and examined the scene. After a short word with his DE's he looked across at me, walked over and to my complete surprise clapped me on the shoulder!

"Well done, John," he said. "Damned good bit of work. Shows you're out there doing your job. Imagine what the guv'nor would have said if they'd got away with it!"

I imagined what he would have said had he known that I had very nearly cycled by! There is a very thin line between success and failure, and an equally thin line between a clap on the back and being shot at dawn.

I suppose that a job of such proportions would have demanded at least two or three men to carry it out. Where had they been when I cycled by? There is little doubt they had seen me go past, pause, and then turn 'round and enter the service road. And what had they done? Taken to their heels! There was no other explanation for it.

The lorry was quickly identified as having been stolen and the job was professionally carried out with every item expertly loaded. So why hadn't they simply clobbered me in that dark alley and carried on with what they were doing? I shall never know, for we never caught them, but what other reason could there be for taking to their heels except for the sight of my uniform?

An interesting sequel came later when the Romford Recorder blazed the news that a 'police swoop' had foiled a daring raid and that thousands of pounds' worth of stolen property had been recovered. I must confess that I had never considered myself on my bike at five-thirty in the morning as constituting a police swoop, but it must be right, for there it was in black and white!

The parade of shops in Main Road, Gidea Park. Stanwood Radios was on the extreme left. The service road I used is on the extreme right (out of picture).

Talking as I am about ridiculous situations and carefree attitudes, I remember one morning on early turn passing the Squirrels Head pub at Gidea Park (the pub is still there but much changed from the old two-up-two-down weather-boarded building it then was). As I glanced in at the car-park at the side, I saw that it was empty apart from a solitary motor bike. My curiosity aroused, I cycled down and had a look. It was a 250cc BSA Bantam. Pulling out my stolen vehicle card, I checked its index number against the various entries I had made from the daily 'informations' (teleprinter messages) brought up from Romford each night. And lo and behold, there it was!

I cannot now remember whether there was an ignition key still in it or whether it started without one, but I knew enough to depress the clutch lever and give the kick-start a thump with my foot. It started straightaway. At that moment, Gordon Betteridge cycled in on his way to one of his points.

"It's nicked," I said, and showed him the vehicle card.

"Good for you," said Gordon, for it was always a bit of a feather in the cap to trace a stolen vehicle. "The only snag is," he said, "it's got to go back to the nick." For in those days, fingerprint officers rarely examined vehicles in-situ unless they had been used in really serious crime like murder or robbery. He would not want to come out to this tiddler.

"Can you drive motorbikes?" I said. Gordon shook his head.

"No, can you?"

"Well, it started all right. Let's see what happens." With that, I engaged the clutch and gently put my foot on what I thought was the gear lever. It clicked into place and I slowly released the clutch. As it began to move, I de-clutched. "It's okay," I said. "Jump on and we'll see if we can get it back." Gordon looked a trifle apprehensive.

"Are you sure you can drive this – and what about our bikes?"

With an air of authority I did not feel, I replied, "No problem, we'll get the area car to bring us back. Jump on."

Moments later, we were making our way out of the car-park and turning right towards Gallows Corner.

"This is good," I shouted over my shoulder as we gathered speed along Upper Brentwood Road. From its rather high-pitched tone, one could almost say strangulated, the engine was telling me it was time to change gear – and I didn't know how! I didn't even know which gear we were in. Finally, after a lot of fiddling with the clutch and foot-lever, I eventually found it and away we went at increased speed.

It then dawned on me that when we got to Main Road where we had to turn right to Gallows Corner, we would almost certainly have to stop for traffic at the junction. How do you stop these things? I fiddled around with my foot but couldn't find anything that felt like a brake pedal. I then gingerly applied the hand-brake. It worked. Arriving at the junction, I was relieved to find my prayers answered for there was hardly any traffic about (it was, after all, only seven fifteen in the morning). Would Gallows Corner roundabout be the same? Not likely. Up we roared and round we went (without changing gear), weaving our way through gaps in the traffic, our helmets still firmly fixed and capes streaming behind us as motorists stared in disbelief. Now for the crunch of actually stopping the thing for the nick was just across the road. Like an expert, I leaned the bike over to enter the service road and then at the right moment slapped on the hand-brake. Still in gear the engine stalled and we came to a stop.

Gordon, being pillion, got off first and wiped his forehead with his hand. "I thought you said you could ride motor-bikes," he said. I laughed.

"I didn't actually say I could ride them, did I, only that it would be no problem. And I got you here, didn't I?"

Gordon swung round. "Are you telling me you have never ridden a motorbike before?"

"Never in my life," I said. Gordon walked into the nick shaking his head. The first thing he did was to tell the sergeant what we had done (he had to because we had left our bikes behind and needed the area car to take us back for them) and I remember the skipper laughing about it. I can't somehow see that sort of behaviour being tolerated nowadays. But it still took a long while for me to live it down, and I have never ridden a motorbike since.

Perhaps another example of how slightly mad we were in those days occurred, of all places, at Romford swimming baths. I do not know whether it was pressure from our side or plain, simple magnanimity on theirs but every Tuesday evening the baths were closed to the public and turned over for the exclusive use of policemen and their families. It was a good idea from our point of view for it encouraged us to take advantage of the facility and in turn helped keep us fit. On the evening in question, I picked up Bill Bould, who was both a Romford Sergeant and my next-door neighbour, in my latest acquisition, a 1950 Ford Prefect. Once at the baths, I met a few mates; Bert Howard, Gordon Betteridge and others and soon we were skylarking about. Part of this entailed 'dive-bombing' our skipper, Gerry Wilmott, from the top board. Gordon and Bert, in the tradition of dive-bombing, did it by curling up in a ball to make an almighty splash alongside the victim. I followed suit but eventually, being a clever-dick, decided to introduce some finesse into the subject by diving straight down to see how near I could get without actually touching him.

This would have worked well except for one thing; at five feet eleven I had completely forgotten that the water was only five feet eight! Going down in a perfect vertical dive I missed Gerry by two inches, and a second later was hitting the bottom of the pool with a mighty crack. I remember quite distinctly my forehead hitting the bottom and then nothing more until I found myself on the surface. Making for the edge of the pool, I realised that my wrists were not working as they should – in fact, they were completely numb! It was quite obvious then that I had done some serious damage.

I swam to the side and told my mates that I had had enough and was going to get dressed. Eventually, after waiting for Bill Bould, we made our way outside and into the car for the trip home. By then feeling was coming back into my right wrist but my left was still useless and I found that the only way I could change gear was by reaching across with my right hand.

Bill, of course, couldn't fail to notice and asked what the matter was so I told him. "You had better get off to Harold Wood and get it looked at," he said. I told him I was on night duty, due to report in just under an hour, so I would drop off at the nick first and warn them.

I managed to complete a rather uncomfortable journey home, drop Bill off, pop indoors to tell Joan what had happened, and then drive off to the hospital. After a little wait, my wrists were X-rayed and I was told I had broken the left one. Before long it had been plastered from finger-tips to elbow and I was allowed to leave. How I drove home with only my finger-tips I don't know for my right wrist was still practically useless.

In fact, I told them this when they plastered the left wrist but they simply said it would wear off, it wasn't broken.

By the time I had confirmed with the nick that I was now off sick I was pretty late getting home. I don't remember Joan's reaction, but I don't think she was particularly surprised. It was only in getting off to bed that I discovered just how difficult it is getting undressed with one hand.

We had not been in bed long before the pain in my right wrist started to worsen, so much so that I went into the other bed in order not to keep Joan awake. Within the hour though, I suppose it must have been about one a.m., I was rolling about in so much pain that Joan got up, walked down the road to the 'phone box and telephoned the hospital.

"Well, send him down," they said, "and we'll have a look at him!"

Now Joan, deprived of her sleep, concerned about me, and in no mood to suffer fools gladly, replied that as she could not drive, and I was in no state to do so, how could I be expected to 'get down there'? The only thing they could suggest was dosing me with aspirin.

A couple of hours later I was still no better, in fact the pain was worsening all the time. Once more, Joan got out of bed and telephoned the hospital. They were no more helpful than before, saying that at that time of night there was no radiologist on duty and that I had better come back in the morning. In the meantime, if she could organise transport they would prescribe morphine tablets or something similar. Somewhat in despair, Joan walked the few yards from the telephone box to Plough Corner nick, where in those days was a direct line telephone recessed in the wall for any member of the public who wanted a policeman quickly. The phone connected the caller to Romford nick as soon as the receiver was lifted (I was going to suggest there should be more such facilities available nowadays, but I suppose they would only be vandalised).

Anyway, Joan used this phone and told Romford the story. In a matter of minutes, the area car was on its way to the hospital where it picked up the tablets and delivered them to us. That was service for you.

The following morning, Joan again telephoned the hospital and explained that I had to get down there, that I could not drive and neither could she. Would they send an ambulance pretty damned quick? They did. Arriving there, a nurse examined my wrist and had another look at the X-rays. She then called another nurse, whom I took to be the sister, and pointed to something on the X-ray. The sister almost exploded and went stomping off – presumably to see somebody, for it later transpired that whoever had examined my X-rays in the first place had completely missed the fact that my right wrist was broken too! How they had missed it I don't know but the sister was having a field day with the staff. A few minutes later, the sister returned and examined the plaster on my left arm.

Turning my hand over, palm uppermost, she stared long and hard at a large plaster patch in the centre of my hand.

With a ferocious look, she suddenly took hold of the patch and ripped it off with a hugely theatrical gesture before bearing it away, held high in the air like a trophy. I just knew that her next victim was to be the plasterer.

Once again I was taken to the plaster room where, as I sat on a hard chair with both arms now on a table-top, I dreamed of that black nurse leaning over me with a measure of brandy, but it was not to be. Instead, I was being clinically treated – or perhaps mistreated, whichever way you look at it.

As I left that place for the second time in twenty-four hours, albeit with both arms now firmly encased, the thought occurred to me that it was going to be even more difficult getting un-dressed now. And how, I wondered, was I to use the loo?

Chapter Five

It goes without saying that not everything we did resulted in laughter. We all experienced in full measure every facet of this multifaceted life, the pain shared with road accident victims, particularly children, the domestic situations we were called in to deal with, the grief of sudden deaths and suicides, the families who seemed doomed in life always to lurch from one catastrophe to another. One of the worst jobs, so far as I was concerned, was having to call on unsuspecting wives or mothers to break the news that their husband or child was dead. It cannot, of course, be done without pain and we were always told to knock up the neighbours first, tell them the job we had to do and ask them to come round in five minutes to make a cup of tea or to lend a shoulder to cry on.

But with all this there were the many occasions when we were able to help people, sometimes going considerably out of our way to do so, and a phone call the following day or a letter of thanks made everything worthwhile. This gesture of courtesy rather back-fired on us one night though when Bert Howard and I had met up on our walk back to the nick for the midnight cup of tea. As we passed a block of flats which were immediately opposite the nick we came upon the figure of a man lying '*vino collapso*' on the pavement. He was an obvious City gent, pin-stripe suit, collar and tie etc. and although conscious he was obviously too far gone to make it the last few yards home to his flat where, he told us, he lived alone. Without another thought in our heads Bert and I helped him to his feet and up the stairs to his flat where we took off his shoes, loosened his tie and put him to bed. He smiled his thanks and waved his hand weakly as we left. A couple of days later, he wrote a charming letter of thanks. Jim Barningham called us in and told us to 'read and note'. Rather pleased with the thought that we had made another convert we were not prepared for the roasting that followed.

"Right," said Jim, "now just consider for a moment. If you had arrested him for being drunk and incapable, he would have been placed safely in a cell and regular checks kept on him all night. He would then have been released in the morning to face a couple of pounds' fine. Think of the consequences of what you did. How were you to know that he would not be sick during the night, as many drunks are, and then choke to death on his own vomit, as many drunks do? Who would be to blame? Would you want that on your conscience?"

From being rather miffed at first with the ticking off, the more we thought about it the more we realised the wisdom of Jim's words, and the fact that the law is not always an ass – it just has to be understood.

I was going to include in the list of negative categories the subject of boredom, but although I sometimes found the job tedious, I never really found it boring. Boredom, I found, was always an attitude of mind and so long as you kept your eyes and ears open the most tedious job often took on a new interest. One particular instance springs to mind. Harold Hill had been plagued for some time with burglaries, all the work of one man for the MO was the same in every case.

When everything else had failed, the powers-that-be decided the only way to catch the villain was to flood the area with policemen every night until he was caught. Not only did it promise to be a long job but an uncomfortable one too for it was mid-winter with freezing nights. Not only this but our instructions were somewhat bizarre too, brought about by the fact that the burglar never broke into the fronts or sides of houses, always the back doors or windows. On that estate practically all the houses backed onto one another which helped us considerably as it turned out, for our orders were to quietly (after midnight) make our way down the side of the allotted house and stand silently in the shadows of the back garden where we could maintain an uninterrupted view not only of those houses but the ones opposite too. If we saw matey-boy, we had discretion as to whether we tackled him ourself or whistled up (literally) the officer stationed a block or so away. Sounded all very well in theory.

The first night brought that theory crashing ignominiously about our ears, for we should have known that news of these burglaries had spread across the entire estate and householders had taken it upon themselves to make it as difficult as possible to gain entry into their back gardens. Those of us who simply found the gates locked climbed over them as best we could. Others though were far less fortunate. One officer opened a booby-trapped gate and got a bucket of freezing water upended on him. Another pushed over a pedal cycle which had been left balanced delicately against the gate, waking up the entire household in the process, another found a dustbin and other junk similarly balanced. Yet another was set upon by a dog and had to run for his life. Another, who had successfully navigated his way without incident failed to notice a small garden pond until he fell into it. The stories of mis-adventure were legion but eventually we all settled down to some very uncomfortable nights standing in back porchways staring at puddles and watching them freeze. That job was exceedingly tedious, armed though we were with flasks of coffee or hot soup, and with nothing but our thoughts (mostly of a warm bed) to keep us company. If we as much as closed our eyes at three thirty in the morning, then we did so sure in the knowledge of what would happen if the burglar hit one of the houses we were watching.

Fortunately, it all paid off in the end for one of the watching officers actually stood there in his garden and saw the gate open, the figure move silently in and start work on a kitchen window. The burglar, who was in his early twenties, nearly died of shock when the officer stepped out of the shadows and felt his collar. He had no option but to give himself up and go without so much as a whimper. Neither did it take him very long to admit a total of 128 burglaries. That was a good arrest!

Doreen Smy! Now, there's a name I shall never forget. She was a true Eastender, as Cockney as they come. In her middle or late twenties, she was slim, dark-haired, reasonably good-looking and a decent mother to her three or four kids. She had been in trouble herself for thieving and prostitution but had called it a day. Her husband Peter though was still active and always going away for short stretches.

She lived in Keats Avenue, just up the road from the nick, and the first time I met her was when I was called by the local post office who were alleging that Doreen had forged an entry in a family allowance book. I called on her and she was as good as gold about it. I took a statement under caution which was her full confession.

Eventually, I got her to court by the simple expedient of driving her there myself in my little old Ford Prefect. Not only did I give evidence against her but I button-holed the prosecutor beforehand to ensure that he gave the court both sides of her story

– Peter was still in prison, she had four young kids on social security, was struggling to pay the rent etc. I don't know why but I simply felt sorry for her. The upshot was that despite her record she escaped with a fine of £10.

That, I thought, was the end of the matter. Not a bit of it! A few weeks later as I came on duty for late turn (two p.m.) I found a message that Doreen wanted to speak to 'Johnny'. She would speak to no one else, she said. Half an hour later, I was knocking on her door. She invited me in and sat down on a settee patting the cushion beside her. No chance, I took an armchair. "Well, what's up then, Doreen?" I said. She smiled.

"You know Peter's back, do you?" she said.

"Yes," I said. I knew he had been released a couple of weeks before.

"Well, I can't be long about it," she said, "but do you happen to have had any garages done lately?"

Taken by surprise at this, I had to admit that a garage had been done only a night or two back when a number of tyres had been stolen.

"That's what I thought, darlin'," she said, "don't look now for gawd's sake but they're up in me loft. Don't come yourself but send some-one else round, all right?"

Twenty-four hours later, Peter was back in custody wondering what had hit him. Needless to say, my DE at the nick was delighted and wanted to know how I had done it. There were one or two extremely rude suggestions from my mates.

A little while later, after Peter had been safely tucked away, I called on Doreen and asked why she had shopped her husband like that.

"Well, darlin'," she replied, "you can see how many kids I got and I don't want no more. Peter's a good enough bloke but he's got one failing... I have to have a rest from him every now and again."

I left the house convinced she was having me on, or that she had a boyfriend and did not want Peter around to spoil things.

Sometime later, I was out on my beat when the phone rang at my point. The sergeant told me that Doreen had been in again and would not say what it was about. My first question was, "Has Peter been released?" Yes, he was out again. A few minutes later, I was knocking on her door.

"What's up, Doreen?" I asked.

"Have you had a club or something like that done recently?" she asked.

"Yes," I said. "Gidea Park Cricket Club was done a couple of nights ago." This obviously came as no surprise to her.

"Send someone 'round, there's bags of cigarettes up in the loft again!"

One of the last dealings I had with Doreen found her on the receiving end for a change. The gasman had gone 'round to empty her metre and found the padlock missing and the cash-box empty.

"A job for you, John," my skipper said.

I went up to Keats Avenue and got no reply so stuck a note through her letterbox to come and see me.

Within an hour, she was at the nick confessing the dastardly deed. The DE at the time was Derek Wyatt (who, when I last heard of him years later, had risen to DCI).

I told him Doreen wanted to tell us all about it. "Do you want to make a statement under caution, Doreen?" he asked.

Yes, she didn't mind.

I shall never forget that statement, bound as it was under strict rules of evidence to make it admissible. Doreen was no great shakes at recounting a story (not one that would stand up in court anyway) and we made one or two botched starts.

Finally, Derek gave up and got me to write the statement at his dictation while Doreen nodded her head from time to time in agreement – totally illegal but she was quite happy with the arrangement! She went to court, of course, and despite the strictures made by the chairman of the bench on her previous appearance, namely that this was her last chance and with her record if she reoffended, she would certainly go to prison, she got away with yet another fine! I often wonder what happened to her, and swear that to this day I have no idea why she chose me for her confidant.

Something on a lighter vein. One bright, sunny afternoon, I was cycling along the Southend Arterial Road towards Rise Park, just north of Romford, when I glanced over and saw a group of people sitting around what looked like a campfire in the middle of a field. My immediate thought was that they were gypsies, with whom we were constantly plagued, but on closer examination I realised they were nothing of the kind.

I walked my bike through the gate and tramped across to where they sat. Two Dormobiles were parked nearby and around the campfire were about a dozen men, women and children, all decidedly Mediterranean in appearance. I then saw, hardly believing my eyes, one of the men slowly turning a spit over the fire, and there on the spit sizzling away and smelling quite delicious was a whole lamb! Scattered around on the grass were a dozen or so containers piled high with salads, bread and other strange and anonymous Middle-Eastern goodies.

The adults turned and watched my approach. For my part, I was expecting the usual reaction, the apprehensive glance or the muttering under the breath one always encountered among gipsies. I was quite unprepared for the reception I received though, for as the full majesty of the law descended upon them they stood up and greeted me with waves and smiles! Then, shuffling 'round they made it plain I was to join them at the fireside.

More than a little nonplussed I did the hackneyed, "What's going on 'ere then," to discover that they were a Turkish Cypriot family from North London on a day's outing. The time had come for lunch and this, they thought, looked like a particularly fine spot.

"But do you have permission to be on the farmer's land lighting fires?" They looked puzzled.

"But we do no harm, eh? When we go, we clear everything up and cover the fire, no problem." They smiled again disarmingly. "Come, sit down, eat with us, it is good," they said.

I happened to know that the owner of that field was not a farmer at all but someone who lived in London and only came down occasionally.

"Well, as a matter of fact," I ventured, "I spent some time in Cyprus with the army. I was very fond of the Turks." That did it. One of the men stood up clasping a huge carving knife. *Oh my God,* I thought, *I understood they were Turkish. Are they Greek?*

Stepping towards the fire though he leaned over and carved off a huge slice of hot, dripping, unbelievably aromatic lamb. Putting it on a plate with a flourish, he then piled it high with salad and olives, and then on another plate a goodly portion of what was for me a nostalgic memory – goat's cheese. Someone passed me a hunk of crusty bread and a glass of sharp red wine, then beckoned me to sit with them. What could I do? Being British I did the only sensible thing, I sat down cross-legged on the grass and enjoyed it!

At the end of the meal, one of them passed me what looked like a thin stick of celery. He too was biting chunks off a piece he was holding. "Good for cleansing the palate," he said. "Go on, try it." It really tasted quite good, a little bit on the sweet side and yet with a tinge of bitterness too.

"This is good," I declared. "What is it?"

He smiled and put his fore finger to the side of his nose. Getting up he walked over to a huge clump of thistles, chose a thick stem, cut it, peeled it and presented it to me. I stared at him.

"I have been eating thistles?" He nodded vigorously.

"Good, no?" I had to admit it was! These people, like those I had met in their native land, really were hospitable folk.

Talking of the A127 reminds me of an incident which taught me a salutary lesson in countryside law. Along this very stretch of road I was once again cycling my beat when I looked across and saw in the middle of a field very similar to that in which I had been so royally entertained, the figure of a man bending over with a spade. Beside him on the ground was an old sack.

I approached and asked him what he was doing. He was fairly elderly, probably in his sixties, and spoke broad Essex.

"Digging for horse-radish, boy," he said. I looked in his sack and found it about a quarter full.

"Do you own this field?" I asked. It was not such a stupid question as it sounds for although he looked as if he didn't have two ha'pennies to rub together, there was always the possibility that he might. In the event, however, he shook his head.

"No, 'course I don't," he said.

I continued, "Do you have permission to dig here then?" He looked at me as if I was from another planet.

"What 'arm is there in digging for a spot of horse-radish?" he asked.

My days of intensive learning at Eynsham now came to the fore. "You're under arrest," I said. "Larceny of growing crops." Taking his elbow (and sack) I walked him with hardly a protest back to the nick.

Jim Barningham was on duty when I wheeled in the dangerous felon.

"What's all this then, John?" he said, looking the old boy up and down with obvious sympathy for he was a staunch chapel man. It occurred to me that I might just blind this wise old sergeant (well, he was at the time considerably older than me!) with some obscure law.

"Larceny of growing crops, Sarge," I said, and explained what I had seen. He looked at me with a jaundiced eye.

"Come into my office," he said. There he turned to me. "Right, now let's be precise, was it a field full of cultivated horseradish, or was it growing wild?"

I had to confess that I couldn't see any sign of cultivation but the horseradish was there nevertheless, the old boy knew where to look for it.

"Well, I'll tell you where to look," he said. "Moriarty first and then Stones (legal text-books). And while you are at it, I'll go and tell him to sling his hook." With that he walked out to where the old boy was patiently waiting and told him that out of the goodness of his heart he had decided not to proceed with the charge. He then handed him the sack and told him he could go!

"Larceny of growing crops means just what it says," he told me, "crops under cultivation. What you found him with was growing wild. Now," he emphasized, "if someone else had dug them up, they would pass into their possession, but not legal ownership. If they then left a sackful in the field and someone came along and took that sack, then it would be theft!"

"Quirky old law, ain't it." I decided I still had much to learn.

The mention of Bob's all-night cafe a few pages back reminds me of an incident which occurred there in the early hours of one morning. I was strolling past checking the nearby factories when I saw about thirty motorbikes outside, which was rather unusual because it was a pretty sleazy transport cafe mostly frequented by lorry drivers. I then heard a right hullabaloo going on inside. Looking through the window I saw about fifty leather-jacketed youngsters apparently making free with everything inside. I walked in and looked around. After the initial silence which greeted my arrival there came a hubbub of conversation as I made my way to the counter where I expected to find the night manager. There was no sign of him.

I leaned over the counter. There he was lying on the floor in a sound sleep with an empty gin bottle still clutched in his hand! I quickly discovered that the bikers had arrived en masse and finding no one there to serve them had simply helped themselves.

I started off firmly enough, telling them all to sling their hooks but the result was embarrassingly dismal. They simply sat with silly grins on their faces daring me to take them on. In the short silence that followed, a silence broken only by the snoring of the comatose manager, a battle of wills developed which I knew I could not afford to lose. I repeated the order and warned them of the consequences if they chose to disobey. They chose to disobey. "Right," I said, and walked over to the telephone on the opposite wall. No sooner had I turned my back than a hail of pork pies and pastries flew through the air. I spun 'round and the barrage ceased. It was then that I realised that of the total missiles aimed only two or three had actually hit me. At that range none should have missed. It was obvious that my uniform still generated a basic element of fear or respect in their bragging little souls and that it was now only bravado which kept their leather-covered backsides glued to their chairs.

Picking up the phone, I dialled 999 and briefly explained the situation. Nowadays, such a call would be made by a single button press on the personal radio to automatically transmit that an officer requires immediate assistance, this will send every car and man racing to the scene. The result was no different then and within minutes two area cars and the inspector's Hillman Minx screeched to a halt outside.

The inspector opened the door and looked inside – the place was a shambles. "Righto, lads, let's get 'em out," was all that was needed for the half a dozen of us to get in there. Heavily outnumbered though we were, the odds were evened when we found that only a handful were willing to do serious battle and before long even they were being thrown bodily out of the door. Just to add a little insult to their injury, there was outside the cafe door a very large and very dirty puddle gracing the unmade surface of the car-park. Most had to pick themselves up out of that before making off.

Some of us, of course, sported the usual bumps and bruises but so too did they – and with honours even and not a single arrest made, it showed that not everything we dealt with had to end up in court.

There was another memorable occasion in Gidea Park one night as I cycled slowly along one of the more elegant avenues of that Romford suburb. We always switched off our lights at that time of the morning in order to blend into the darkness, flicking them on again only if a car came into view. That way we generally had the advantage of a few precious seconds if the unexpected should crop up.

On this particular night, I noticed a large American Buick

standing at the kerb outside a particularly fine house. It was facing me on the other side of the road and inside were two shadowy figures. I swung across the road approaching it head-on (a fatal error I never repeated) and switched on my lights, at the same time taking out my torch and shining it directly at the driver and his mate. They visibly jumped and a moment later the engine roared into life. The car shot straight forward and with me firmly fixed in the centre of its sights I had little alternative but to bail out. Swerving hard to my right, I jumped off my bike but still managed to shine my torch at the car as it sped away. They had obviously been up to no good but at least I now had an index number to go on and there could not be that many Buicks in Essex.

I cycled back to the nick and telephoned headquarters for the registered owner. We were then years away from PNC (Police National Computer) and if a registered owner was required at night, you had to satisfy the Information Room Inspector that the matter was urgent enough for him to contact Chelmsford to get a PC to go 'round to County Hall, open up the records office, find the right file and telephone the result back. Of course, on this occasion the incident was not considered urgent enough that it couldn't wait until morning. I left a message with early turn to sort things out for me.

A couple of days later, I got a call to go that evening to Barking Police Station as the Mets had arrested the driver but did not know what charge to hold him on! I turned up in due course and was ushered into the CID office where a DE told me that in response to our message he had nicked the driver.

He was now sitting in the next room, very truculent and saying nothing. I explained my interest in him. "Oh! well, that gives us something to work on then," he said, and disappeared into the next room. A few minutes later, he returned and beckoned me in. There at a solitary table sat a character in his early twenties.

The DE turned to me and winked. "Is this the bloke you saw in the car the other night?"

I had no idea, I hadn't seen him for more than a second or two. Nevertheless, "Yes, that's him all right," I said confidently, and the look on the suspect's face confirmed it for me.

The DE went on, "Well, he's the owner of the Buick and we say he was the driver. Now you've confirmed it. Until now though he's been saying nothing, but I've had a word in his ear and told him there's a possibility of a deal being worked, but it's got to have your agreement." I nodded. "If you agree not to press the charge of attempted murder of a police officer, then he'll agree to being a little more co-operative about what he was doing in your neck of the woods."

Now, I was stunned. I had never regarded the incident as anything more than a villain trying to avoid a few awkward questions, but looking at it through his eyes the way he had driven that night certainly had its possibilities. With a great show of reluctance and a few words about having to square it with my guv'nor, I finally agreed.

As it happened, the outcome was a total anti-climax. He was an active burglar with plenty of form. He was also out looking at a few houses that night although he was not daft enough to admit it in as many words, and proving 'loitering with intent' would be nigh on impossible. This being the real world and not television fantasy with Perry Mason or Colombo providing a crescendo of brilliant detection, I had to content myself with nothing more than a few road traffic offences. However, I left Barking that night sure in the knowledge that I had prevented some heavy burglaries.

One incident I particularly remember occurred while I was still a probationer and served as a salutary reminder that we were not infallible; in fact, the affair was an almighty 'cock up!'

Palmer & Harvey, a Romford-based tobacco wholesaler, reported their suspicions when they received a huge order for cigarettes running into several thousands of pounds, particularly as the customer instructed that the order should be delivered to a private house in Rush Green. The police quickly established that the client was a very well-known Romford criminal.

Since he had only just come out of prison, it was obvious that he did not have the wherewithal to pay for the delivery and plans were made for Detective Constable Bob Quinnel (stationed with me at Plough Corner) to pose as an employee of the company when the delivery was made. The villain's house was to be quietly and discreetly surrounded and as the cartons were delivered the DE was to make a signal by removing his cap and replacing it for us to move in. So far, so good.

On the day in question, I happened to be observer in the Romford area car with instructions that as this was a CID job we were to remain in reserve for use only in an emergency. The lorry load of cigarettes duly arrived and the crew began carrying them down the front garden path and through the front door of the house. As the minutes ticked by, the impatient observers waited for the signal from the undercover police officer.

After what seemed an age, and only as the last case went in did he signal, and suddenly it was all systems go as police swept in from all directions – except it seemed from the back of the house which was exactly where the goods and the villains had disappeared! It was a childishly classic case of in through the front door and out of the back. Someone had blundered!

For the next ten or fifteen minutes, the air was blue with radio traffic. The area car in which I was observer was called to search a particular sector for the suspect van while others, both CID and uniformed, spread out in ever-widening circles in a desperate search for the fugitives.

At this point a tiny thing sticks in my memory. It was raining at the time and while my driver threw the car around the streets I sat with ears glued to the radio and eyes everywhere. Suddenly, there was a crack as the offside windscreen wiper- blade flew off and disappeared over the roof of the car. My driver, his mind totally absorbed in what he was doing, took not the slightest notice. As the minutes ticked by the wiper arm continued to sweep across the screen, at first producing only a minutely scratched arc in the glass but then as we swept from one sector to another I stared fascinated as the arm gouged deeper and deeper into the glass. As I watched all the activity going on around me, I reconciled myself to the fact that the price of a new windscreen would be of little consequence to the overall cost of this operation if it failed.

Despite all our endeavours the villains got clean away and we were finally recalled to base for de-briefing. There the recriminations began and already the guv'nor, a detective inspector, was distancing himself from responsibility for the fiasco by claiming that his orders had not been carried out. Whether there was any truth in this or not I don't know as I had not been in on the original briefing, but whatever impressions of him were left in the minds of the men after de-briefing were magnified many months later when Palmer & Harvey sued the Essex Police in the High Court for the loss of that consignment.

It appeared to be of little consequence that the villains had by then been arrested and imprisoned for the theft, for Palmer &

Harvey were still massively out of pocket. We who were not called to give evidence followed the case as closely as we were able and it became apparent to us that the weight of blame was filtering slowly and inexorably down through the ranks onto the shoulders of the unfortunate DE Quinnell.

At the end of the day, judgement was of course, awarded against the police but was worded in such a way that the DE was made to believe that he personally would have to bear the full burden of costs and compensation. Nobody, it seemed, bothered to explain to him that in law he was the 'servant acting on his master's instructions' (the chief constable). I well remember his walking into the Plough Corner nick looking totally shattered.

A deep depression remained with him for some weeks, despite the fact that we all rallied 'round to persuade him he had nothing to worry about, but no amount of persuasion could convince him that the county would pick up the tab. Then late one morning while I was on office duty the sergeant asked me whether I had seen DE Quinnell. I replied that I had not seen him since the previous day. We contacted his wife but all she could say was that he had gone out the previous evening and had not returned. She assumed he was tied up on something important with the job but was now beginning to get worried about him. When we told her we had no idea where he was, she began to panic.

This phone call signalled the start of a concentrated search for the missing detective and eventually, after another day or so, a confidential circulation was made to all forces that he was missing. Three days later came a telephone call from the Sussex Police to the effect that they had come across a man wandering around in a dazed state who claimed to be a police officer and who indeed carried a warrant card to that effect. Within a couple of hours, a car had picked up Bob and brought him home. He had, of course, suffered a nervous breakdown. Only now did the county seem to appreciate what he had been through and he was given extended sick leave. He recovered in due course and was eventually posted well away from the area which held too many memories for him.

We had some good guv'nors and one or two poor ones. One of the decent ones was John Dighton, then a Romford Inspector but later to become ch/superintendent at Clacton. I knew little about him personally except that he served, so I was told, in the Marines during the war. Certainly, his chest bore two rows of medal ribbons so he must have seen some extensive action. I found him to be a very quiet man, reserved, almost shy. He rarely gave more than a brief, wintry smile to show there was any warmth about him and appeared to have little sense of humour. These though were mere surface impressions which belied a much tougher character beneath.

I remember a few anecdotes about him. One particular night, he met a Collier Row PC at his point and during conversation learned that the officer had the job of serving a summons that evening on a notoriously unstable character who lived with his family in a caravan. John Dighton told the PC that he would drive him to the caravan and wait outside – just in case. The inevitable happened, the PC was invited in but within minutes an almighty argument developed during which the caravan-dweller set about the unfortunate officer. All the PC could remember was lying on his back with the man getting the better of him.

There then came an almighty crack, the man's eyes glazed and he fell semi-conscious onto the officer. Standing over them was Dighton with a heavy torch in his hand. He had hit the man so hard that the torch now resembled a banana.

"Well, that's ruined that," he said ruefully. "Let's get him down to the nick," and with that they bundled the man into the car and took him off.

Another occasion involving John Dighton occurred while I was waiting to give evidence at Romford magistrates court, which then formed part of the police station in South Street. Sitting with me in the foyer was DE Fred Stannard of Harold Hill (later to become det/ch/inspector).

The normally peaceful atmosphere of that foyer was disturbed by a group of Harold Hill teenagers making complete nuisances of themselves, shouting, skylarking about and upsetting other members of the public who were already apprehensive enough about their own forthcoming ordeals. Finally, being in uniform, I got up and had words with them. They quietened down for a few moments but the ringleader, who was about nineteen, started up again. I warned him once more, this time telling him that he would be arrested for breach of the peace if he continued. An obvious braggart, he could not afford to lose face so decided to call my bluff. A minute or two later, Fred and I were walking him up the side of the building to the police station.

Even on this short walk, Fred had to tell him to keep his mouth shut or he would get a thick ear. We marched him into the charge room and a few moments later John Dighton entered. As I tried to outline the charge, I was constantly interrupted by the arrogant kid, so much so that the inspector too had to tell him to keep quiet and listen. He then started to shout that he had been threatened with a thumping, and turning to Fred he sneered, "You're not so brave now with your guv'nor standing there, are you?"

Now, fortunately, I had at that moment gone into the

adjoining office for something but heard everything that was going on. According to Fred, who told me about it afterwards, as soon as the prisoner made this challenge about a thumping, John Dighton glanced at Fred and then quite deliberately turned his back on them. Fred walloped the youth, not with his fist but the flat of his hand.

"You saw that! You saw that!" screamed the offended youth.

Dighton turned 'round and calmly said, "Saw what? I saw nothing, what happened…?"

Another personal encounter with John Dighton came when one of the PCs at Plough Corner retired and threw a party at his home. We were all invited but as luck would have it our shift was on nights which meant that we would have to leave at nine o'clock to get changed for duty at ten. The late turn lads kindly offered to stay on until ten-thirty, without overtime of course, so that we could at least enjoy some of the evening. This unusual arrangement had been sanctioned by Romford.

We duly turned up and began to enjoy ourselves, one of the attractions being an enormous punch bowl prepared by our host. Now bearing in mind that we did not then drink anything like as much or as often as we seem to nowadays, suffice it to say that we found the punch particularly tasty, and by the time it came for us to depart for duty we were all more than three sheets to the wind.

Getting to the nick at ten thirty, we thanked the late turn lads and got out on our beats. My first point was at eleven o'clock in Gidea Park. For my part, I found great difficulty in performing the simple task of cycling in a straight line but reassured myself that if left to my own devices and no major catastrophe occurred during the first hour or so, I would be all right.

Now it was not often that Romford inspectors troubled us

with visits at night, especially when they knew our sergeants were on with us, but it was not unknown. I cycled as steadily as I could through Gidea Park and arriving at the point in Upper Brentwood Road I propped my bike against the phone box to settle back and wait the regulation ten minutes.

Only a few minutes had gone by when I turned at the sound of a car drawing up. A black Hillman Minx. It had to be, didn't it? Out climbed Inspector Dighton. I saluted and gave him the usual, "All right, sir". He returned the salute.

"How was the party then?" he asked.

I told him that everything had gone well, that we had all enjoyed ourselves and were grateful to Romford for allowing us the extra half-hour. I thought I was being pretty successful too in keeping my words from slurring.

We chatted amiably for two or three minutes more before he finally declared, "Right, put me one in here then please." This was police jargon for me to record his visit in my pocket book and for him to sign the entry as proof of his visit. I got out my pocket book and began to write but the more I tried the more I seemed to sway. My pencil too chose that particular moment to misbehave, steadfastly refusing as pencils do, to write in a straight line. I glanced at the inspector, for I wasn't that far gone that I didn't know what was happening! There was a moment or two of silence before he suddenly pulled his car keys out of his pocket.

He gave a little wave of his hand and said, "Don't bother now, I must be off. I'll sign you up sometime during the week. Have a quiet night!" With that, he strolled back to his car, gave me another wave and drove off! Now there was a gentleman.

Chapter Six

It was in March 1963 that Joan and I discussed the question of moving out into the country on detached beat. We were both 'country people' at heart and I felt that after four years in Romford it would not only be a rewarding and satisfying experience to work a country beat but the children would also benefit from a different environment – not, I hasten to add, that they were in any way affected by Romford or Harold Hill, they were still too young for that, but we simply felt that a few years in the country would do us all good.

In those days, detached beats were as scarce as hen's teeth and if you wanted one it was a question of putting your name down and waiting for pot luck. How things have changed over the years, for nowadays rural beats are advertised ad nauseum and officers have almost to be bribed to go out onto them!

Why, I don't really know, for we found our four years on detachment an absolute delight and the children (now adults) still regard our old beat near Ongar with deep affection, almost as 'home'.

Some months had passed after my report went in when I read on standing orders that the detached officer at Moreton, PC Alf Bonnage, was retiring. Moreton? Where's Moreton? I had to look on the map at the nick to find this tiny village just three miles from Ongar. I told Joan that it would shortly become vacant and did she feel like running out there to have a look.

A day or so later we motored out, reached the Shelley

cross-roads at Ongar, turned left at the Red Cow pub and drove out into lush, green countryside. A couple of miles later, we slowly descended a hill to see the village before us. Over a steep hump-back bridge we went and into the village itself. We turned left at the White Hart and ran out into countryside almost immediately. Returning to the same junction we turned right at the Nags Head and again ran out into countryside.

That was Moreton? Wondering what a bobby would do there to keep himself busy, I took heart from the fact that he also covered five or six other smaller villages around. We fell in love not only with the village but the countryside which surrounded it. The police house too was modern with an integral garage and purpose-built office – unlike some which still existed where the front room also served as an office.

An added attraction to what we had already seen were the marvellous views to be had across the countryside from both the front and rear of the house. We thought back to Romford and Harold Hill and decided there was no contest.

The very next day, I sent another report winging to headquarters stating that I was aware of PC Bonnage's retirement and could I please be considered for the Moreton beat. Weeks went by, in fact so far as I can recall, it was October before I received the news that we were moving to Moreton within the month.

The November day we moved in to our new house and surroundings could not have been worse. There was half a gale blowing and rain slanting down across the village. I remember the removal men trying to carry a wardrobe up the garden path and being blown sideways across the front lawn. We managed somehow to complete the operation only to find that while we had electricity, it controlled only the lighting and cooker (there was no gas), and the heating came courtesy of open fires in every room and a solid fuel boiler in the kitchen. We had not thought to order fuel either for the boiler or the fires.

To the rescue came the Mackmans, Alec and Rip, whom we had first met at Harold Hill. They had come out onto detached beat a short while before and were comfortably established on the adjoining beat at High Ongar. Within minutes though, they arrived with a life-saving sack of coal in the boot of their car!

I was given the regulation three days to move in, that is one day for the outward move, one day to move in and one day to sort things out. After that it was business as usual. My sergeant was to be George Cant of Ongar who came out and visited us when we arrived. He was a nice enough bloke, I believe another ex-Marine, only a few years short of retirement. He lived at Fyfield. During furniture removal and straightening up, he ran through the various things I would need to know about the office, the beat, my duties, and the sub-division (Ongar).

On the office wall was a framed map of Moreton beat which I studied in some detail. It covered a very sizeable area from Ongar in the south to Potter Street (Harlow) in the north, from North Weald in the west, and Fyfield in the east. In addition to Moreton itself, the beat covered the Lavers which comprised Little Laver, High Laver and Magdalen Laver, Bobbingworth and Matching Green. With the exception of Matching Green, which was certainly larger than Moreton, the others were really no more than scattered communities set in lush, green, rolling countryside. All were connected by narrow, twisting roads which really were nothing more than lanes, for few of them would allow two cars to pass without careful manoeuvring. Dotted all about were farms, scattered centuries-old cottages and fine country houses.

My duties consisted of five hours' discretionary duty a day followed by three hours' set patrol in the evening. This sounded, on the face of it, a doddle compared with the eight hours of set duty I was used to. It was not all quite what it was cracked up to be though. In the first place I was on duty, or rather on call, twenty-four hours a day, and I could not leave my beat without first informing Ongar. If I had to work over the eight hours I was compensated by time off – no paid overtime then. Of those five hours, I was expected to man the office for a set period and then go out and attend to my beat. The remaining three hours' cycle patrol was on a fixed system which comprised eight p.m. to 11 p.m. one day, nine p.m. to twelve a.m. the next, ten p.m. to one a.m. the following day, and five a.m. to eight a.m. the day after. Twice in every eight days there were MC discretionaries, which meant I could please myself with what I worked – provided that I saw the pubs out and the village quiet, which of course put paid to any thought of an early night. These set evening patrols had already been worked out and were in printed form, called a list, so that anyone at Ongar or Harlow (our Div. HQ) could tell at a glance what a particular officer was working that day and the point at which he could be found.

The patrols and the points I had to attend were specifically designed to ensure that the officer covered his entire beat. Thrown in for good measure were the conference points which were always sited where two beats met. These were designed to ensure that officers from those beats met at a specified time to 'exchange intelligence'. In practice, it turned out to be a convivial chat with a lot of laughter. My conference points were at Matching Green where I met the Matching Tye officer, Bobbingworth where I met the North Weald officer, and Shelley Post Office where I met my old mate Alec Mackman, the officer for High Ongar. There, Mack and I would chat and crack jokes to such a degree that the sub-postmaster eventually complained to Ongar that we were keeping him awake at night! Opposite the post office was the Shelley fish-shop. That meeting was the last night point for both of us and once the regulation wait of ten minutes was up we would walk over, buy fish and chips, stuff them in our saddle-bags and race off home before it got cold. Mack's was always warmer because he had just over a mile to travel against my two and a half!

But here I am running away with myself.

Ongar Police Station, sub-divisional station under Harlow. I served in the Ongar Sub-Div from 1963-67. Built 1855. Demolished 1965. Present Station built on same site 1966.

Ongar Police Station. Stands on the site of the original 1855 station. Its style is typical of the uninspiring architecture which spread like a rash across the county during the 1960s, just a smaller version of Harold Hill and many more.

Ongar: a view of the High Street. Still a pleasant country town with far too many modern building around it now – but where is there not?

During his visit, George Cant pointed out that my first working day would include a five a.m. to eight a.m. patrol, which meant of course that I would work only five hours that day and then a five a.m. to eight a.m. patrol the following morning, this early patrol being part of the previous day's duty. Thus, on the one day I would work only five hours followed by eleven hours the next. Queer system, but we got used to it.

I hardly slept a wink that night, so concerned was I at getting up at four-thirty to be out at five. I was convinced too that George would make a point of coming out himself to meet me just to see how reliable I was. With this in mind, I had decided to reconnoitre the route to my three points in daylight, the first being at five thirty a.m. at Bobbingworth, the second at six thirty a.m. at Shelley post office, and the third at seven thirty a.m. back at Moreton.

I rose uncomfortably and still half asleep to a pitch black, silent as the grave, freezing morning. I looked out of the window into a void broken only by hedgerows and trees laden down with a hoar frost the like of which I had never seen before. Getting dressed, I moved about carefully so as not to disturb Joan or the children, and at precisely five a.m. let myself out of the house. The roads were totally silent and deserted, the front light on my bike making little impression in the inky blackness stretching out ahead of me. I had forgotten how urban life had spoiled us with its street lighting.

Within minutes, I glanced down and saw that the front of my overcoat was white as my breath froze, and already my fingers were numb despite good quality leather gloves. I pressed on a mile, two miles, I should be getting near my point by now. The phone box, I knew, was right on the corner of this road as it joined the main Ongar to Epping road. Arriving there finally, I looked about for the phone box. Where was it? Damn it, it had gone! I looked up and down the deserted road, nothing. But it was there yesterday! I walked a hundred yards each way but still no sign of it. Finally, glancing at my watch I realised I had committed my first cardinal sin – missing a point, and the first one on my new beat too. God help me if the sergeant was standing there waiting!

I mounted my bike and slowly turned towards Ongar for my six thirty a.m. at Shelley knowing there was no chance of my missing that one, it was in a built-up area and surrounded by street lighting! Not only that but it was less than half a mile from Ongar nick and there was a distinct possibility of the sergeant being there waiting for me demanding to know what had happened at Bobbingworth.

Arriving safely, I strained my eyes for any sign of a visitor. Nothing. I parked up again and waited, relief growing with every minute as I realised that had he paid a fruitless visit to Bobbingworth there was no way he would have missed my second. After the usual ten-minute wait, I made my way back to Moreton where again I received no visit.

Instead of getting straight back home, I walked over to the village post office and with some trepidation asked the postmaster whether he might have heard anything about the GPO hi-jacking the Bobbingworth phone box overnight. I was not too surprised at the puzzled look on his face as he replied that he had heard nothing about it.

It was only an hour later when I got my car out and re-traced my route in daylight that I solved the mystery. Half a mile short of my destination my road bent sharply to the right while another even more minor road sneaked craftily off to the left to weave its way drunkenly down to join the Ongar Road half a mile further down. In the darkness, I had missed the bend and taken the wrong turning… but then you had already guessed that, hadn't you?

I felt duty-bound to pop into Moreton post office to reassure my friend, in case he had been worried that someone had stolen a valuable TK, that it was still safe and sound. It occurred to me as I left that he was quite probably also wondering what the village had done to deserve me.

Moreton: and that's all there is!

One of my first introductions to rural policing was cattle registers. What on earth were they? Well, once a quarter I had to call on all farmers, smallholders and even the old lady who kept a pig in her back garden, to examine and sign their cattle registers – a daily record (for the larger ones that is) of all purchases, sales and movement of livestock. New arrivals had also to be kept separate from the rest for twenty-eight days – always assuming, of course, that you knew the difference between one breed of pig and another in order to spot whether the right ones were indeed being segregated.

Moreton: the village policeman's house is on the right, c1900, long before architect-designed police houses were ever thought of. The village post office lies just beyond and was where I reported the theft of the Bobbingworth telephone kiosk: The post office is now, alas, a private house.

Moreton: The Nags Head, (became known as Moreton Massey but is currently The Nags Head).

My arrival to check this quarantine brought forth many a smile as I glanced knowingly at a sty full of Essex Saddle-backs when I should have been examining Yorkshire Whites!

Experience soon taught me the difference though. During my routine visits, all I had to do was check whether the record was up-to-date, confirm that no sales or purchases had been made during a 'prohibition' period, i.e. an outbreak of swine-fever or foot-and-mouth, and then sign the record. It occurred to me that a farmer would surely not make an entry in his register if he had bought or sold illegally, but the only way to check this was to call him a liar to his face and then go out and physically count every head of livestock he had.

This, in fact, never happened as every farmer I knew was as honest as the day – I think.

Our house at Moreton was detached and standing on the site of what had been a row of seventeenth-century cottages. Five still remained, the one next door to us was occupied by a Mr and Mrs Perry, and a row of four stood about fifty yards away on our other side. Obviously our house had been built on the site of a semi-detached pair of cottages, for alongside us was the rubble remains of one. It was not until much later when the site was well and truly covered in brambles, weeds and stinging nettles, and we were asking who to contact to clear them, that Mrs Perry calmly informed us that the land upon which the two cottages had stood had been bought by the police authority not only to build our house but another one too if the need should arise. The overgrown site was therefore our responsibility!

Joan and I discussed what to do with it and decided it would be a good idea to keep chickens on it. It would need fencing in, of course, and a decent chicken house. Now, it so happened that a short while later, I had had dealings with a villager for fraud as a result of which he was sent down for six months. He lived in a large bungalow at Pedlars End on the Bobbingworth approach to Moreton. What was he going to do with all the six-foot-high chicken wire he had in his garden, I asked.

"Nothing," he said. "If you want it, you're welcome to it – I shan't need it where I'm going!"

Joan and I set forth with a will, and hand cleared everything on the site beside our house, and within a short while I had enclosed it with the chicken wire. The next thing was the chicken house. Fred Gemmill at Wood Farm had, I noticed, a couple of old chicken houses on his land. Each about twenty feet long by four feet wide with sliding roof and proper roosting and nesting boxes they would be ideal.

"How much do you want for one of them?" I asked Fred.

"Give me a couple of quid," he said. I thought for a bit.

"That seems reasonable, but there's only one snag, how do I get it home?"

"No problem," said Fred, "I'll bring it along tomorrow on my low-loader."

True to his word, the following day his tractor pulled up outside the police house and he and I manhandled the heavy thing onto the spare plot. That was a fair two quids' worth and we were in business! All I had to do now was find the chickens.

A couple of days later, I was chatting to Tom and Muriel Surridge, licensees of the Nags Head, about the problem. "I know where you can find some good layers," said Tom. "Up in my field near Matching Green. But they've gone a bit wild, you'll have to catch 'em if you want to bring 'em home. I'll give you a hand if you like, and what you catch will be yours. We'll buy whatever surplus eggs you have and sell 'em over our bar." I asked how many chickens there were.

"About twenty or more," he replied.

A day or two later, armed with a number of hessian sacks, I drove up to the field with Tom. Unfortunately, it was very late afternoon and as I looked around Tom remarked, "They'll be roosting by now," and pointed up into some trees. There sure enough were a couple of dozen fine black hens snoring away in the higher branches.

"Best time to catch 'em," said Tom, "while they are all dozy. You climb up and knock 'em off their perches and I'll catch 'em in the sacks."

I was extremely dubious but nevertheless climbed the trees and scrambled out along the branches. Sure enough, what I couldn't catch I frightened off and one by one Tom caught about half a dozen before the rest took fright and flew too far off.

"Have to come back tomorrow," said Tom. "That's all we'll get today." Bearing home my spoils I resolved to make another trip the next day.

As it happened, Tom was not able to come with me then so I set off with my sacks to capture a few more. I waited until later in the evening and caught most of them asleep. They clucked and flapped, pecked and scratched for all they were worth but I managed to catch about a dozen before my bleeding wounds told me I should call it a day. Putting the bulging sacks into my car, a newly acquired Morris Isis, I set off back to Moreton.

Before long, however, I heard a squawk and then a flapping of wings as first one and then another worked its way loose from its prison. Thinking they would be perfectly safe while I had the doors and windows shut, I let them get on with it. As I approached the village though a number of them had decided to make themselves comfortable by perching in precarious rows along my back window and the back of the bench-seat of the car.

I simply ignored them and drove on. Ignored them that is until I arrived at Moreton, where I was met with stares of incredulity from villagers who really did not want to believe that a dignified representative of the law was in the habit of taking chickens out for a ride!

An interesting sequel to the chicken saga occurred sometime later. Despite the fact that I had by then about thirty birds, I found one to be missing. After a brief but fruitless search I assumed, since they were still semi-wild, that it had wandered off or got run over. About a fortnight later, Joan woke me up from a deep sleep at around two o'clock in the morning.

"Listen," she whispered, "there's something going on in the hen run." I listened. There, sure enough, was the sound of frantic clucking. "Do you think it's someone trying to steal the chickens?" she said.

"More likely a fox has got in there by the sound of it," I replied knowledgeably.

Unfortunately, I did not have a shotgun then although one was later given to me on 'permanent loan'. What on earth my neighbours would have thought of a twelve-bore going off under their windows at that time of the morning I shudder to think. Nevertheless, I put on my dressing gown and went down to the office for my torch and truncheon. *If I can't shoot it, I might give it a hefty whack,* I thought.

Creeping out into the garden, I quietly let myself into the chicken run and made my way towards the sound of threshing wings and fierce clucking. I was surprised to find that it wasn't coming from the hen-house at all but from the middle of a dense bank of stinging nettles and brambles. The bulky hen-house barred my way so I was left with no alternative but to climb over it. Reminding myself to be careful as the sloping roof, only three feet off the ground, was slippery with green moss, I made my way toward the sound of combat not daring to switch on my torch for fear of frightening off the intruder. Reaching the spot I carefully parted the stinging nettles with my truncheon and then switched on the torch. I couldn't believe my eyes. I had found the missing hen sitting on an improvised nest deep in that jungle of weeds. What was more she was sitting on a dozen eggs laid during the time she had gone 'missing'. And there, the source of all the fuss and bother, was a hedgehog doing his damnedest to get to the eggs and being fiercely repelled at every turn!

I was a bit reticent at the thought of picking up the prickly offender, they are well-known for being lousy with fleas, so I made life very uncomfortable for him by flashing my torch in his eyes and prodding him with my truncheon until at last he decided to call it a night and ambled away.

Picking up the angry hen, and receiving numerous painful pecks for my trouble, I deposited her back with her rudely awakened companions in the hen-house. Returning to the makeshift nest I stood looking at the clutch of eggs wondering what to do. If I left them, every hedgehog in the area would have a field day. Fortunately my dressing-gown had two rather large pockets, and within a minute or two I had filled them, fervently hoping that the infertile eggs had not addled under that stupid hen.

Reaching the hen-house I was faced with the difficult task of climbing back whilst trying at the same time to protect a dozen valuable eggs. I did not succeed, of course. Losing my grip I found myself sliding uncontrollably and ignominiously for a fall, feeling and hearing the awful squelch of breaking eggs as I did so.

Stomping back indoors roundly cursing hens, hedgehogs and

country-life in general I poured the sticky, glutinous mess from my pockets while a sympathetic Joan fell about laughing.

As if to salve my battered pride over this domestic disaster, an interesting event followed involving Joan and her then-boss, John May of Bovinger Lodge, for whom she worked as a secretary. One of the many contracts he had was as a script-writer for the radio programme 'The Archers'. When, next day, she recounted to him the saga of the hedgehog he simply could not believe it. Assured by her that it was true, he declared what an interesting 'country life' anecdote it would make for weaving into the series.

Sure enough, a few weeks later he told her to switch on at a certain time and there for the entire nation to enjoy was old Walter Gabriel recounting to his cronies what had happened to him the previous night when one of his chickens encountered a hedgehog.

As expected, I found detached beat work to be far removed from that of urban areas – especially Romford and Harold Hill! It was often inconvenient and uncomfortable, the permanent split shift ensuring that you were on or available for most of the time, so much so that we soon found it politic to get out as much as possible on rest days otherwise they just turned into duty-days in plain clothes. It was nothing to spend half of the rest-day answering the phone or sorting out someone's problem.

The good people who lived on my beat were generally very kind and always willing to pass the time of day. I made a point of never cycling past anyone but always stopping for a chat. It was sound policy too for if that person was a stranger, there was always the chance of picking up some tit-bit of information. At best, there were good arrests made as a result of information thus obtained, and at least there was the build-up of knowledge and confidence which was so often to prove invaluable both in the detection of crime and domestic situations.

One of the things I found was that the country bobby was expected to be a jack-of-all-trades, an adviser to families in need, a speaker at local village schools or parish meetings, a good darts player at the local and a chucker-out at closing time, a confidant to wayward wives or girlfriends (men never seemed to unburden their souls as women did), a sympathetic ear for farmers whose world revolved around the weather and harvest yields, and above all an authority on law. It made no difference if the subject was civil law, you were expected to know the answer. Above all was the necessity to maintain trust, to listen without criticism, to treat confidences as sacred, yet remain firm in what you considered your duty, although this did not always correspond to what the law of the land might say about it. Countryfolk too were more willing to accept 'summary justice', it was much simpler than being dragged all the way into Epping for their misdemeanours to be aired in open court. In all, rural policing had much more of a 'family' feel about it and involved a great deal more than riding around on a bike all day.

But back to amusing anecdotes which is what this is all about. Running up from Moreton to Matching Green there are three roads, High Laver Road in the west, Little Laver Road to the east, and Watery Lane in the centre. Travelling from Moreton, I would normally take the Little Laver Road simply because it was the shortest and most direct route. If I had plenty of time to make my conference point with the Matching Tye PC, I would opt to branch left off Little Laver Road and approach Matching via Watery Lane. It was a narrow lane which over the centuries had resisted change by the simple expedient of turning itself into a river in winter. Our Victorian forebears with their wooden wheeled carts must have found it completely impassable in bad weather, and even now the only concession made to modern transport is an indifferent surface and a sign at each end which reads, 'Unsuitable in wet weather'.

On a particularly wet night, I found myself with plenty of time to get to Matching Green so decided to walk up Watery Lane rather than cycle. I was wearing my police raincoat with its white fluorescent belt – the only concession made then to road safety at night.

Observing the rules of the road, I was wheeling my bike along the offside of the road to face the non-existent oncoming traffic. I was about halfway up the lane and surveying the already filled ditches overflowing into the road when I heard the sound of a motorcycle engine coming up from behind. I moved even closer to my right to allow the rider plenty of room to pass. Indeed, so confident was I that I did not even bother to look behind as he approached.

Suddenly, there was a squeal of brakes, a swishing noise of tyres sliding on the wet road, a thump, and then an almighty splash! I spun 'round and for a second saw nothing. Then with a spluttering and a stuttering there emerged from the ditch on my right what looked like the head and shoulders of Neptune, but was in reality a very bedraggled motor-cyclist.

As he climbed out, I felt entitled to ask what on earth had possessed him to choose that ditch and not the one on my left. Had he not seen me? 'Oh! Yes,' he replied, he had seen me all right, in fact he had recognised me as his local bobby. He had also seen the lights on my bike and had noticed my fluorescent belt. He stood looking down at the racing water which had now totally engulfed his machine.

"Bloody silly really," he said. "I saw you and then your bike but for some reason assumed you were riding it. I pulled over to the right to overtake you..." There were no hard feelings on his part, and declaring that he would have to return the next day when the flood had subsided, he walked amiably with me the rest of the way to the Green.

Talking of Matching reminds me of an incident which occurred there one night as I made my ten thirty p.m. point. It is a lovely village with a medieval green surrounded by houses and cottages of all descriptions and age, where cricket was, and still is, played in front of the Chequers pub. The landlord, like two or three others on my patch, was always grateful to see me about closing time, for he wasn't overly forceful in turning his customers out and actually welcomed my walking through his bars calling time. In doing so, of course, any criticism or comment made by customers being hurried along would naturally be blamed on me and not him! For this small service I was treated to a convivial pint. But I digress.

On this particular night, I made my ten-thirty point looking across to the Chequers. It was lively with music, singing and laughter, all the usual sounds associated with village life. Licensing hours finished at ten thirty and drinking-up time extended it to ten forty. I finished my point and strolled across with my bike. Propping it up against the front of the pub, I checked my watch and saw that it was coming up to ten forty-five. Just the right time for chucking out. I walked in and was greeted with a cheery wave by the guv'nor who then turned his eyes meaningfully towards the public bar. I walked in and found a merry party going on with no sign of anyone wanting to call it a day. Tactfully, I told everyone that it was high time they found homes for themselves, and within a few minutes they had all drifted off as good as gold. I stood out front and saw them away

– including three or four noisy youngsters getting into a red and black mini. Now with everything quiet I returned and shared a pint with the guv'nor before saying goodnight.

As I was getting onto my bike, I realised straightaway that something was wrong. Checking it, I quickly found that both tyres had been let down! Looking around, I saw that all was dark and deserted. It was a matter of only two or three minutes before I was on my way again but I resolved not to let this one go.

A few nights later, I had the same point to make, and there lo and behold was the red and black mini parked outside the Chequers. This time I did not advertise myself by going in but strolled quietly up, had a good look 'round and then bent down. Within a minute, the front offside tyre was practically flat, and then thinking that they would have a spare, I let the front nearside tyre down for good measure. Quietly, I mounted my bike and disappeared into the darkness.

A week or so later, I was at the Chequers again, this time about midday. During my chat with the guv'nor, I asked as innocently as I could, "Do you know anything about a car's tyres being let down a week or two back? I've heard word about it." He knew exactly what I was talking about.

"Oh! Yes," he said. "There was quite a to-do about that, the lady had to ring her husband to come and get her."

With mounting horror now, I said, "Lady? What lady? Wasn't the car a red mini with a black roof?" He nodded.

"Yes, but there are two in the village, one owned by a lad in his teens and the other is hers. A garage had to come out the next day with a spare wheel. I just don't know what the world's coming to, I really don't." I solemnly agreed with him and promised to do what I could. Perhaps the lads got to hear of it and wondered too…

There are a number of amusing incidents involving my local pubs. One such was at the John Barleycorn at Threshers Bush (sometimes called Thrushes Bush, I never found out which was the right name) at the far extremity of my beat bordering Potter Street, Harlow. Once again the landlord, Jim Smith, preferred my clearing his bars than himself, and there was always a chicken sandwich and a pint in it for me afterwards. It was a long slog up to the John Barleycorn, about four miles, which is all right in good weather but pretty miserable when it isn't. There was no phone box outside the pub, for like one or two other points on my beat without phone boxes, the pub's telephone number was held at the nick (and Harlow) so that if needed, I could always be contacted via the landlord. My night point there was ten forty-five p.m., which did not give me a lot of time to bolt down a sandwich before getting away again to my next point at Bobbingworth for eleven-thirty. Fortunately, having slogged uphill nearly all the way to the John Barleycorn, it was downhill all the way to Bobbingworth, and the speeds that I attained when pushed for my next point were quite phenomenal – as my little grand-daughter would now say, I Billy-whizzed all the way!

On this particular night as I stood quietly outside the pub, I could hear the sounds of great revelry within, a live group were playing drums, saxophone, piano etc. with everyone apparently having a great time. But with my point starting at ten forty, the pub should already be cleared out. I looked in through the windows and saw the bar packed with customers. *Was there an extension tonight?* I wondered. Normally, when extensions were granted, I received a copy which of course avoided embarrassment, but I had received nothing. I checked my watch, it was ten fifty p.m. and my regulation ten-minute wait was up. I looked in again convinced that Jim would not be so blatant as to let things go on like this, but the place was still popping – and there amongst the revellers was my own Chief Inspector Horne from Harlow along with the detective chief inspector, their wives and families.

I knew if I turned a blind eye and sloped off, the chief inspector would certainly (knowing my luck) discover that I had made the point and done nothing about it. I was left with only one course of action. I marched into the pub, making my way through the crowd which parted like the Red Sea at the sight of my uniform, and leaned across the counter (quite deliberately pretending not to notice my two senior officers as I did so).

"Mr Smith!" I called formally along the bar. He looked up.

"Mr Woodgate," he replied equally formally.

"Have you got an extension tonight?" I asked. His eyes flickered around, all had gone very quiet.

"Well – er– no, not exactly," he replied.

"What is 'not exactly'?" I asked. He glanced at my guv'nors who I had still not 'seen'.

"No, no extension, Mr Woodgate," he replied.

"Then clear your bars, Mr Smith!" I said sternly, and walked out. No chicken sandwich tonight!

As I stood outside by the door, the revellers streamed out like rats from a sinking ship. Saying goodnight to them as they went I suddenly 'recognised' the two chief inspectors with their families. I nodded and said "Good evening" to them both and they nodded back in return. Grinning to myself, I got on my bike and made my way to the next point. That, I thought, was the end of it. No way!

A few nights later, I was making an early evening point at the John Barleycorn. Bang on the appointed time, a car approached and out got Chief Inspector Horne! That was the first time he had ever visited me. I saluted with the usual, "All right, sir", and he returned the salute. We chatted inconsequentially for a minute or two before he suddenly said, "I'd like to see your pocket book please."

Now, of course, he was quite entitled to ask for it but very few of them did except to sign the point entry. I handed it over and saw him flick back the pages until he found my last point at the Barleycorn. He almost sighed with relief when he saw that I had written, '10.45 p.m. entered John Barleycorn PH In order'. He handed the book back.

"You keep a very tidy pocket-book, Woodgate."

"Thank you, sir," I replied, but with deep suspicion. A moment's silence, and then,

"About the other night (*Aha!* I thought). My wife gave me hell on the way home." I looked at him innocently.

"Hell, sir?"

He went on, "Yes, of course, she did. All the way home it was. The shame of it! Drinking after hours and then being turned out by one of your own men. She gave me some stick I can tell you." He paused for a moment. "On the other hand, though, I would like you to know how impressed I was with the way you handled it, very firm and polite, a pleasure to see!" I shall never know whether he really meant it or not!

Talking of having my pocket book examined reminds me of an unusual little incident at the Green Man pub at Magdalen Laver – a tiny community of no more than a dozen or so cottages and the pub. It was so off the beaten track that it was almost by accident that visitors ever found it. The landlord could not have made much of a living there and the general decor of the pub reflected it. Nevertheless, there must have been some sort of regular patronage or he would have gone bust. The Green Man was not on my usual route home but every now and again, as I was obliged to visit every pub on my patch at least once a month, I would make the effort to pop in.

I remember visiting the John Barleycorn that Sunday evening and then turning off on my way home to call in at the Green Man. It was about nine-thirty when I arrived. There was a customer standing at the bar and three more sitting 'round a table playing what looked suspiciously like poker. The licensee was standing sorrowfully behind the bar, his chin propped on his hands, watching the game. I gave the usual, "Evening all," and took a look around. No one took much notice of me. I looked at the three players. It certainly wasn't crib they were playing, but I nevertheless took pity on the licensee thinking that if I turfed those three out he might just as well shut up shop.

The following morning at about half-past nine, my sergeant, George Cant, rang me from Ongar.

"Everything all right last night?" he said. I confirmed that it had been. "Can you come in and see me – now," he said.

Somewhat bemused, I replied that I would be in in about twenty minutes.

Still wondering what it was all about, I cycled the two and a half miles and walked into his office.

"What's up, Sarge?" I asked. He looked up at me.

"You said it was all quiet last night?" I confirmed it again. "Did you visit the Green Man at Magdalen Laver?" I replied that I had. "How many were in there?" he asked.

I said, "About three or four, it was pretty dead, why?" He held out his hand.

"Let's have a look at your pocket book." I handed it over and stood patiently while he went through it. After a moment or two, he read out loud my entry for the previous evening, "Nine thirty p.m. visited Green Man PH, in order." He looked up at me. "And was it in order?"

Feeling distinctly apprehensive now, I said, "Well, that's what I've written, Sarge. Why, what's this all about?" He smiled a long slow, conspiratorial smile.

"What it's about is that you saw a game of poker going on and did nothing about it, that's what it's about."

Now, playing poker in pubs, along with most other gambling games, except crib and dominoes, is illegal. I stared back at him but he went on, "The Chief Super got a phone call at Harlow this morning from someone he knows who told him all about it, and he has asked me to look into it. But before you say any more, let me tell you that the informant is a local builder whom the chief dislikes intensely. He is expecting a satisfactory reply. So what was it they were playing last night"?" Now it didn't take a house to fall on me to make the prompt reply.

"Crib, Sarge, without a doubt."

George leaned back. "Now that's what I told the guv'nor it probably was. That's all. But next time just be a damn sight more careful who is about before turning your back on illegal games!" I thanked him and walked out.

There really are some 'orrible characters about, I thought.

There was another such character in Ongar High Street one Friday evening in April 1964. I was in the town doing a four-hour foot patrol as they were short-handed that day, when I came across a Hillman Minx stationary about four feet from the curb, it's engine still running and the driver's door wide open. I was looking around for whoever had abandoned it when a passer-by came up and said, "If you're looking for the driver he's in there," pointing to the public toilets immediately opposite.

I waited for a few moments and then saw the figure of Fred

Padfield a local farmer in his sixties and notorious drunk, staggering out of the toilets. He just about made it to a tree standing a few feet away before having to grab it to steady himself, wrapping only one arm around the trunk because he was minus the other (lost some years previously when he had brushed against an oncoming lorry while his arm was out of the car window with his fingers drumming on the roof!). He then tottered across the road to his car. I let him get in and then asked whether he intended driving himself home. He stared at me with totally blood-shot eyes and slurred something to the effect that he was. I arrested him then and there.

On arriving at the nick, a matter of only fifty yards away, I ushered him in. Fred stumbled to the counter, cannoned off and then literally rolled along it before hitting the wall at the end. He was spaced out! Now this was long before anyone had ever thought about breathalysers and the police surgeon had to be called out to examine the driver and determine whether he was fit to drive. It was as simple as that. His word and the arresting officer's evidence was enough. There was, however, one small snag; the driver had the right to call in his own doctor too, and that is precisely what Fred did.

In due course, Dr Burgess arrived from his home nearby and commenced his examination. What this entailed had us gasping at the farce of it. First, Fred was asked what day of the week it was, and in this he had no difficulty for it was market-day in Chelmsford and that was where he had been! The doctor then took out a penny from his pocket and asked Fred to identify it.

Well done, Fred! Putting the coin on the floor, he was then asked to pick it up, which he did with the greatest of difficulty. Finally, with one or two more simple questions answered, Dr Burgess declared that while Fred had had a drink or two, he was quite capable of driving! He then left, no doubt conscious of the stares of disbelief we were giving him.

Appalled, George Cant declared that Fred was going nowhere and that we would wait for the police surgeon to arrive from goodness knows where. While we were waiting, George explained to me the position we would be in if the police doctor certified Fred as unfit to drive. We would have one doctor testifying against the other which would introduce enough doubt in the minds of the magistrates for them to acquit Fred.

Eventually at ten o'clock, an hour or more after the arrest, the police surgeon who rejoiced in the Anglo-Saxon name of Rydlewski arrived. Even after that time lapse he had little difficulty in declaring Fred unfit. It was then decided that I should take Fred home, put him into the arms of his long suffering family and then submit a report to headquarters asking for guidance.

It came as no surprise that no further action was taken although I had some small consolation in wondering what size bill Fred must have received from his doctor for that little service. In this respect, I was not sorry to see the breathalyser introduced four years later.

Amongst the aggravation there were gentler, kinder things I came across. Cycling home fairly late at night from my Shelley point, I came to a sharp left-hand bend in the road just past Wood Farm. Looking to my right, I saw a number of gypsy caravans parked in the field and a group sitting 'round a bright campfire. I recognised them immediately as the Bartons, not strictly Romany but caravan dwellers all their lives who scraped a living off scrap iron.

Normally speaking, we chatted to them and then gave them twenty-four hours to quit, which they usually managed to stretch to seventy-two hours after finding mysterious faults developing in their motors.

The Bartons were harmless enough, in fact I had got to know them all pretty well. The old man was perhaps in his fifties, skinny, exceedingly dirty and with a mouthful of rotten teeth. He obviously never washed himself or his clothes and within a ten-foot radius his foul odour was enough to make a 'townie' gag. A veritable old man Steptoe. I always recognised Mum too for she was about the same age and looked, dressed and smelled the same as her husband. They had obviously not allowed such mutual repellent to stand in their way for they had at least nine kids, and it was these that always baffled me, for although I was assured that all were brothers and sisters, they ranged in age from three to their middle thirties. As half of them were congenital idiots, I put it down to more than a touch of incest in the family – a lot more goes on in the country than meets the eye.

He and his family were always polite, in fact excessively so, calling me 'sir' every third or fourth word, but then I suppose they thought that the more respectful they were the more chance there was of cadging an extra day before being moved on.

On this particular night, I stopped off to have a word with them, there was no question of giving them their marching orders because they were camped in a farmer's field, and until I heard from the farmer whether or not he had given permission (which they assured me, of course, he had!) I could do nothing about it.

They were sitting on logs around the campfire, having no doubt just feasted on poached rabbit or hedgehog, and were now engrossed in the task of making clothes pegs for the women and girls to take out the next day. It was very much a combined effort and I watched fascinated as this rural, centuries-old craft was enacted before me. The men had previously selected suitable lengths of ash which they had stripped of its bark and then cut into six- or eight-inch lengths. Using very sharp knives, they split each length down the middle and then proceeded to whittle each into a peg shape. At this stage, I learned, it was important to keep the two halves together for no two pieces ever split exactly the same and when fitted together must do so accurately for strength. While this was going on, the youngsters occupied themselves with metal shears cutting narrow strips off old one-gallon oil cans. Once the pegs had been cut into shape, the women placed the two halves together, wrapped the metal strips firmly around the head and tapped in a small nail to secure it. Hey presto. One peg!

Now, I couldn't just sit there watching. I had to have a go, so tossing my cape back across my shoulders and pushing my helmet to the back of my head, I sat down and allowed myself to be taught the finer points of this rustic art. Within half an hour, I was making reasonably fine pegs and within three quarters I was turning out specimens fit for any clothes line. When the time came for me to go, my hosts insisted on presenting me with the bunch I had made which, at a shilling a dozen, was poor return for an hour's work, but I cycled home well content.

It was only the following day I learned that the villagers were talking of their policeman-turned gypsy, for so engrossed had I been that I had not noticed a number of cars slowing down for the bend, their headlights catching a well-defined figure sitting by a campfire whittling away. At least I had the consolation of knowing that my pegs would last longer than theirs and were a lot cheaper too.

Chapter Seven

As was to be expected, we were never particularly plagued with poachers at Romford and only minimally so at Harold Hill, the few calls we got usually turning out to be 'no trace on arrival'. It was a different proposition at Moreton though for both mine and the adjoining beats were ninety-five per cent open countryside where game abounded and where farmers and gamekeepers with twelve-bores crooked over their arms were a common sight. It was not surprising then, after four years, that the little I had gleaned at Eynsham of a very complicated set of game laws (or at least I found them so!) had wasted away. Introduced during the extreme social upheavals of the early nineteenth century when the taking of a rabbit represented food for a hungry family (and transportation to Botany Bay), it had now become little more than a sport carrying a nominal fine. The old legislation remained though, and of the draconian punishments meted out by our early Victorian forebears only one had survived – the confiscation of the means by which the game was taken, and that as often as not involved the confiscation of very expensive shotguns!

One of my first tasks was to re-read the game laws. What constituted night poaching, day poaching, trespass in pursuit, the use of dogs, nets, ferrets, gins, guns, vehicles, and the law on stopping, searching and seizing suspects. One of the first things I learned from the more experienced officers was that proof of poaching had to be presented to the court, not only the equipment used but the animal or bird itself. On the other hand, magistrates had long since discouraged the practice of setting out in serried ranks rabbits or pheasants which had died a month or two back, and which tended to turn a court into a Watership Down mortuary. They were instead quite happy to view the more clinical sight of a set of paws for each rabbit taken and a pair of feet for each pheasant.

The gamekeeper for the land on which poachers were taken was always offered the game by the arresting officer, for this represented nothing more than the legal return of stolen property. He for his part had more than he could deal with anyway so he simply handed them back to the officer 'to be disposed of'!

One night at about ten thirty, I was standing at my point on the main Ongar Road, when my peaceful reverie were shattered by the sound of a shotgun blast some distance away towards Blake Hall. I looked across the fields and a few moments later saw a pair of car headlights coming from Toot Hill towards the main road. I gauged that by the time the car reached the junction I could be there to meet it (after all it was downhill all the way!). My estimate was good and I stopped a little Standard Ten as it reached the junction. Shining my torch inside, I saw there was the driver, his wife nursing a baby in the passenger seat and another kiddie asleep in the back. No sign of any game and all very normal and innocent.

"Did you hear the sound of a shot as you came through?" I asked.

The driver shook his head. "No, nothing, did you?" he asked his wife. She too shook her head.

"Now that's very peculiar," I said, "because I heard it clearly half a mile away, but you have just come past the spot and heard nothing." He still denied hearing a thing, so I walked round to the boot. It was locked.

"Give me the key," I said.

"I can't," he replied. "It needs a special allen key and I haven't got one."

I returned to the driver. "Out you get."

He looked startled. "Why, what have I done?"

His wife chipped in with something like the police should have better things to do, but he got out anyway. I looked down at the driving seat, then reaching in picked up the stock, butt and double-barrel of a very expensive-looking twelve-bore shotgun.

"That must have been pretty uncomfortable sitting on that lot," I said.

His reply was classical, "Oh Gawd, that's torn it."

In the glove compartment was a box of Eley cartridges which I seized to go with the shotgun.

I put the barrel and stock on the roof of the car and retained hold of the butt (just in case). I then turned to him. "Right, now we'll have a look in the boot."

He spread his hands. "Honest to God I can't open it, I haven't got the key, and there's nothing in there anyway." I searched him and the car. No key. Determined not to let him get away with it, I climbed into the back of the car and prised forward the back-rest of the rear seat. Remarkably, it gave about six inches. Reaching in with my hand I felt around inside the boot. I pulled out a cold rabbit, then another, and then a very warm pheasant. I showed these to him.

"Oh! That's easily explained," he said, "and you can check up on it if you like. I've been out shooting with a party this afternoon at Marden Ash. They're legitimate kills, they are."

I pointed out that the rabbits were cold and stiff while the pheasant was still warm and oozing blood. He was trapped and knew it.

"Okay then, fair deals. I did shoot it a few minutes ago. You did well there, mate!"

I thanked him nicely and then told him I was seizing the lot including the shotgun and ammunition.

"What! That gun ain't mine, it's my brother's. He gave over three hundred quid for it. He'll kill me!"

Telling him that was something he would have to sort out with the court, or failing that his brother, I loaded the game and ammunition into my saddle bag, reassembled the shotgun and tied it to the cross-bar of my bike (well, what else could I have done with it?).

A month later, I met him again at Epping Court where he pleaded guilty to night-poaching. Ironically, the chairman of the magistrates was Major Nigel Capel-Cure of Blake Hall, upon whose land the pheasant had been taken. With such a vested interest, he naturally stood down but his colleagues fined the culprit handsomely and confiscated the shotgun despite eloquent appeals for its return. That was an expensive bird.

On another occasion, in a wood just outside Moreton, I was called by a gamekeeper who was sure that a poacher was operating there. We agreed that I should stand at one end while he beat his way through to drive the poacher out onto the road where I waited.

It was a successful little operation and I nabbed the intruder as he came out carrying a couple of sacks. He gave himself up very quietly and handed over his nets and booty. I opened one sack to find three or four freshly killed rabbits, but as I put my hand into the other sack he kindly warned me off saying that it contained his ferrets who were waiting patiently to sink their nasty little fangs into me! I thanked him but still opened the sack (somewhat gingerly I hasten to add) to check the truth of the matter. He was telling the truth. I still confiscated everything else with the exception of those ferrets which could not in law be seized.

By far the greatest majority of poachers 'came quietly' like this one, almost as if it were a code of honour to do so. But then they were the country boys who looked upon having their collars felt as an occupational hazard. From what I heard the city boys (and city means London) had quite different ideas, but fortunately I had very few dealings with them 'capes'. The good old bobby's cape was certainly the most old-fashioned and yet the most useful item of clothing ever issued. Made from fine quality melton, it was thick enough to keep you warm, heavy enough to be almost waterproof, and hanging as it did straight from the shoulders it kept the arms free and mobile. When not in use, it folded into a narrow strip making it easy to carry over one's shoulder or to slip conveniently over a cycle's handlebars. In those days practically every policeman carried one, but now it seems to have given way to the raincoat. We had raincoats, of course, and good quality they were too. The only drawback was the heavy rubberised lining which did not 'breathe' and thus left you sweating on a warm but showery day. Subsequent issues were of gaberdine and much more comfortable.

One advantage of the cape was that it came below the level of your hands. You were therefore able to walk around with your hands in your pockets and nobody would notice, and they were useful too for a quiet smoke in a shop doorway. I still have my original issue cape to this day.

One incident which demonstrates its versatility – and danger – occurred at Moreton as I was standing at my point outside the White Hart pub. It was quite late at night and this was to be my last point before getting off home. As I stood looking around at the near deserted village, the pub door opened and out came one of the regulars with a pint in his hand.

Holding it out, he said, "Here you are, John, you look as if you could do with it'!"

I glanced around quickly and took it with thanks. I did not hurry over it because the glass was easily concealed if anyone should happen by, which, of course, was exactly what happened. The skipper's car pulled up alongside me and out stepped George Cant!

I greeted him in the usual way and we chatted for a few minutes, my fingers tightly wrapped around the glass of ale. *This is typical Woodgate luck,* I thought, *all the times I've stood here and nobody's offered me a pint, and now as soon as they do George has to turn up! And what happens when he asks me to put the point in my book for him to sign, do I get him to hold the glass while I write?*

Another minute or two passed before he suddenly announced that he hadn't visited my office for some time and that he would come out the next morning to do my books. He would, he said, sign my pocket-book then!

With a huge sigh of relief, I wished him a very good night and watched as his car disappeared through the village. The rest of that pint was sheer nectar.

The avoidance of getting caught (by our own people that is) was something that all of us had to perfect in time. There were so many little things that today would be tolerated but then would, and often did, result in disciplinary charges.

One PC stationed at Abridge was suspected of leaving his home at ten-past five in the morning (instead of five) to make his first point in the village at five fifteen. The fact that he would probably more than make up for this during the day was not considered. No less a personage than Inspector Payne of Ongar took it upon himself to hide up every time this PC had a five a.m. patrol to note the exact time he left home. Having got his evidence, he confronted the man one morning at ten past five and put him on a charge for neglect of duty. This could easily have been dealt with by a ticking off – a view which was also held by no less a personage than the Chief Constable who admonished the PC and then instructed the inspector to remain behind for a few words!

This sort of behaviour only served to widen the chasm between 'them and us' and increased manyfold the artful measures we took to avoid getting caught. One rather extreme example immediately springs to mind. One of my nine p.m. – twelve a.m. patrols finished with an eleven thirty p.m. point at Moreton, a mere two hundred yards from my house. As I had not been visited at any of my three points, the likelihood of running into 'authority' was now remote. I felt it safe to wander off home a few minutes early.

It had been teeming with rain the whole evening and I was more than relieved to get out of my wet things. Joan was upstairs checking on the sleeping children when she suddenly came to the top of the stairs and called down quietly, "There's a car outside, just sitting there."

I went up and glanced out of the bedroom window. There, sure enough, in the darkness was a pair of side-lights! It was Pete Cousins, a relief-sergeant from Stanford Rivers who was doing a stint in Ongar. He had either arrived too late for my point or was waiting to see whether he could catch me getting home early. I checked my watch, it was still only ten to midnight.

Telling Joan that I would be popping out for a few minutes, I went back downstairs and put on my still soaking leggings, raincoat, helmet and gloves. I left by the back door picking up my bike as I went. Wheeling it down the back garden, I heaved it over the barbed wire fence into the field. To save time, I decided to ride the bike, without lights, of course, the two or three hundred yards along the back of our houses until I came to a five-bar gate which I knew would let me out onto the road. Bumping along in the dark was uncomfortable enough but nothing compared to what happened next. Forgetting all about a deep ditch which ran at right angles across the field to feed Cripsey Brook I suddenly felt the bike nose-dive and I went with it straight into the ditch!

I was now splattered in mud as well as being wet through. Cursing mightily in the darkness, I hauled myself out and reached the five-bar gate. It was locked. By now I was in no mood for niceties. Picking up the bike, I hurled it bodily over the gate and heard it crash onto the roadway. With some difficulty, for the farmer had kindly wound barbed-wire along the top of the gate, I climbed over, picked up my bike, and rode as calmly as my heaving breath would allow up to where the sergeant sat comfortably in his car. Fortunately, it was still raining and with the skipper not willing to lower his window more than an inch or two, he could not see the state I was in. That this also left me standing out in the rain was, of course, of little consequence. Far better a wet PC than a wet car seat! He explained he had 'missed' my point and in order not to suffer a wasted journey had decided to meet me on my way home! He then looked a bit puzzled.

"Your last point was in the village, what are you doing coming in from the opposite direction?" My circumnavigation of the field had brought me out further down the road away from the village.

Even I was surprised at my immediate and confident reply,

that the local rector was away on holiday and I was checking the rectory before turning in. He then said, "But I came down that way past the rectory and didn't see you."

"No, you wouldn't," I replied. "I was 'round the back of the house."

He nodded. "Oh yes, I suppose so."

I then looked at my watch and announced that as it was now after midnight, I was on overtime! With a cheery wave, he bade me good night and drove off.

Looking back on these incidents, and there were many similar to this, I marvel at the level of discipline imposed and accepted. I really thought nothing of going to such lengths to escape capture, and so inculcated were we in both military and police discipline I cannot remember ever thinking how ridiculous some of it was, the satisfaction came from bucking the system.

After a short while at Moreton, I soon twigged how much easier it would be getting to a point in bad weather if I put my bike in the boot of the car, parked up a couple of hundred yards from the point and then cycled the rest of the way. This worked well until one particular morning at six thirty George Cant turned up in his car, made my point, and then announced that as my next rendezvous was at Shelley (Ongar), and as I looked wet through, why didn't I get myself off to Ongar nick and make a pot of tea? By the time he had met the constable on the adjoining beat, the tea would be nicely brewed. What could I say in the face of such generosity?

I cycled the three miles into Ongar, made the rotten tea, cycled to my Shelley point and then all the way back to where I had left my car, wondering as I did so whether George had ever played the same trick with his sergeant…

That this was an old trick was established sometime later

when I was chatting to a very old retired policeman. On telling him this, he suddenly burst out laughing and said that the same thing had happened to him. Way back before the First World War they walked everywhere, town or country it didn't matter which for bicycles were not allowed for beat use. Of course, that did not mean they were not used, for he did the same with his bike as I with my car, the only difference being that he could hide his more easily behind a hedge. On this particular occasion, his inspector turned up for the point driving the divisional horse and trap. "Hop aboard," he said generously, "I'll give you a lift to your next point."

It was three miles away!

Two or three miles out of Moreton, at Little Laver, there stands a very grand house called White Lodge. It is best described perhaps as a mini-mansion set in acres of gardens with an impressive driveway leading from the road. It was owned then by Mr and Mrs John Lebus, of Lebus Furniture, then a very big name in quality furniture. They had two children; Richard, who was then about fourteen, and Barbara about two years older. Both were away at boarding school most of the time. Richard subsequently went to Eton, later qualified as a doctor and went to live and practice in America. I cannot remember what happened to Barbara but no doubt she 'married well' and settled down somewhere.

Mr and Mrs Lebus were a pleasant couple who, if they saw me cycling by on my rounds, would always wave me in for a cup or glass of something. I was particularly fond of him for he was unaffected by his obvious wealth and would chat away on quite a man-to-man basis. Mrs Lebus, whilst equally pleasant, had a tendency not to forget her position, rather like a more mature Penelope Keith in 'To the Manor Born' – except that Mrs L lived in the big house and not the lodge!

Whenever they had a particularly big party – and by this I mean the entire house and grounds taken over by a couple of hundred guests – they would ask me to station myself at the gates to keep an eye open for traffic congestion and then walk around the grounds to keep an eye on things. I did not mind the latter as I knew I would always end up in the kitchen where a large tray of sandwiches and drinks would be laid out for me. It was the former which rather made me a candidate for socialist style class-levelling as pimply faced youths of undeniable pedigree with the mandatory fluffy bird at their side would sweep into the drive in Daddy's MG or Jag, giving me a cursory wave as they did so, before wheel-spinning up the drive in a shower of gravel. Now, with the maturity of many more years I smile at myself as I remember how I ground my teeth at these obviously well-heeled types while contemplating the £77-a-month I was then earning!

One particular day, Mrs L telephoned to ask if I would mind popping up during the evening to discuss a certain future event. This turned out to be her daughter's coming-out party (so she must by then have been eighteen). I turned up on my humble bike and she showed me into what I suppose must have been the drawing room, although it covered about the same area as our house. There I was surprised to find a couple of lady guests, an ice-bucket of champagne and a tray with toast and caviar! For the first time in my life I tasted this Rolls Royce of delicacies – and took an instant liking to it. We toasted (no pun intended) Barbara's forthcoming birthday and eventually got round to discussing the arrangements.

Sometime later, and by now considerably merrier than when we had started, Mrs L asked whether I would like to finish with 'a little whisky'. I would have agreed to anything at that stage.

She went to the drinks cabinet, selected a fine bottle of single malt, a crystal glass tumbler (naturally) and then proceeded to fill it! I looked upon its brimming surface with some trepidation but decided it would be boorish of me to comment. The conversation continued until, I don't know how much later, I saw her blurred figure approaching and felt my glass being refilled...

About midnight that night, Joan answered a feeble knocking at our back door where she found me sitting on the doorstep murmuring, 'Silly bitch, silly bitch'. Bearing in mind that she had no idea what had happened, her calmness and compassion was positively angelic. Helping me upstairs, she could only marvel at how I had managed to cycle four miles in that state without falling into a ditch.

The culmination of those discussions resulted in just about the biggest 'bash' I have ever seen. Although ostensibly an eighteenth birthday party, it represented much more a 'coming out' or entry into society. I believe it was about this time that the queen abolished the annual Queen Charlotte's Ball, an age-old institution of privilege and snobbery at which the great families of the day spent small fortunes for their debutante daughters to get invited to the ball, and with only one object in mind; to curtsey briefly before the queen. That was enough to launch them firmly into society.

Sleepy Little Laver was to see something only a little less grand than Queen Charlotte's that night, but enough to have eyes popping and tongues wagging for weeks afterwards. A company from Denmark which had come over to measure up the house and garden now arrived with an enormous made-to-measure marquee which fitted exactly over the back of the house. Its interior was draped in pink and white, its floor laid with parquet and enormous pink and white floral displays decorated its walls. The main house was similarly decorated throughout with the same pink and white floral arrangement.

For those who wished to stroll about the grounds, concealed flood-lighting lit up not only the trees and lawns but the entire house too. I had popped up during the early evening for a last-minute check to find Mr L as excited as a boy with a new train set. Having shown me around the inside of the house, he conducted me through the marquee and out onto the floodlit lawns. Then to my complete surprise, he put his arm about my shoulder as if it were the most natural thing in the world and we continued to stroll and chat. That man certainly knew how to charm.

I shall not go into detail except to say that the evening was an outstanding success, and although I was there on duty I was treated with every courtesy and respect. There was the inevitable pile of food in the kitchen, exactly the same as was being served to the guests, with quantities of wine or whatever else you wished. And there later in the evening, Barbara and Richard, along with an extremely pretty blonde Danish au-pair girl, joined us. Richard was particularly taken with my truncheon and handcuffs and at one stage actually paraded around the house brandishing them. A little later, with the sound of the band coming through quite clearly from upstairs, we held our own impromptu party. The Danish girl confessed that she could not dance but that did not stop us for a moment and before long we – cooks, gardeners, cleaners, son, daughter, au-pair and uniformed bobby – were enjoying ourselves every bit as much as those upstairs.

In the cold light of day, I wondered how much that evening had cost. I had no idea of course except to say that I heard that the marquee alone had set them back four thousand pounds – a huge sum now but a fortune in those days. And all for one eighteen-year-old girl.

Chapter Eight

I had been at Moreton about nine months or so when I received a phone call from Ongar that the Chief Constable John (later Sir John) Nightingale, was making his rounds and would be calling on me that day at eleven thirty. Now, the chief in those days was about on the same level as God and a visit from him to a large station was always preceded by a session of sweeping, polishing, tidying and cleaning. Every now and again though, he would catch everyone on the hop with a sudden and unannounced visit. That sorted a few of the guv'nors out.

He, like his predecessor Sir Jonathan Peel, made a point of visiting every station in the county from Divisional Headquarters to the lowliest detached beat at least once a year. It was a gesture which most of us on one-man beats appreciated for it ensured that no one felt abandoned or forgotten, and it also gave an opportunity for any gripes or grievances to be aired on a man-to-man basis.

This of course was my first experience of having him visit me personally. I had seen him before on a number of occasions but always surrounded by divisional brass. Nevertheless, I gave the office a clean, my desk a good polish, and checked all the records and books that he was likely to ask for.

At exactly eleven thirty, his chauffeur-driven car drew up outside and I waited at the office door as he walked slowly up the garden path. He paused for a moment to peer intently at what I had to admit was an exceptionally fine display of mixed dahlias, and then again at an indifferent clump of chrysanthemums in the bed below the office window.

I welcomed him in and asked, as I would any visiting sergeant or inspector, whether he would like a tea or coffee. He politely declined, sat himself at my desk and indicated for me to take one of the other chairs. We chatted for a few minutes during which time I became painfully aware that he knew an awful lot about me and my hitherto fairly short career (it was only later that I was told that he made a habit of looking through one's personal file before visiting). He then went on to check the usual books, the duty roster, crime returns, pocket-book etc., which I had carefully laid out for him, and then asked if I had any problems I wanted to discuss.

I told him I was very happy, of course, which seemed to please him and he got up and walked around the office looking at the various 'wanted' posters and police gazettes. All fairly routine stuff. He then caught me off guard by opening up the stationery cupboard, which I had previously taken pains to tidy, and examined the contents. Murmuring something about it being nice and tidy, he then bent down and opened the two small cupboards under the office counter. Now, I was quite convinced that a man of his stature would never demean himself by nosing around cupboards, and with the knowledge of what lay within I waited with bated breath for there, staring back at him, were a couple of rabbits and half a sack of potatoes delivered only that morning by an obliging farmer! He closed the doors, walked across to the window and then commented, "Squire of the parish already, I see."

That was the only reference he made to what he had seen and he quickly changed the subject by saying, "But there's one thing you haven't got the hang of yet though. Come outside." Mystified at what he could be on about, I followed him out into the front garden where he stood looking at the bed of chrysanths. "Do you ever prune these?" he asked. I had to confess that I had not touched them since my arrival. "Right, now this is what you do..." and with his chauffeur looking interestedly on he demonstrated exactly how, when and where chrysanths should be pruned to give the best show.

As he left, I decided that so far as I was concerned he was certainly a man's man (a view I never altered over the next fifteen or so years he was our chief). I then walked back into the office to telephone the usual warning to the next beat that he was on his way.

The Reverend Weir was a nice old boy. In his late sixties or early seventies, he administered to a declining congregation at our centuries-old village church. I well remember our youngest daughter Diane, who was then only a few months old, being christened by him one bitterly cold and foggy November day in 1963, just weeks after our arrival at Moreton. She had not been christened at the usual age because of health problems but she was over them now and was a lusty, healthy, bawling infant.

It was a family occasion with aunts, uncles, nephews and nieces coming down, not just for the ceremony but to see for themselves something of our new surroundings. Notwithstanding the beauty of the countryside, there is nothing more dismal than a bare, unadorned, unheated church on an already darkening Sunday afternoon in November. The only truly comfortable one amongst us was Diane whom Joan had sensibly wrapped in layers of blankets while we foregathered shivering in the pews as we awaited the arrival of Mr Weir.

A few moments later, the door opened and he bustled in. Making straight for the font he raised its canopy and beckoned us round. Satisfied that we were gathered, he plunged his hand into his cassock and produced, like a rabbit from a hat, a rubber hot-water bottle which he promptly unscrewed and upended into the font! Whether he had blessed it before drawing it from his kitchen tap I don't know but he justified this rather bizarre behaviour by declaring that he was not going to be responsible for giving Diane her first cold!

With all the years which have elapsed since the christening, these few facts were brought to mind only as I prepared to recount a quite different but equally amusing story involving the same Reverend Weir.

One morning, I was in my office when I received a telephone call from Moreton gravel pits, about half a mile across the fields from where I sat. The foreman asked if I could get up there straightaway as they had found a body. It was only when I exclaimed something like, "Bloody Norah" that he retracted his statement. It was not so much a body, he said, but a skeleton. Two minutes later, I was on my way.

On arrival, I was met by the foreman who conducted me across a muddy stretch of churned up soil to where a mechanical digger was standing poised in mid-stroke. "Just there," he said. I followed his pointing finger and there sure enough, staring up at us forlornly through empty sockets was a perfect human skull. Nearby were the scattered remains of other human bones.

Crouching down, I examined what turned out to be an almost complete skeleton. Then as I carefully brushed away the surface with my hands I discovered more bones, far more in fact than any self-respecting skeleton should boast.

I questioned the foreman and digger-driver and discovered that nowhere else in the pits had any similar discovery been made, and that this find had come to light only as the JCB began pushing topsoil into a worked-out pit.

"So the bones were in the topsoil then?" I suggested.

"Must have been," he replied.

My next question was obvious, "Where had the topsoil come from?"

Telling me to wait, he went off to his hut and came back with some papers.

"Yes, that load was from Whitechapel." I looked at him.

"London's Whitechapel?" He nodded. As I thought about it, a glimmering of a solution was already beginning to form in my mind. Getting hold of a carboard box, I packed away two skulls and an assortment of bones.

"Don't touch anything until you hear from me," I ordered. "I'll get back later."

Returning to my office, I telephoned the news to Ongar and then got in touch with Doctor Margaret Tuck at St Margaret's Hospital, Epping. I had had previous dealings with her in her role as pathologist when I had brought in various bodies which had met unexplained or violent ends. She was a tall, slim woman in her middle fifties, and although outwardly pleasant her face in repose wore a drawn, mournful look, a face which I always considered befitted her calling – rather like an undertaker. I had witnessed one or two of her post-mortems and had always been intrigued by the fact that she constantly smoked cigars over the bodies, whether as a result of her being a confirmed if unconventional smoker or just simply to disguise the smell of the unfortunate victims I never found out.

She was certainly interested to hear my story (I suppose it made a pleasant change from the usual mangled remains that were placed before her), and asked me to deliver them straightaway, which I did. The following day, I went back as arranged and she handed over both the box and her report. Her examination showed that the skulls were pre-dental and not less than three hundred years old. A swift historical calculation put that at the time of the great plague of London in 1665.

Returning to Moreton with the bones and report, I made a few 'phone calls to the Metropolitan Police giving them the location supplied by the lorry driver. Someone there with a sense of history must have got his finger out for within twenty-four hours they rang back to confirm that the spot in Whitechapel had indeed been a common burial pit for the victims of the Plague.

I was now left with a box of remains. What to do with them? Displaying a rather macabre sense of humour, I exhibited the most complete skull in my office, the rest being packed away in a cupboard. Before long though the village schoolmaster got to hear about it, undoubtedly through my children who were his pupils, and on learning how they came into my possession he asked if he could borrow them for history lessons! I was only too happy to get rid of them.

Unfortunately, this state of affairs did not last long. Being a church school, the vicar always called in to take daily prayers. Before long, he was knocking at my door asking what on earth I thought I was doing giving away bones like that. Was I not aware, he said, that these were the remains of honest, God-fearing Christian folk who had died awful deaths before being slung unceremoniously into those ghastly burial pits? For my part I could not disagree on either religious or historical grounds except to venture an opinion that we did not really know who we were dealing with. They could have been Christian, Jew, Greek Orthodox or atheist. He gave me a withering stare.

"What on earth does that matter! Whoever they were, they deserved a decent burial. With your permission, I shall take them away and give them that!" He really was rather annoyed.

Thus to this day, somewhere in that churchyard lie the mortal remains of just a few Londoners who had probably never in their lives ventured more than a mile or so from the teeming squalid streets of East London, and had certainly never heard of a little Essex village called Moreton.

Moreton: the 14th century Black Hall on the right and the village store beyond.

I always looked with mixed feelings upon the quarterly visits to farms and small-holdings to sign the cattle registers. It was a pleasant chore in fine weather but a bit of a bind in the winter for not every farmyard then was metalled as they seem to be now. In fact, I recall a small farm on the Shelley Road whose yard was always six inches deep in winter mud and to visit without a pair of wellies was simply asking for trouble. That particular farm, by the way, is now long gone and what was once a centuries-old but ramshackle farmhouse is now an exceedingly fine house with ornamental gardens which owe much to the fact that they were planted on generations of manure!

In addition to the larger farms there were the smallholdings where perhaps only a single pig was kept and no livestock movements were ever made. Nevertheless, the book still had to be kept, examined and signed. One such, a lovely old dear who lived in Pedlars End, Moreton, always kept her record in an old school exercise book hanging on a hook just inside the kitchen door. Page after page bore nothing but countless signatures of Alf Bennage (my predecessor) and never a single movement of livestock to disturb its perfect symmetry. She was probably in her seventies then and lived alone in a very old weather-boarded cottage with a single pig of great age in the back garden. I often asked how she could justify the expense of keeping it and she would always say that perhaps one day she would have it slaughtered. As I got to know her better, though, I realised it was in fact her pet!

Although every third month, March, June, September and December heralded the mandatory visits we could in fact call at any time to examine the records. So far as the old lady was concerned, I would pop in at least once a month just for a chat.

I like to think she enjoyed these visits for she was lonely and loved talking of years gone by. I found her tales of the steam-driven yesteryears fascinating. She wasn't a country girl in the true sense of the word but had, believe it or not, spent all her life travelling with fairs, as had her father and grandfather before her. She had nevertheless picked up one or two very pleasant country skills not least of which was the making of fine country wines. Berries, fruits and leaves were always picked fresh from the field and hedgerow and turned into the most delicious wine which she stored in half-gallon stone jars in her pantry. She had only one failing though, she would insist on serving liberal quantities in half-pint glasses. I quickly learned, having one day reeled away from her cottage after a surfeit of rhubarb wine only to bump into my sergeant, to time my visits for the end of my tour of duty rather than the beginning!

That apart, there were more serious aspects of our duty in respect of animal husbandry. The dreaded epidemics which today we seem to hear very little about were principally swine fever, foot and mouth and fowl pest. All heartily feared by the farmer and a matter approaching a national calamity for the government. Fortunately, there were not too many outbreaks but those that did occur brought a lot of work for the police insofar as livestock farms had to be isolated with no entry or exit for pedestrians or vehicles which had not first been disinfected, and all movements of animals were banned without movement licences.

I well remember one particular instance when I was instructed to oversee the disposal of the carcass of a cow which had died of foot and mouth at a farm just outside Moreton. Once again, nothing I had learned at training college or my years at Romford had prepared me for the task of 'overseeing' such a job, and when I asked the Ongar skipper what it was I was supposed to oversee, he replied airily, "Rely on the farmer, he knows what to do…" Such then was the depth of our instruction in those days.

I duly turned up at the farm in question and gum-booted my way across a field to a meadow where a JCB had already excavated a pit about ten-feet square and eight-feet deep. Kindling was piled into the bottom followed by bulks of timber and old railway sleepers, and on top of this was poured a drum of waste oil. All this was then set alight.

Once the timber was well underway coal was brought up and tipped in bit by bit until a fine blaze had taken hold.

At that point, I turned and saw a tractor trundling towards us dragging behind it the carcass of the unfortunate cow. Behind it came a mechanical shovel, its wheels carefully lined up on either side of the track left by the animal. Its blade was lowered and it was scooping up a healthy layer of topsoil.

Once filled, it ran up to the pit and dumped the contents into the flames before returning to take up its position behind the dead animal. So virulent was foot and mouth disease that not a trace of any contact made by that animal was left for healthy cattle to walk or graze over.

Finally, the carcass was tipped over into the flames and more coal piled on top. At this point, I was told that as the rest of the operation was now routine and that the funeral pyre would be kept going for something like another six hours, I could wander off and get some lunch. If I returned about four o'clock, I could witness the final sealing.

On my return, the fire had died down and all that remained in the bottom of the pit was a thick layer of grey ash. The JCB returned and carefully filled it in. Then, just to be on the safe side, a wire fence was erected around the pit to prevent other livestock coming into contact with it. That then was how they dealt with a diseased animal in the sixties. Positively Victorian in its application but nevertheless extremely effective. I wonder what they do nowadays.

Our life at Moreton was generally agreed to have been one of the happiest times we, as a family, had spent together. For me it was four and a half years of varied police-work among some of the nicest, most genuine people it has been my pleasure to serve. For Joan, a home-loving Mum only happy in the knowledge that her family was happy, there was a rekindling of that part of her childhood spent in rural Dorset. Now she added to her many talents by slipping into the role of unpaid police secretary, telephonist and enquiry officer. She would also say, office cleaner, for she was paid the princely sum of five shillings a month to keep the police office spick and span!

She supplemented our income to a considerable degree by working at the offices of C & A Gould, corn and seed merchants of Moreton Mill, about half a mile outside the village. Within yards of where she sat was the original post windmill which had stood on that spot for over two hundred years. An act of official vandalism took place shortly after our arrival when it was pulled down 'for safety reasons'. There she worked and mixed happily with a variety of girls until accepting a job (for which she was both trained and qualified) as secretary to an author, John May, who lived in a lovely old farmhouse at Bovinger, about a mile from Moreton.

For the children, the village and countryside was a delight with never a fear, as regrettably there must be nowadays, for their personal safety, and they roamed at will with their friends to come home tired out and filthy from top to bottom.

The village school, little more than a hundred yards from our door was, and undoubtedly still is, a typical little church school built, if I remember the wording on the old plaque over the door, in 1821. Attached to it was the headmaster's house where Mr and Mrs Clarke devoted so much of their lives, reminding me as they did so of a couplet from an Oliver Goldsmith poem, *"There in his noisy mansion, skill'd to rule, the village master taught his little school."*

The three Woodgate children were to have something of a shock one day when Diane, then aged four, decided that she had had enough of waiting for her brothers and sister to come home. Marching into one of the classrooms, she told Mrs Clarke in no uncertain terms that she wanted to join her sister at school! In answer to the question, "And what does your mummy and daddy have to say about it?", she lied remarkably fluently for one so young by declaring that Daddy was out on duty and Mummy couldn't be found! To her credit, Mrs Clarke smiled, took her hand and walked her into Sharon's class plonking her down beside her startled nine-year-old sister before telephoning a frantic Mum to tell us what she had done. From that day, Diane went to school whenever the fancy took her! That was real country life.

Another little memory of the time comes to mind. David, at about the age of nine or ten, asked me what it was I did when I went out at five in the morning. I told him that it was necessary for a policeman to be seen at all hours of the day and night, and that sometimes things happened at five o'clock when most people didn't expect to see a policeman around. In theory, that was a good reply; in practice, I found next to nothing to excite my interest at such a God-forsaken hour, but I lived in hope that my presence was having a deterrent effect on someone somewhere!

Moreton: the village school past and present 1820 and 1960. It was here that Diane gate-crashed the classes in her eagerness to learn.

What was once the playground is now grassed over.

The upshot of all this was that David asked if he could come with me on my 'dawn patrol'. I did not dismiss the idea out of hand imagining that being woken at four forty-five in the morning would have a salutary effect on his enthusiasm. On the morning in question, I shook him out of a sound sleep to say that he had fifteen minutes to get up and dress. My first surprise came when he leaped out of bed full of energy and raring to go. That certainly never happened on a school day!

At exactly five o'clock, we let ourselves out of the silent house, and with me on my sturdy police Raleigh and him on his diminutive child's cycle, we rode out of Moreton bound for High Laver. He knew that at our three points we must keep our eyes peeled in case the sergeant turned up for a visit. If he did, then David must do a fast disappearing trick behind the nearest hedge or tree as I hadn't worked out what to say if he found me turning what should be a serious patrol into a family outing.

David gazed at his first sun as it rose over the fields and meadows, and listened as the dawn chorus grew from a few faint twitterings to a crescendo of sound over a slowly awakening countryside. His eyes looked afresh now at silent fields and copses, lonely hedgerows and still-silent cottages as we made our way silently along the twisting road to the Lavers. For him, it was an adventure. He loved it and wanted to play it again. In fact, he did, for I would often invite him to ride with me, mostly on routine patrols but sometimes to help take measurements of roads and junctions for accidents I was dealing with.

In every walk of life, one meets interesting characters, and Moreton was no exception. One in particular will always remain in my memory for I visited him many times, fascinated by his tales of village life fifty years before. PC Frank Marriott had joined the Essex Constabulary, as it was then called, in 1899. Prior to that, he had emigrated to Canada with his brother and set up a smallholding some miles from the nearest town. For several years, they tilled the soil and broke their backs in a veritable wilderness to grow fruit and vegetables for the market of that town. A horse and cart was all they had for transport, and a rough wooden cabin provided a modicum of comfort and shelter.

He well remembered, he told me, one particularly ferocious winter's day when, on preparing to leave town for his journey home, he was advised to get a room for the night as a blizzard was in the offing. Being young and headstrong, he ignored what turned out to be sound advice for halfway back the blizzard struck as only Canadian blizzards can. He put his head down and knowing the horse was familiar with the journey home left him to it.

Within a short space of time, he realised he could no longer move his hands, then his arms, then his legs. He slowly and inexorably lost consciousness. Hours later, he opened his eyes and found himself wrapped up in blankets and lying on the floor of his cabin in front of a roaring log fire. It was not long before he learned that the faithful old horse had made it back safely and had stopped in front of the cabin door – all this in a blinding blizzard with no road to follow! His brother had found him unconscious and frozen solid in the cart. Half-dragging and half-rolling him into the cabin, he had spent hours slowly thawing him out. It was at that stage that they both decided that Canada was not for them and returned to England.

Arriving back, he decided the permanence and stability offered by the police rather more attractive than Arctic winters and joined the Essex Constabulary. One day towards the end of his basic training at head-quarters (which had only just been built and therefore dates the story to 1903), he stood surveying the wide expanse of lawns which swept across the front of the handsome red-brick buildings. Hearing the sound of footsteps he turned and saw the figure of the chief constable, Captain Showers, approaching. Whipping up a smart salute he was surprised to find the chief stopping for a chat. On learning of his horticultural experiences in Canada, Showers suddenly clapped his hands and declared Frank to be an ideal candidate for the job of digging flowers beds in the lawns! He would arrange with division for his temporary secondment to headquarters staff for as long as it would take him to complete the job. What power!

On a cold November day in 1919, Frank Marriott found himself posted from Eastwood to Moreton. The actual move proved to be something of a problem for he had by then acquired a number of goats and he was told in no uncertain terms by the removal men that goats did not constitute furniture and household effects. He would have to arrange alternative transport for them. He asked around but found that the cost of transporting them would be beyond his pocket. On the day of the move, therefore, as his furniture was trundled along the quiet country roads in a horse-drawn pantechnicon, he followed behind on foot with his goats! That journey must have been in the region of twenty-five miles so he had a very long walk that day.

He quickly found that the idyllic little village of Moreton was not all that it appeared to be on the surface, for at harvest time it was the centre for traction engine gangs, bands of labourers, many of them gipsies, who roamed the countryside looking for casual work that was always available at that time of year.

Unfortunately, it was quite common for many of them to repair to the White Hart or Nags Head (The Moreton Massey as it has now been inexplicably re-named) to drink away all their hard earned pay. Apart from the normal tankards, beer would also to be dispensed in half-gallon earthenware jugs which was a great favourite with the serious drinkers. The upshot was that fights would break out in the pubs and spill out into the village. In fact, he told me that it was no uncommon sight to see blood running down the road in streams towards Cripsey Brook on a Saturday night.

The lone village bobby, 'physical' though he had to be in those days, was sometimes no match for those drunken roughs, and a number of officers were seriously hurt in these fights. Eventually, one of them (I do not know whether it was Marriott or one of his predecessors) hit upon a drastic but perfectly legal form of protection which had been introduced as far back as the 1880s following the murder of Inspector Simmons at Romford. The Force had then purchased over twenty .38 revolvers and allocated them to divisions for use by officers on night duty on dangerous beats. That facility had never been revoked and the guns were still available.

Frank Marriott kept his revolver, holster and ammunition in the drawer of his hallstand at the police house by the humpbacked bridge. He not only described it to me, along with the regulations governing its use, but showed me a photograph of himself in uniform wearing it. This had a salutary effect on the rougher elements and the village became a much quieter place as a result.

He told me many a tale to show how much the job had changed in just fifty years. Although most of the population like today respected the uniform and what it stood for, there were always some who just had to see how far they could push the local bobby before getting a clip round the ear. In those days, it rarely went far beyond that, and the recipient of this form of summary justice walked away sure in the knowledge of what to expect if he misbehaved again. Even so, there was always a small minority of trouble-makers.

One such group of village lads were in the habit of taking their stone jars of ale up into a hayloft which opened onto the roadway beside the row of red-brick cottages which still stand next to the White Hart. There was a meadow and a telephone box (the Moreton point) there in my time but a *cul-de-sac* of houses now stands on the spot. Apparently, these lads – often four or five in number – were in the habit of sitting in the hayloft with their legs swinging over the edge, "insulting the ladies as they walked by, and other unseemly behaviour." In the end, Frank had to sort them out. Climbing up into the loft he proceeded to give them all a good hiding, in the process of which one of the louts fell (or was knocked, for Frank only smiled and winked his eye when I asked which!) out of the loft and onto the road below, breaking his leg in the process. No word of criticism was ever levelled at Frank, indeed the villagers proclaimed that he had only done his duty, and the lads when they sobered up acknowledged that they had deserved what they got! What would happen today?

Drunkenness was just as much of a problem then as it is now and the method employed in dealing with them rested entirely on how far away you were from your sub-divisional station, for this was where they were supposed to be taken for charging. The physical effort and inconvenience involved in walking a drunken and often violent prisoner two and a half miles to Ongar, followed by the walk back, was out of all proportion to the five shillings' fine which was usually levied. To offset this reluctance to take prisoners in, the authorities paid constables two pence a mile for their trouble. For Frank, this would have earned him nearly a shilling a prisoner, but as he said, it was still too much trouble! Like most of his colleagues he preferred to deal with them summarily, a total drunk was dumped behind the nearest hedgerow to sleep if off, and the violent drunk given a few hefty clouts to teach him his manners before being handed over to his mates to be taken home."

He finally retired from the force in 1924 and built himself a bungalow on the right-hand side of Ongar Road, opposite the row of council houses which run up from the bridge on the edge of the village. There he raised goats, pigs, chickens and any other livestock which could turn a little profit. He also grew fruit and vegetables in his large garden, his wife made jam, and all the surplus was sold in the village to augment his pension. His daughter, who never married, became a teacher at the village school and retired many years later to look after him. When we left the village in 1968, he was well into his nineties and still living in the same house, now rather dilapidated over the years. He died a couple of years later having drawn his police pension for over forty years!

I apologise for dealing at some length with such a facet of village life when, after all, I set out to relate my own amusing experiences. The Frank Marriotts of this world though fascinated me beyond measure, and I can only hope that it has done the same for you.

After four and a half years, and under gentle but persistent pressure from section sergeant to divisional superintendent to go for promotion, Joan and I talked long and hard on all its pros and cons. As a family, we were happy and settled, the children contented with school and friends, Joan working for a most considerate employer who allowed her flexi-time in order to look after our needs, and I had settled down into an equally happy routine. If we moved, where would it be? Grays? Harwich? Tilbury? God help us!

In the end, it was decided that nothing would be lost by my sitting the exams, particularly as the act of promotion depended on the success of personal interviews before the promotion board (after all, one could be brilliantly clever but a total twit). Getting the exam under my belt committed us to nothing and we would still have all the time needed to decide what we wanted to do.

The exam consisted of three papers; education (maths and English), police duties (internal procedures and disciplinary regulations) and crime and traffic law.

I don't know whether they run such a scheme now but it was then possible, for not too considerable a fee, to enrol at the Harlow College of Further Education for a course in English, maths and examination technique. For my part, the latter was particularly fascinating for it demonstrated what was for me an unknown art – the ability to examine a subject, break it down and produce a coherent solution. No examiner, we were told, could thus fail to notice our complete grasp of the subject followed by its faultless presentation! Such a discovery was always worth a few extra marks which in the end could make the difference between success or failure. This was all new to me, schooled as I had been in South London where not even the eleven-plus had been available to us, but it worked!

My weekly stints at Harlow were fascinating and I revelled in every minute of it. Along with the majority my weakest subject was maths, but to my astonishment after the first week or so something seemed to click and things started to flow. I felt a growing confidence that I had never experienced at school. The credit for this burst of light on the road to Damascus went to our tutor whose patience was endless and whose ability to put over his subject faultless.

At the end of the course, there was an examination followed by a critical analysis of our work which served only to further increase one's self-confidence.

Following this, I immediately applied for a place on the two-week pre-promotion course at headquarters, a course which in itself required an entrance exam to qualify for admission and was carefully timed to end only days before the all-important home office promotion exam. Twenty-one of us were selected and from the first morning, we were left under no illusion as to the intensity of what lay before us. Day in, day out, our instructors pounded us with criminal and traffic law, police procedures and regulations, and at night we studied the following day's subjects. This, the most gruelling fortnight I had experienced since joining the police, bore full fruit however, for of the twenty-one selected nineteen of us passed.

It is only natural I suppose that this would have an effect on our discussions about leaving Moreton, and almost overnight the scales of decision tipped suddenly in favour of the move. Another event occurred though which really took the matter out of our hands. David, who was now eleven, had passed his eleven plus and been allocated a place at Netteswell Comprehensive School in Harlow. To attend, he had to cycle to Matching Green (just under three miles), leave his cycle with a friend, and then catch the school bus to Harlow. This trek in all weathers served only to highlight our isolated rural position and forced us to consider the same problem when the other three children reached the same age.

We decided to 'go for it'.

A short while later, in best uniform with razor-sharp creases, I sat with a dozen other hopefuls in an ante-room at headquarters waiting to be interviewed by the chief constable who was accompanied by two or three divisional superintendents.

One small peculiarity I remember was that we all sat with our helmets on our laps. When your name was called, you stood up, put on your helmet, walked into the chief's office, saluted, took your helmet off and sat down. At the end of the interview, the procedure was reversed, and smartly of course!

I remember being told on very good authority that one particular constable, totally flustered by the occasion and the questions put to him, so forgot himself as to put his helmet on back-to-front when it came to saluting his farewell to the board! It must only have been a momentary oversight for the fit of a helmet is quite different when back-to-front, but he still managed to do it.

My interview was surprisingly easy-going with only two or three questions about, 'what would you do if…'. Most of it seemed to concentrate on where I had served, with whom, and what I had done. I remember being stumped for a diplomatic answer when the chief asked whether I had any leanings toward

CID work. Unable to think of a reasonable sounding lie, I think I impressed them with my honesty rather than my ambition when I replied that I had spent the required month of my probation as CID aide in Romford and that as far as I was concerned it had put me off CID work for life! This brought smiles to their faces and a short while later, I was asked to show in the next candidate. True to my word, I never ventured near the CID for the rest of my service.

A month or so later, my boss from Harlow, Chief Superintendent Vickers, paid me what I thought was a routine office visit.

After going through my books, he sat back and accepted the traditional cup of tea that Joan brought in. As she turned to go though, he said, "Wait a minute, I've got something here you might be interested in." He put his hand in his pocket and took out a pair of bright new silver chevrons. Handing them to me he said, "Well done, Sergeant! You move to Chelmsford in a fortnight." It was November 1967.

Outside Chelmsford Police Station 1985

Chelmsford Police Station. Replaced Police offices in the Shire Hall. Built 1905. Vacated in 1969.

Chelmsford Police Station Built 1969.

Chapter Nine

Like every other family moving to a new home in a strange town we drove over to Chelmsford as soon as we were told where we were to live. It was a dreary, drizzly day and I found myself singularly unimpressed with an equally dreary, dismal county town. I distinctly remember saying to Joan, "Don't bother to unpack, we won't be staying that long."
Had I known that twenty-five years later I would be penning these words no more than two miles from that very same town centre…

Looking back, it was a pretty awful-looking place. The only two buildings of any architectural worth were the Shire Hall and the Corn Exchange, the latter now long since demolished to make way for the present shopping precinct and that monstrosity of a multi-storey carpark. On the same site was the cattle market, a forlorn empty expanse of iron-railed pens about which the litter of market day blew in all directions.

The narrow Tindal Street served the market folk with its four pubs, all within a space of a hundred yards or so, the Spotted Dog, the Blue Dolphin, the White Hart and one other I cannot now remember.

The dual-carriageway which now runs from the railway arches to the army and navy roundabout, effectively splitting the town in two, did not exist then. Instead, Old Moulsham commenced at the Stone Bridge over the river with Friars Place to the right and Baddow Road to the left, signalling the start of alterations which have now changed Chelmsford out of all recognition.

Our move to 33 Peel Road (the use of the name Peel showed original thinking) at Springfield started out catastrophically. The road of identical council style semi-detached houses was given over entirely to police and prison officers, and while some were obviously well-cared for, others showed signs of indifferent occupation.

On a particularly nasty November day, we let ourselves in and walked through to the kitchen, our footsteps echoing hollowly throughout the empty, bare-boarded house. Our first impression was that it was filthy and our second confirmed it. The gas stove in the kitchen hadn't seen a cloth or cleaner in years and black grease abounded on every surface, inside and out. I glanced up the stairs and saw folds of wallpaper hanging down in huge strips. The other rooms too bore the same mute testimony to total neglect. The house, I knew, had been vacated by a detective inspector, a man renowned for his sartorial elegance with beautiful suits and snow-white shirts adorned with snazzy bow-ties. The impeccable appearance he showed the world certainly belied everything that lay before us that day.

My anger was such that, new sergeant or no new sergeant, I was not going to have this, and within a few minutes I was on the phone to what turned out to be (had I known it then) the best man for dealing with such a situation, Chief Inspector Ray Long at Chelmsford. I told him what we had found, and that my wife was in tears, which she was. He only spoke once. "Stay where you are, I'll be up immediately." Within ten or fifteen minutes, he was at the house and walking slowly from room to room surveying what passed for decor. He was not a happy man and when Ray Long was unhappy, things tended to happen rather quickly.

He completed his tour, carrying with him the house-inspection sheet which had supposedly been completed and signed by an examining inspector to the effect that he had visited the house with the outgoing tenant and had found everything clean and respectable, the decorations up to standard and all the appliances similarly clean and in working order. It took little imagination to work out who Ray Long's first victim was to be!

He was especially nice to Joan and apologised for the fact that our first day in Chelmsford should have started so badly. At the door, he turned to me and said, "Let's face facts. You have every right to complain by way of a report to the chief constable, but as a newly promoted sergeant, the last thing you need is any sort of reputation as a stirrer. I have more clout than you, so if you are willing to move in and leave the rest to me, I promise immediate action. Will you agree to this?" Knowing that what he had said was perfectly true I agreed.

Within twenty-four hours, the county architect had visited and promised emergency decorations throughout. I later got to hear that my predecessor had been called before our guv'nor, Chief Superintendent Wilf Partis, and had spent a very uncomfortable time with him. Bearing in mind that only five years previously when we had vacated our house at Gallows Corner the examining officer, Chief Inspector Ambrose, had practically used a magnifying glass, actually running his finger along the tops of doors and picture rails. That's how strict some of them were and how I imagined them all to be.

I spent the first few days as a newly promoted sergeant acclimatising myself to the new surroundings and to the somewhat daunting task of being responsible for a shift of up to a dozen men. Each of the four shifts (earlies, lates, nights and rest days) had two supervisors, one the patrol sergeant and the other the duty sergeant. As the names imply, the former was expected to be out on the streets supervising the men while the latter remained in the station dealing with the paper-work, the reception, booking procedure and charging of prisoners. A few months after my arrival, he also found himself responsible for the radio network out on the streets, for personal radios had just been introduced.

I found the work fascinating and at such a busy station the guv'nors, assuming that forty-eight hours was more than enough to turn a constable into a sergeant, left you to it and it then became a policy of 'sink or swim'. To give them their due though I did not meet a single guv'nor who would not back you to the hilt if you made a cock-up of something. This did not mean that a sound rollicking was never administered, it was just done behind closed doors, good for discipline and all that. This only served to make me more determined to learn quickly and to try at any rate to make the right decision first time. I always said, and always meant it, that it was the best rank in the force. Lowly enough never to be out of touch and yet sufficiently elevated to be able to pass the buck! I loved it.

I hadn't been at Chelmsford very long when, on a quiet Sunday morning just before seven o'clock, I was cruising around the town centre and received a call on my personal radio to attend a domestic at a house in the Mildmay Road area. Now domestics are commonplace, even on Christmas Day, but seven o'clock on a Sunday morning took some believing.

I was at the address within a couple of minutes and there, lo and behold, was a particularly pretty young blonde in her early twenties standing in her front garden – stark naked. Not a stitch. Unable to believe what I was seeing, I checked the house-number again just to be sure, and then trying hard to maintain an expressionless countenance (as if I ran into this sort of thing every day of the week) asked her what the dickens she thought she was doing.

She explained that she had had a ding-dong argument with her husband the night before and had stormed out. She had visited a friend to cry on her shoulder only to be told that she was just leaving to go to a party, but would she like to go with her? Of course, she did, and the party lasted all night.

Arriving home at about six-thirty, she got undressed and slipped into bed. This woke the husband who demanded, not unnaturally, to know where she had been. An almighty row developed and he threw her out of the house – starkers.

Ever gallant, I took my raincoat from the police car and wrapped it 'round her, telling her to sit in the car while I spoke to the husband. I spent the next few minutes arguing the toss but the old man would have none of it.

"Tell her to go back to her precious friends," was all I could get out of him.

"Well, at least pass out some clothes for her," I pleaded.

"No way!"

I was left with little alternative but to tell her that I was taking her back to the station where she could wait until her old man had cooled down. By now she was back on the pavement again, having got out of the car to hear what was being said. At that moment, the beat PC turned up having heard the call to me and deciding to give me a hand if the 'domestic' got rough. The look on his face when he saw me chatting to a totally starkers blonde with a police raincoat draped over her was something to behold. I was cautious enough to tell him that he was travelling back to the nick with us, just in case.

A tragic sequel occurred about six months later when, on

arriving for duty, I learned that a blonde woman in her early twenties had been found drowned in the Boreham gravel pits.

Her name, of course, instantly rang a bell and I told the CID of the domestic I had attended. They treated the affair as possible murder and brought in the husband for questioning but he had a cast-iron alibi. The fact that he was a very well-known local scrap-dealer with a bit of a record went against him for a time but eventually a careful examination of the scene showed only one set of footprints (hers) leading to the edge of the pit. Murder could never be proved and suicide was recorded at the inquest.

Yet another interesting sequel occurred involving this same man, named Miller. The inspector called me to the control room at the nick to tell me that Miller had just been disqualified for a year at the Shire Hall Quarter Sessions and that he had driven to court. Knowing him, there was every likelihood that he would use his car to get home! We jumped into a car and within minutes were at the Shire Hall in time to see Miller driving down the High Street in his Jaguar.

Our Cortina would normally have been no match for his car but fairly heavy traffic favoured us and we stayed close behind as he weaved in and out in an effort to shake us off. Finally, rounding a corner in the Mildmay Road area we came across his Jag hastily abandoned at an angle to the kerb. There was no sign of him.

We started a foot search with the inspector taking one side of the road while I took the other. Only a moment or two later, a man walked past me, and without turning his head, said out of the corner of his mouth, "He's down the alleyway," and walked on. Off I went down the alleyway and there sure enough was matey-boy crouched in a doorway.

"Come on," I said, and he came, as good as gold.

Three weeks later, he appeared again before Chelmsford Court where, with little alternative, he pleaded guilty to driving whilst disqualified. He was to find that his trip home was to cost him a further twelve months' ban and a fine of £100, a heavy fine indeed for its day.

One of the jobs of shift sergeant I found most rewarding involved the guiding and instruction of new recruits from Eynsham. There they were, all bulled up to the nines, their minds bursting with theoretical knowledge, very eager to get stuck in, but totally lacking in practical experience – quite understandable, of course. Most were excellent, some were more than a trifle lacking.

One of the 'excellents' was someone who later became a very good friend and who rose (at the time of writing) to Detective Chief Inspector. On the morning I first met him, my shift were sitting round the parade-room table entering up their 'informations' when I walked in with the usual file under my arm. I looked around and saw the new face staring at me. His uniform was razor-creased, his boots shone like glass, he looked as if he had just stepped out of a band-box. "And you are?" I asked, knowing full well who he was.

He leapt to his feet and barked, "Robert Edward Miller, 1188, SARGE!" Now, this was straight out of the army manual of drill and brought smiles to all assembled.

"You're ex-army then," I asked.

"No, Sarge" he replied, leaving me wondering whether Eynsham were now turning out guardsmen. In fact, he had served for several years in the army cadet corps at Dagenham and it showed! Not once, in all the years I knew him, did he ever let his standards drop, whether in uniform or out, his boots or shoes were always bulled to perfection and his dress immaculate. It was always a pleasure patrolling the streets with him. His initial reaction to my question lived on, however, for whenever a sergeant required a certain PC at the nick it was standard practice simply to yell his name (no tannoys in those days) for him to respond. Whenever I wanted Bob, I would call, 'ROBERT EDWARD, 1188!'

One of the less capable – no let's face it, idiots – was a youngster called Darling. Yes, that was his name and it was most apt. How on earth he had managed to get through Eynsham without being told to pack his bags was a mystery. He talked like a darling, walked like a darling and behaved like a darling. I was out walking with him in Duke Street one night when I saw an approaching car with only one headlight.

"Have a word with him," I said.

Darling edged towards the kerb rather hesitantly and then at the last moment leaped out in front of the poor motorist, raising his arm in a classic training school 'stop' position. Though beautifully executed, it was certainly thirty yards too late and as the driver slammed his foot down, the car skidded on full lock right up to the frozen figure of PC Darling. I closed my eyes waiting for the inevitable bang and the sound of breaking glass. Opening them again, I saw an irate driver and a PC too speechless with shock to answer. I growled a couple of unprintable words in Darling's ear and then spent the next two minutes smoothing the ruffled feathers of the motorist before gently ticking him off about his lights.

Quite apart from this, Darling's sins and omissions were manifold and he only lasted another couple of months before being 'persuaded' to accept that whatever talents he may have lay elsewhere. The next time I saw him, he was the assistant manager at the Odeon cinema in Baddow Road. It has now been demolished, but I can't help wondering whether it simply fell about his ears.

Another of my lads displayed a somewhat questionable, though certainly entrepreneurial skill, whenever I gave him front-office duty on nights. He would slip out to his car and return with a couple of gallon-cans of petrol. Now, hardly a night went by without at least one panicky motorist calling to ask directions to the nearest all-night petrol station. In those days, there were only two; the Widford White Horse (now demolished) and the Oasis at Springfield. The PC would direct him, of course, but then casually add that he just so happened to have a spare gallon. He found most motorists would gratefully slip him an extra five bob for his 'trouble'.

At the bottom of the High Street, by the Stone Bridge over the river, lay Caters building, then the tallest in town. It had a peculiar setup at the rear for one could drive halfway up the six or seven storeys by way of a winding service road and then complete the journey to the roof on foot. I have stood up there many a time at three or four o'clock in the morning, looking out over the peaceful sleeping town or watching the dawn break on the horizon. It was also the favourite spot for our more adventurous PO's who would make the climb armed with a milk bottle. As the sergeant passed below, an accurately aimed bottle would suddenly shatter a few feet behind him. I never heard of a sergeant being hit by one of these missiles so I suppose the lads must have put in some practice on passing members of the public. Whether it was considered that my sense of humour had perhaps not fully acclimatised itself to Chelmsford's way of life I don't know, but I was put wise to this initiation at an early stage and thereafter always took care to cross to the other side of the road when passing Caters. Even today, I find myself glancing up at the top whenever I pass.

One of the necessary duties of a police officer, and one which understandably most members of the public are happy to leave to them, involves death in all its forms. From cot-deaths to road accidents, suicides to murders, the commonplace and the bizarre are all part and parcel of a policeman's lot. By commonplace I mean natural deaths which occur at home and for which, although a doctor may well have attended, he cannot legally issue a death-certificate if he has not seen the patient within two weeks of death. In all such cases, the police must attend, examine the body for any injury, obtain statements from whoever found the body, and the next of kin, and then arrange for its removal to the mortuary for a post-mortem examination.

In my early years, the officer had to attend the post-mortem to identify the corpse to the pathologist and to be on-hand should anything suspicious be found. To get us used to the sight of bodies, both 'clean' and otherwise, all probationers were required to attend Oldchurch Hospital to witness two or three routine PM's. The only advance information you would get of this would be when, having signed on in the duty roster, the sergeant would write alongside your name 'PM 10.30 a.m.', and that was that.

I must confess to experiencing more than a little apprehension before going in for my first one or two but consoled myself with the thought that everyone must do it and I would soon get used to it. I never did really but once you had managed to divorce your mind from the thought that it was a human body lying there you were all right.

Presenting yourself at the appointed hour, you introduced yourself to the pathologist's assistant who had already prepared the subject for examination and who entreated you that if you felt sick during the proceedings, then you should leave the room immediately – before not after! Although often queasy, I was thankfully never ill, for once underway my nerves settled and I found myself taking an inordinate interest in what was going on, even so far as peering over to study something the pathologist had discovered or listening as he pointed out various conditions which had affected the deceased or had actually caused his death.

Apart from the railway line death at Romford, most of those I had dealt with had been fairly clean. The next 'nasty' occurred during my first summer at Chelmsford when I was out on motor patrol. It was a particularly hot day when I received a call to attend an address at nearby Melbourne Park where the neighbours were complaining of a particularly nasty smell coming from one of the pre-fabs and had also been thoughtful enough to tell us that they had not seen the elderly occupant for some days. As I made my way across town, it took little imagination to work out what the smell could be.

On my way, I picked up the beat officer, George Campbell, who was then still a probationer. We drew up outside the pre-fab and were met by several neighbours. The smell was certainly awful. Quietly warning George of what was to be expected I knocked a couple of times, just in case, and on receiving no reply I took out my truncheon and broke the window in the front door (in thirty years I had never had to use it on anyone, it was only ever used to break windows!).

Opening the door, the stench came out and hit us; it was awful. There was also a strange humming noise coming from inside.

Holding our hands over our mouths, we checked the various rooms and found that the humming came from swarms of bluebottles which were infesting the place. Finding nothing in the rooms we came to the bathroom, and there lying on the floor was what remained of the male occupant. He was, of course, dead and had been so for some days. In that hot weather, the pre-fab had become a veritable oven and the constant heat had done horrible things to the body. The bluebottles had done the rest.

An unusual incident concerning death occurred during my first year at Chelmsford. I walked in one day and did my usual check of the detention sheets. There, I saw that a prisoner had been booked in as 'detained for his own safety'. It seems he had been wandering about talking to himself, walking out into traffic and generally risking life and limb wherever he went. I had a look at him and saw he had rolled himself up in a ball in the corner of his cell ignoring the bed and blankets that were available. I asked him if he felt all right but he just stared back at me with a totally blank expression.

I cannot remember now whether we got the doctor out to him or not, I expect we did, for we all agreed that he was high on drugs. In those days, drugs were nowhere near as commonplace as they are now and all we could do was to keep a close eye on him. Eventually, he appeared to have returned to normal and we released him.

The following day, a call came in that there was a body in the river by the Stone Bridge. Off we went and there sure enough was the body of a man drifting face-down with the current.

Hauling him out we found that it was the same man we had had in the previous day. Since there was no evidence of foul play, we assumed that he had either succumbed to the depression that so often accompanies drug taking or was so 'high' that he thought he was Jesus walking on water. That is not a heartless comment to make for there were cases where the addict, convinced that he was Batman, would fling himself off a building to prove it.

Before I close the subject of death, for the time-being at any rate, I must mention one unusual incident which occurred at Chelmsford Prison. At about eight o'clock one morning, the Duty Inspector told me to get off to the prison as one of the inmates had hanged himself. I had never dealt with a prison suicide before and considering the number there must be throughout the country I wondered why I was being asked to deal with this one.

I was there within a few minutes and was immediately struck by the almost deferential treatment I received from all members of staff from assistant governor down. An officer, who had been allocated as my assistant, stressed that anything I wanted would be given and that I had free rein to go anywhere I liked in the prison.

My first port of call was, of course, the deceased's cell. Believing that by then the body would have been removed to the prison mortuary I was somewhat surprised to find it still lying on the cell floor. Lifting the blanket which had been placed over it, I saw that the deceased was a West Indian in his middle twenties. The ligature, which was still 'round his neck, consisted of the deceased's tie and trousers belt which had been tied tightly together with the tie forming the noose.

The other end had been tied to the bracket of a shelf on the wall over a free-standing radiator, and was thus no more than four feet from the floor! I spoke to the officer who had found him and learned that the prisoner had knelt on the floor in front of the radiator and had simply allowed the weight of his body to strangle him. 'Strangle' is the wrong word really for although I was assured that this was not an impossible way to die, it was unusual in that the deceased could, of course, reverse the process simply by standing up. That he was determined to die was therefore not in doubt and it was only later that I learned that hanging in any form is not simply a matter of cutting off the air supply, if sufficient pressure such as the weight of one's own body is brought to bear around the neck it is the lack of blood flow to the brain which causes death – often within eight seconds!

I saw that there was only one bed in the cell and it was confirmed that the prisoner had the place to himself. I made the routine check for other injuries but could find nothing. Asking whether there was anything about this death that had struck them as unusual, I was more than surprised to learn that the prisoner, along with other West Indian inmates, was heavily into the occult and the whisper was that he had had the finger pointed at him!

The news certainly took me aback for I knew no more than the next man about 'juju' and my immediate reaction was to pooh-pooh the idea, but the prison officers were serious! It transpired that the deceased's mental condition had been such that he had been allocated this single observation cell where at night a dull red light shone from the ceiling to facilitate the regular checks that had to be made. Looking up, I saw there was no bulb in the fixture. A prison officer produced it saying that the prisoner had apparently climbed onto his chair, unscrewed the protective surround (presumably with a small coin) and taken out the bulb. He obviously had no intention of being disturbed and resuscitated.

After checking the night visit reports of the duty officers to ascertain how often he had been visited, I was satisfied that no other person had had access to him after lights-out. I was now faced with the ridiculous task of interviewing the other West Indians involved in this so-called occult ring. I got nowhere, they simply laughed it off. "It's crazy, man!"

A week later, I visited the prison again, this time for the inquest, and found that the deceased's entire family had arrived from North London. I imagined there would be all sorts of protest and reaction from them, prison neglect or brutality, that sort of thing, particularly when I pointed out to the court how easy it had been to remove the observation light from the ceiling, and how easily a prisoner's tie and belt could be used to form a noose. But they conducted themselves with great dignity and were in turn treated with sympathy and courtesy by the prison staff. They, along with the coroner, were satisfied that it was a straightforward, if somewhat bizarre, suicide and that was what the verdict turned out to be.

One of my earliest duties at Chelmsford involved the assize court at the Shire Hall. Justice in those days was meted out at the magistrates court for fairly minor offences which carried a maximum penalty of six months or £500 fine. The more serious cases, involving correspondingly higher sentences, went to the Court of Quarter Sessions, and the really serious cases such as murder, armed robbery etc. went to the assize. This was the 'red robe court' presided over by senior judges who visited the town for this purpose about four times a year.

Then with due pomp and splendour, they processed through the streets from the judge's lodgings at a house called Maynetrees, just fifty yards from the police station, to the Shire Hall, accompanied by robed dignitaries including the Lord Lieutenant, the high sheriff, under sheriffs and others.

The task of the police, whose only contribution to the splendour of the occasion was that they wore white gloves, was to escort the procession. The sergeant walked in front, two constables escorted the judges and another two held up traffic to the front and rear.

Once inside, the constables were allocated seats in the upper and lower public galleries of the two courts to keep order. The sergeant remained in court with a three-fold duty, to assist his constables in maintaining order (I never witnessed any such thing but I suppose we had to be there just in case), to assist the judge with any requests he might make, and to take note of any criticism or praise he felt constrained to make in respect of police witnesses. This performance was repeated when the court rose for lunch, was resumed an hour later for the afternoon session, and was repeated again at the end of the day when everyone returned to Maynetrees. Needless to say, with two assizes running the cost in terms of police manpower was considerable. Consequently, a few years later, the whole rigmarole was abolished and the honourable gentlemen now don their traditional black overcoats and bowler hats and walk like everyone else to court.

Talking of courts reminds me of an occasion when I very nearly came to grief because of a prisoner. Now, prisoners come in all shapes and sizes, some are easy to handle, some are not, and others can be downright dangerous. One quickly learns how to cope. Of all prisoners though, an angry Irishman is bad news, an angry drunken Irishman very bad news, and an angry, drunken, fighting navvy of an Irishman is something to avoid at all costs – and I say that with deference to my O'Leary ancestors.

Most people, of course, can avoid such a beast by ignoring him and walking away. It's more difficult for a policeman though, and impossible when that policeman is a sergeant in his own police station!

Such a confrontation took place at Chelmsford in the days when the station stood on the corner of New Street and Waterloo Lane. I was chatting to the front office constable when a visitor turned up at the public counter. One glance was enough to tell me that he had taken too much Liffey water and his thick Irish brogue confirmed it as he demanded to use our toilet. I told him that the nearest public toilet was just down Waterloo Lane, two minutes' walk away. No, he said, he couldn't wait that long, he wanted to use ours. No, I said, he would have to wait until he got down Waterloo Lane. He continued with his demands while I continued to refuse him.

"Right," he said, "in that case…" and undoing his trousers he promptly urinated on the spot against the public counter.

I remember standing there for a moment or two thinking, *I don't believe he's doing this*. Then – and this was the only thing I could think of doing – I grabbed a mop and bucket (kept handy for cleaning out the cells) and thrust them at him, ordering him to clear up the mess. Had he done so there would have been no story to tell and he would have saved himself, and me, a lot of grief. As it was, he picked up the mop and bucket and threw them at me!

Within seconds, we were at each other hammer and tongs; I to drag him into the police station and he to enjoy a good fight. As he was in his forties, a good fifteen years older than me, about five-feet six inches tall and of slim wiry build, I could be forgiven for thinking that I could handle him. Not a bit of it! With the front-office constable looking on to see fair play I quickly discovered that I was getting the worst of it. Finally, as I felt Paddy's fingers gouge into my eyes, the almost-disinterested constable decided it was time to lend a hand. For Paddy that should have been bad news, but in fact a second opponent only served to whip up his Irish dander and the doubling of enemy forces served only to make the fight more interesting! A minute or two later, the Seventh Cavalry arrived in the shape of Ron Groves, the burly station sergeant. That finally had some effect as we struggled to get Paddy to the cells. I was, I must confess, a mite angry by now and it was only as he continued to struggle that I hit him very hard two or three times in the body. As I glanced at my skinned knuckles, I thought, *If that doesn't slow him down, nothing will.* It didn't!

There was now only one way to deal with him. "Get the cuffs out of the control room," I shouted, and the constable dashed off. A few moments later, he returned and while two of us forced Paddy's arms behind his back the third slapped the ratchet cuffs unceremoniously on his wrists before dumping him in a cell. That was that, we thought, he can stay there until he cools off.

About five minutes later, the cell buzzer went (he must have pressed it with his forehead because he was still 'cuffed'). I went along and lowered the flap to see Paddy standing there facing me. Without a word, he spat straight at my face.

Fortunately, he missed but it was a sure sign that his spirit had not been cowed. I re-locked the flap and returned to my office.

About ten minutes later, the buzzer sounded again. I told the front office man to ignore it. Another five minutes and off it went again. We still ignored it. Finally, it became so persistent that I went along myself. Gently lowering the flap I stood to one side before glancing in.

Paddy, for what turned out to be sound reasoning, was standing on the far side of the cell well out of spitting range.

"Can you take me cuffs off now, sor?" he said. I looked closely and distrustfully at him. "They're hurting me, sor," he said, and turned his back to show me his hands.

I could not believe it. His fingers had swollen to the size of small bananas and were fast turning black! So much for ratchet cuffs being hurriedly applied.

"Right," I said, "behave yourself and I'll get them off you."

Knowing that if I didn't relieve him immediately, I would be in big trouble, to say nothing of him, I returned to the control room for the key. No key!

"Where are the ratchet-cuff keys?" I shouted. The front office man arrived at the double. He had no idea. Ron Groves arrived.

"Gawd 'elp us," he said. "I know where they are, on their way to Brixton. You remember we packed a prisoner off on remand today? The escort took the other set of cuffs and the keys – plural. We've got no key."

Within a minute, I was on the radio to all personnel out on the streets with ratchet cuffs to get back on the double. No dice, not a key fitted Paddy's cuffs. His hands were now decidedly indigo and I was seeing High Court writs floating before my eyes.

"Get the area car up to headquarters stores and grab every key he can find, and make it damned quick!"

Fortunately, it was still mid-afternoon and the stores would be open. After twenty frustrating minutes, the area car returned with a box-full of keys.

Paddy was now walking around in agonising circles.

"It's all right, it's all right," I said soothingly as I tried key after damned key. Finally, there was a click and the cuffs sprang open.

He stared in total disbelief at what had once passed for a pair of human hands but now looked like a bunch of black bananas. Then, letting out a yell as the circulation returned, he recommenced his circular walk around the cell wringing his hands and swinging his arms like windmills, his oaths abating in time with the blood as it flowed back into his veins.

I venture to think that if that had been anyone else but a tough Irish navvy, I would have been in big trouble. As it was he calmed down and we fed him, gave him a cup of tea, and having restored him to good humour charged him with assaulting me in the execution of my duty before tucking him up for the night. He took it very well really when his senses finally cleared enough for him to recognise that it was he who had started it all in the first place.

The following morning, I attended Chelmsford court where he pleaded guilty to urinating in a public place (the foyer being a public place), and assaulting a police officer. He was given a conditional discharge on the first charge and fined £150 on the second, a pretty whopping fine in the 1960s. To my relief, no mention was made by either side of the handcuffs saga and I console myself with the thought that he must have looked upon it as part of the price one pays for getting, as the Victorian charge sheet would say, 'beastly drunk'.

Chapter Ten

After a year or so at Chelmsford, I began looking around for what might be available in the country. I enjoyed the work in the town, it was certainly varied, but I still hankered after rural police work. Now and again, when the section sergeants at Danbury, Broomfield or Ingatestone went on leave, I would visit their men on their various detached beats. The peace and tranquillity of the countryside still pulled like a magnet and the laid-back yet thoroughly knowledgeable rural officers remained as they had always been, one of the main stays of the force.

After eighteen months or so, I got to hear that Charlie Sams, the skipper at Danbury, was retiring. I lost no time in applying to take over from him. Luck was against me this time though for another Chelmsford Sergeant with more experience got the job. I was daft enough then to think that I had all the qualifications, I had after all served at two divisional stations (Romford and Chelmsford), a sub-divisional station (Harold Hill), a section station (Plough Corner) and detached beat at Moreton. What more did they want? They wanted me to prove myself first.

A few months later, Sergeant Bill Feeke from Ingatestone popped into Chelmsford for one of his routine visits. Whilst chatting to him, he let it slip that he was retiring shortly. My ears pricked up. "Have you put your papers in yet?" I asked.

"No, not yet," he replied. I told him I was more than interested in getting a section station to myself and Ingatestone would be ideal. I asked him, with more than a bit of cheek, to promise that I would be the first to know the moment he put in his papers.

The day arrived when he telephoned to say that they were on their way to headquarters. I straightaway put in a request for a transfer to Ingatestone before my chief super even knew that Bill was retiring! A week or two later, I was told that I had the job. It was then August 1969.

My farewell to D shift and Chelmsford took place at the Saracen's Head, just yards from the police station, and turned out to be not only one of the most memorable nights of my life but one which I doubt would be repeated these days.

We were on nights at the time although I had been given a half-night (six p.m. to two a.m.) to facilitate my house move the next day. At about eight-thirty my shift of eight, along with Inspector Fred Johnson and Chief Inspector Alec Ferguson, gathered in the saloon bar of the Saracen's. We had agreed that an hour or so was enough for an informal farewell. It seemed much less than that when Jim Loader looked at his watch and declared that it was nine forty-five and time for them to go on duty. As I thanked them for coming, it was agreed there was no point in my rushing as the late-turn sergeant would be there to look after things until ten o'clock.

"Oh and by the way," Jim said, "we've left you a drink on the bar." I looked across the room.

Standing there in an orderly line were eight pints along with eight whiskies!

After the initial shock, it did not seem such an insurmountable problem, for a quick calculation told me that the three of us remaining had about two and a half pints and the same in whisky each. The only snag was that we had had a few already and I had another four hours' duty to do. Now, Alec (later to become superintendent) was a Scot, so I felt it right and proper that he should attack the whisky while Fred (who tragically died of a heart attack a couple of years later) and I should make an attempt on the beer.

At about half past ten, we walked with as much dignity as we could muster into the nick. I did the usual check with the front office for outstanding jobs, unusual incidents and whatever prisoners we had in. The office man assured me that all was quiet and there were no prisoners.

"Good," I said. "If anyone wants me, I'll be in number one cell." He grinned and nodded his head in acknowledgement. A minute later, I was stretched out on the plastic coloured mattress in the cell with a blanket over me.

Drifting off beautifully, I was suddenly aware of hands running over me. I jerked awake. "Who's that?"

A voice replied, "Oh! Is that you, John? I was looking for somewhere to put my head down for a bit." It was Fred Johnson.

"Take number two cell," I said. I turned over and was asleep within a minute.

I never really found out where Alec Ferguson got to. Whether he took number three cell or was possessed of a stronger constitution than Fred or I and had managed to get home I do not know.

It seemed I had only been asleep a few minutes when I felt someone shaking my arm. "Come on, Sarge, time to go home." It was the front office man. Dragging myself awake, I asked what time it was. "Ten-to-two," he said. I jumped. I had slept for three hours! Now life in a busy station didn't stand still just because the sergeant was missing.

"What's been happening?" I demanded, a touch of panic creeping into my voice.

"It's all quiet, Sarge," he replied in a tone a mother would use to soothe a fractious child.

"Well, something must have happened," I said.

"Nothing we couldn't cope with, and anyway the patrol skipper took over." A thought occurred to me.

"Where's Mr Johnson?" A long-suffering sigh this time.

"We woke him some time ago. He's checked everything and has gone home."

"Any prisoners?"

"No, Sarge."

I persisted, "Nothing I should know about then?"

Another deep sigh. "Look, you'll be in Ingatestone tomorrow, or rather today, so forget about it."

I walked out of the cell knowing that I was in no fit state to drive and as I turned to suggest that the area car had better come in for me I was met with another resigned look. "It's waiting outside for you now, and when you get home, you'll find your car parked outside the house. I went through your pockets for the keys." What a bunch of lads. It was August 1969 and I was back to rural policing again.

The sergeant's house at Ingatestone incorporated the police office, much as it did at Moreton and most of the rural nicks in the county, except that next-door was a pair of semi-detached houses for the two constables. It meant, of course, that when the PC's went off duty, the sergeant still had the telephone and personal callers to deal with day and night regardless of whether he was on or off duty. Although each of the constables had extensions through to their homes capable of taking incoming calls, it seemed never to have been the practice to disturb them! The skipper was obviously expendable, but I considered it a price worth paying to get back to the type of work I loved.

Sergeant's house, Ingatestone. Ian Pigney and Dave Sawford lived in the two houses on the left.

In fact, this took a considerable toll on both Joan and I for we grew accustomed to the bedside 'phone ringing at all hours of the night, mostly with calls which could easily have waited until morning. As it happened, the Metropolitan Police, whose border was just five miles away on the other side of Brentwood, were the worst offenders for if they had a query, they would simply look us up in the police almanack and call, never dreaming for a moment that there were police stations that actually closed at night! When I tetchily reminded the caller that it was three-thirty in the morning and that he had woken me up to ask if someone-or-other had produced his driving documents, the response was always the same, "Asleep? Aren't you a twenty-four hour nick? I'm sorry, mate, I'll call back in the morning". But by then the damage was done. Over the years, we found we had acclimatized ourselves to sleeping lightly; Joan to wake at the slightest sound from the children, and me to grab the 'phone at its first tinkle so as not to wake the entire household! Many years later, when we moved into our own house at Writtle, we found it difficult settling down at night because it was so quiet.

I recall one such call coming in at about half past midnight, not from the Mets this time but our own information room at headquarters, which was subsequently to cause more than a little consternation for Dave Sawford, my night-duty officer.

"We can't raise Charlie Golf Seven (our call-sign) and we've got a bit of a funny one at Stock," the operator told me.

"What's it all about?" I asked, growing wider awake by the minute.

"We've had a call from a man who says that he has been round to his mother's house and thinks that she has committed suicide."

"Thinks?" I said.

The operator replied that the man was pretty upset and not very helpful, but said that he lived nearby and would return to his mother's house to await police arrival. This was obviously going to be me, I thought.

I told him I would attend the address (about four miles away) and asked him to inform Dave Sawford when he came back on the air. I explained briefly to Joan and got dressed. Going downstairs, I opened a drawer and took out a sharp kitchen knife knowing that if it were a suicide then hanging was the only form of self-destruction that required a tool to deal with it. About twenty minutes later, I drew up outside the lonely cottage in a pitch black lane at Stock. As I walked up the garden path, the figure of a man approached from the house. He was in his early forties, smartly dressed and showing obvious relief at my arrival.

"Round the back," he whispered, although there was not a neighbour for miles. I followed him round to the back door. "There," he said, pointing to something white on the outside of the door. I shone my torch. It was brief and to the point, 'Charles, I am in the garage, Mother', it said.

In the eerie darkness of that garden, a chill ran up my spine, it was almost as if the dead were speaking. I turned to him. "Where's the garage?" He pointed to a lean-to at the side of the cottage.

"She has insisted on living here alone since Dad died last year. There's plenty of family to help but she said she did not want to be a burden. She has also become quite depressed lately."

"Have you looked inside?" I asked. He shook his head emphatically.

"No way, I'm not going in there." It was understandable.

I opened the garage door and walked in, shining my torch around as I did so. I almost bumped into her. She was quite dead, an overturned chair beneath her feet. She had used the clothes-line. I studied her for a few moments, formally that is, for any other sign of injury and to take in the situation should any questions be asked at an inquest. Taking out the kitchen knife, I cut her down and then looked carefully around for any sign of a suicide note. There was nothing. I returned to the garden.

"I'm sorry..." I said, knowing that was all he needed for confirmation.

We returned to the cottage and let ourselves in. It was well-furnished and very clean and tidy. There, in a neat row on the kitchen table were a number of letters to various members of her family, another addressed to the coroner and insurance policies. She was certainly a meticulous lady, and thoughtful too, for leaving the note on the back door and using the garage instead of the house where anyone could have blundered innocently into her.

Telling the son that I needed his formal identification, I

asked for a blanket to cover her up. Returning to the garage I laid it over her and then called him in. I raised a corner of the blanket to expose her face and he nodded in recognition.

Telling him there was no point in causing him extra grief by calling out the undertakers at that hour, I proposed leaving her until morning. He agreed.

As we made our separate ways home, Dave Sawford turned into the lane. He had at long last received the message. Reaching the house, he walked around it a couple of times but found everything in total darkness. He knocked at the door. No reply. He knocked again. Still nothing. Trying the doors, he found them all locked. He went to the garage and tried that. The door opened. Shining his torch inside, he stood transfixed at what was obviously a body covered with a blanket. Raising it, he saw clearly the ligature marks around her neck but no sign of the rope (I had taken it for evidence). How could she have hung herself, cut herself down and then covered herself with a blanket, he thought. It struck him that this looked a lot more serious than just suicide; in fact, far too serious for him to deal with. Returning to his car, he radioed the facts through to information room asking for scenes of crime and senior CID to be turned out. This was going to be a hectic night.

"Is your sergeant there?" asked the operator. Now, this puzzled Dave for as far as he knew I was safely tucked up in bed.

"Negative," he replied, "should he be?"

"Suggest you return to base and ask him," was the reply. "And the next time you leave your vehicle, follow the procedure and sign off with your location." Poor Dave was to became a much chastened man that night.

I had not been at Ingatestone for more than a day or two when, standing in the office looking out across Transport

Meadow (now re-named Seymour Field) towards the by-pass, a memory flashed me back to my early days soon after leaving Eynsham. It was September 1959 and I was on a local procedure course at headquarters before actually taking up duty at Romford. The instructor asked whether anyone wanted to pick up some practical experience acting as observer in a traffic car. Most of us volunteered and I found myself reporting to a Sergeant Reg Watson (who as time went by made it to chief superintendent).

In the yard stood a magnificent gleaming black Wolseley 6/110, complete with red leather upholstery and walnut fascia. We got in and I sat there thinking that this was certainly the most beautiful car I had ever been in, pretty understandable really as very few of us then had had the opportunity of sitting in any sort of car, Wolselely or otherwise. Indeed, of the forty odd on our course at Eynsham, I recollect only two actually owning cars, one Bedfordshire lad had a little Austin A35 while another had the famous bubble-car. The rest of us did what we had always done, bussed or trained it.

Sergeant Watson started up and we purred out onto the road. There the Hillman Minxes, Morris Minors and Austin Devons seemed to pale into insignificance as we glided along the A12 on that peaceful Sunday afternoon. There was, for me at any rate, a warm feeling of safety, comfort and control (and, yes, let's admit it – superiority!) sitting in such a car with its gleaming bodywork, sleek lines and a first-class driver behind the wheel.

I found myself asking lots of questions about the car and its performance, and was astonished to learn that it had already reached the end of its allotted life with us and was due to be sold off the following day.

"But there's nothing wrong with it!" I protested.

"Well, let's see how right you are," said Reg. "We'll give it a last burn-up."

We entered a new stretch of almost empty dual-carriageway, I had no idea where, and he put his foot down. We fairly leapt forward and I watched fascinated as the speedo crept up, 60—70—80. As smooth as silk and with only the sound of rushing air disturbing us as we flew along. 90—100—110—115! He slowly took his foot off.

"Don't want to overdo it," he murmured while I sat there wondering how such a machine could still perform like that at the end of its days.

Looking around at what was for me totally strange countryside, I asked, "Where are we, by the way?"

"Ingatestone by-pass," he said, "The nick's just over there." I had barely heard of the place.

Ingatestone High Street

Before actually taking over at Ingatestone, I followed the usual custom and called a few times on the outgoing sergeant. Much had to be learnt about the section, its problems, its officers, duties, responsibilities etc. On top of this, the two wives met to chat about shops, deliveries and the inevitable measuring up for new curtains. Bill and Mailey or Mayley Feeke (an Irish name I think) were a homely couple in their mid-fifties who were about to embark on a new venture as licensees of The Hound public house at Stradishall, near Eye in Suffolk. Bill was an expert wood carver and fine examples of his craft were everywhere to see. He was also, I later learned, reputed to be the most accomplished poacher in the district, a fact that really set me back on my heels until I was assured that this was known only to a very close circle of friends!

On one of my solo visits, he walked me down to the Star pub in the village. A centuries-old inn of cramped proportions, it's bare-floored interior was straight out of a Dickens novel. No two items of furniture matched and what there was looked as if it had been bought for a song at a local auction. The only item which even suggested comfort was an extremely battered settee which lay along the far wall, its upholstery split and grimed from years of wear. It was difficult to determine whether the oak beams were black with age or suffering from the effects of wood-smoke which billowed out from the huge fireplace over which the date '1610' was carved in the oak lintel. Neither had the walls and ceiling escaped, for both were richly brown with the effects of nicotine.

Singularly unimpressed though I was with the decor, I warmed to the licensee. Les Smith was then a slightly built man who although still in his fifties looked considerably older, a direct result of advanced alcoholism. He was both a gentle man and a gentleman, quietly spoken, polite, respectful and possessing a dry self-deprecating sense of humour which always manifested itself with a twinkle in his watery blue eyes.

I really cannot remember Les ever serving behind the bar, his role being to sit on one of the high stools (public side that is) chatting to and keeping his customers happy. Although undoubtedly a steady and confirmed drinker it is a credit to his constitution that I never saw him the worse for drink, the only real tell-tale sign was that his already-quiet voice got quieter and quieter until you had to press your ear close to his face to hear what he was saying!

Not surprisingly, his wife, Violet, who seemed to spend a lot of her time in the kitchen rather than the bar, kept an eye on his drinking. At one stage, it seemed to be having some effect for he began to take longer and longer over a solitary half-pint. It did not take a keen observer to notice though the quick glance towards the door as he gently slid his glass across the counter with a murmured instruction to, "Put a gold watch in there please." The glass would then be held under the optic for another large whisky to join those already there in his heavily laced beer. I remember too how it seemed to grieve him having to assert his authority when calling 'time', preferring instead to turn to his customers and say, "Come along now, you lovely people."

The section comprised Ingatestone itself (three men), Stock (one man), Margaretting (one man), Writtle (two men), and Roxwell (one man), covering a huge rural area from Chelmsford in the east to Brentwood in the west, and Doddinghurst in the north to Billericay in the south. The one-man beats still boasted pedal cycles while Writtle had a Velocette motor-cycle and Ingatestone a Mini-countryman. I used my own car and was paid a handsome mileage allowance – of one shilling and three farthings a mile (a fraction over five new pence!)

Compared with what I had been used to (with the exception of Moreton, of course) the section, being predominantly rural, was well-behaved and civilised. Most of my officers had served there for years and had got to know every youngster who was ever likely to cause trouble – and they made sure the youngster was aware of that. The result was that identification was often immediate and retribution swift, a hark-back to village life of old. Despite the fact that it was still force policy, although admittedly a dying one by now, to move a man every five years to prevent over-familiarity with his locals, the effect of spending all that time at one station also produced officers with profound and invaluable local knowledge. The powers-that-be could not have it both ways.

Having said that, I never did find out why I was left alone at Ingatestone for the next sixteen years!

I soon discovered that we had some interesting characters

living in the village, some weird, some eccentric. some very rich. For instance, there was Mr Webber, an old man by then who lived in a huge house called 'Ardtully' in Station Lane (now a nursing home). He was, it was said, the original of Webbers jewellers which have branches everywhere if they haven't been taken over by another conglomerate. He was in his seventies then and lived alone except for a housekeeper. One of his passions had been miniature railways – not the type you build in your loft but the one you actually sit on to be taken for a ride. At the height of his interest, he actually built a railway line which wound around his back garden. That garden was certainly big enough, for after his death a portion of it was sold off and three or four regency-style houses were built on it! When I knew it, though, it was sadly neglected and overgrown but the railway line could still be seen, for Webber had had it built on concrete pillars which raised it a couple of feet off the ground.

Just down the road from Ardtully over the level-crossing, there lived James Wentworth-Day. He was another absolute nut. Famous in his day as an author and journalist, he was a typical product of a 'between the wars, well-to-do upbringing'. A descendant of a line of East Anglian squires and land-owners whose portraits hung around his enormous study, he was for the most part a charmingly polite man. Every man has weaknesses though, odd little foibles, and Wentworth-Day's were whisky, a short fuse and Webber from Ardtully. What the origin of the feud was nobody ever really knew, but the talk was that they had fallen out many years back over a woman. The upshot of it was that neither lost an opportunity to complain about the other and both regarded the police as arbiters, but only so long as the decision went in their favour!

I remember James W-D ringing me up one day in a

spluttering rage. Off I went down to his house to find him pacing up and down his study.

"The man's a lunatic!" he yelled. "With all his money who would ever think he would stoop to theft!" I waited patiently for him to cool down.

"Right, what's your problem then?" I asked.

"Webber! Bloody Webber! That's my problem!" I sighed quietly to myself.

"What has he done this time?" I asked.

James glared. "Stolen six bottles of bloody beer, that's what he's done!" I was puzzled.

"But he can afford to buy the brewery, why should he steal six bottles of beer?"

The story came out. Wentworth-Day had purchased the beer at the off-licence in the High Street, the bottles being placed in a plastic carrier-bag. He had then called in at Finchams, the butchers, and who should be just leaving the shop but Webber. Having placed the carrier-bag on the counter while he made his purchases, James turned round and, lo and behold, the bag had gone. For reasons which can easily be imagined he decided not to pursue and confront the dastardly thief – who by then would have been no more than a few yards down the High Street – he returned home and called the police.

Now we really did, even in those halcyon days of the sixties, have better things to do than go running around recovering bottles of beer. However, the Wentworth-Days of this world still carried a lot of clout and it was always policy to show interest, however outrageous the demands. In addition, he was perfectly serious in his allegation and would have been on the phone to the chief constable the moment he thought I was not giving the matter my full and undivided attention.

Five minutes later, I was knocking at the door of Ardtully and being let in by Webber. There on a side-table in his sitting-room was a glass and an empty beer bottle, and beside his armchair the off-licence bag containing the other five. On questioning him, I quickly discovered that the absent-minded old boy had gathered up his purchases at Finchams and returned home only to find that he had an extra bag.

"Hmm! Must have bought 'em, I suppose," he replied.

It occurred to me also with only one other customer in the shop he must have realised who the owner was, but I couldn't prove it.

The upshot was that a few minutes later, I was returning the five remaining bottles to J Wentworth-Day and reimbursing him the cash for the sixth! When I think of it now, I shudder that we allowed ourselves to be demeaned in such a way, but believe it or not the wealthy gentry in those days were still deferred to by country folk – and the rural police, the modern counterparts of a centuries-old tradition whereby the squire did the bidding and everyone jumped. In life, though, everyone pays the price sooner or later and James Wentworth was no exception – tragically so. He was quaffing his usual pint or three in the Star one day and boasting that he was as fit now as he had ever been, certainly fit enough to lift and carry a grown man across the bar – something he was prone to do in his younger days. But alas! He was in his seventies now and the challenger was a big man.

Without a moment's hesitation James stepped forward, wrapped his arms around the man and lifted him clear off his feet. For a moment or two he paused, red in the face, and then slowly let the man go. It had been too much, he collapsed with a 'busted gut' and was taken off to hospital. He died shortly afterwards.

Talking of Station Lane with its grand houses reminds me of

another incident of some worth. I received a telephone call one day from a neighbour of a particularly fine house, I think it was Station House, just a hundred yards down from Ardtully.

He told me the house was empty pending sale. "There's a man on the roof stripping off the tiles," he said.

Within minutes, I was down there and sure enough, on walking 'round the back, there was an extending ladder leading right up onto the roof and a man working away stripping the tiles. I called up to him. He looked genuinely nonplussed at my presence but nevertheless climbed down. "What are you up to?" I asked, which was a silly question because I could see what he was up to.

"I'm under contract to demolish the house," he replied.

"Well, that's the first I've heard of that, this house is on the market," I said. "Where's your contract?" Now I expected him to say, 'It's at home or in the office or with my boss', but, no.

"It's in the van," he said. "I'll show you." Two minutes later, he handed me what appeared to be a genuine contract for demolition for which he, in return for the £5,000 fee, will be free to dispose of all the bricks, tiles, windows, staircases, fireplaces, panelling and assorted contents.

Still not too happy with this, I told him that I intended making further enquiries by radio about his identity (I had taken the police vehicle). With that I pushed one of his arms through the rungs of the ladder and slapped my handcuffs on his wrists. If he wanted to do a runner, he would have to take the forty-foot ladder with him.

Minutes later, I was back again to find him waiting as patiently as secured wrists would allow. Unlocking the cuffs I told him I had verified his identity and that we were going back to the nick. There further questioning disclosed just how far ordinary people were prepared to go to make a fast buck.

It appears he had received a letter from a firm in Buckinghamshire inviting tenders for the demolition of this particular house. He went off and had a look at it, from the outside of course, and thought what a lucrative job it would be. He replied offering to do the job for £5,000. A few days later, he received a phone call from this particular firm saying that it had received quotes from numerous applicants, some of which were better than his. However, and here's the sucker-bait, if he chose to pay the £5,000 in cash rather than by invoice, certain tax problems could be by-passed. Did he want the job? He jumped at it!

"Right," said the caller, "I'll come down to Ingatestone by train and in return for the cash I'll hand over the contract." He fell for it! The caller turned up, took the cash, handed over the 'contract' and caught the next train back to London. The demolition man, if he was to be believed, had no idea who the man was or where he came from, and could only hand over the original advertisement and the bogus contract.

All the enquiries I made with the Buckinghamshire Police drew a complete blank. Someone had walked off with a cool five thousand pounds for the cost of preparing one dud contract and the return fare from Liverpool Street to Ingatestone. I wondered how many others he had got away with.

Chief Inspector Hugh Brown was our rural chief inspector, responsible for the smooth running of the division's three sections – Ingatestone, Broomfield and Danbury. He was an ex-Scots Guardsman who had been captured by the Italians at Tobruk in 1941. After appalling treatment and near-starvation, he was shipped off to Italy and later handed over to the Germans when Italy (described by Churchill as "the weak under-belly of

Europe') capitulated. He spent the rest of the war toiling in copper mines. It was, as one can imagine, desperately hard work on rations that rarely reached subsistence level.

It was often said by those who lived through the war that so-and-so had a 'good war', meaning that he had been in a reserved occupation and had never been called up for active service. Conversely, there were those who had had a 'bad war', who had suffered out of all proportion to their contribution. 'Jock' Brown was certainly one of the latter, returning in 1945 very much the worse for wear. Yet, amazingly, and despite all the hardships he suffered, he emerged at the end of it a secret admirer of Hitler in respect of what he did for Germany during the 1930s, for the disciplined manner in which the German armies had fought, and for the odd little acts of compassion and kindness he was shown by his captors. I often wondered whether he ever mentioned these 'heresies' to his senior officers. I wouldn't be surprised, for he was the type that would and hang the consequences! He certainly made no secret of his feelings to me during our many conversations together. In fact, I put him down as a quiet fascist!

There were times when his language was quite ripe, ripe enough indeed to get him into trouble sometimes. On one of his trips to visit us at Ingatestone, he stopped off at some roadworks and blasted the navvies, as only he could, for failing to keep their road signs clean. Finishing his tirade he bent down, tore up a handful of wet grass and proceeded to show them how to clean road signs without the aid of water and cloth!

On another occasion, he had dealings with a rather wealthy and well-positioned lady who ran a riding school at Norton Heath, not far from Ingatestone, the like of which left her speechless with shock. She spent little time in complaining to the chief constable who ordered Jock to call on her and apologise for his temper and bad language. He visited me immediately afterwards at Ingatestone and far from keeping such humiliation to himself, as I think most of us would have done, he made no bones about it. He was wrong, he had lost his temper and had paid the penalty for it!

There was always one thing I dreaded with Jock, and that was visits to licensed premises – pubs, that is. Every pub on every beat in the section had to be visited once a month by the local beat bobby. This entailed his walking in unannounced and having a look 'round for any infractions of the law, mostly under-age drinking, gambling etc. Such a visit took no more than a few seconds to look around the bar before passing on to the next. However, the sergeant was supposed to visit all the pubs in his section, and this was an absolute bind for I had about thirty pubs! Every now and again, Jock would ring to say that he fancied doing a few that night, which meant of course that I would have to accompany him. Not for him a few moments standing inside the door, he turned it into a full-scale inspection. He would enter to the momentary hush which always greeted the sight of a police uniform (particularly a chief inspector and sergeant), stand looking around and then walk slowly through, pausing to talk to one or two customers before going through to the next bar and so on. I always breathed a sigh of relief when we left.

For a dour Scot, though, he was not without a certain sense of humour. On one memorable night, we visited the Cross Keys pub on the Roxwell Road. There, as we walked in, we came upon five customers playing cards at a table, in the centre of which was a wooden bowl containing a sizeable amount of cash. There was the usual hush as Jock stood looking at the players who had suddenly ceased their game. The seconds ticked by as he looked from one to the other.

"And what's this you're playing then?" he asked. They looked at each other.

One of them elected himself spokesman and replied, "Cribbage," which is the only card game permitted in pubs. Now Jock was obviously a card-player, which I was not.

"Och, aye," he said. "I play crib too but I must say I have never seen it played five-handed. I am going to learn something tonight. Right now, teach me five-handed crib then." Now, no one in the middle of a good poker game can possibly convert it to crib, but they tried, they really tried!

A minute or too later, Jock interrupted them. "What's that pot of money doing on the table then?"

They looked at each other before the spokesman blurted out, "It's the kitty for the next 'round of drinks." Jock nodded. A few moments later, he interrupted them again.

"If you're playing crib, don't you need a crib-board?"

That was the final crushing blow to their hopes. With a frantic flurry, a crib-board was suddenly produced from under the table. But then, they simply sat there looking at each other. They were beaten and knew it.

Jock turned to me. "John, would you find the licensee, please?"

A few moments later, the two were in earnest conversation at the bar with the landlord being left in no doubt as to where his licence stood. On the way back to our car, Jock suddenly said, "Well, I proved one thing tonight, you can't play crib with a poker hand," and burst into peals of laughter.

He and I always got on famously, and I was privileged to share many a wee dram which he always kept in his office cupboard.

Some years later (1989) he, now retired, came along to my

retirement party at Chelmsford nick. I made a little speech of course, and with as full an accent as I could muster, I finished by recounting this incident at the Cross Keys. He sat there laughing until the tears ran down his face.

"It's true," he exclaimed, "absolutely true. But, John, your accent was Glaswegian and I'm from Edinburgh!"

Chapter Eleven

I was always blessed with having on my shifts, both at Chelmsford and Ingatestone, a far greater majority of good lads than mediocre. All were either experienced, or if inexperienced possessors of sound common sense which is the main requisite for a good policeman.

On my arrival at Ingatestone, I had PC Ian Pigney living next-door, and PC Dave Sawford next-door but one, both with a good number of years' service. At Stock was PC Jim Baxter with something like twenty years' service. At Margaretting was my ex-next-door neighbour from Peel Road, Chelmsford, PC Ron Taylor. At Writtle were PC's Len Train and Tony Parker, while at Roxwell was Neville Leach. Every one of them thoroughly dependable.

There was little in the way of personality clashes between them, except perhaps for the two at Writtle. It quickly came to my notice that they did not always see eye-to-eye, so much so that on one particular day they had a heated argument in the office which resulted in Len laying out Tony with a single punch!

It was not very long afterwards that I heard from Tony that Len was not pulling his weight. I got the story from him and as a result of what he told me, I went out on a number of nights to see for myself what Len was up to. It was precisely nothing – which was the cause of Tony's complaint.

True enough, I saw Len come out of his house (which was attached to the office via a connecting door), sign on in the duty roster, and then go back indoors for the rest of the evening! I kept a record of what I had seen, interviewed him, examined his pocket-book and duty roster which both showed entries for work I could prove he had not done. I then put him on a charge for neglect and making false entries. He received a severe reprimand.

Len eventually got his own back though when, on coming out for day duty (nine a.m. to five p.m.), he found the rear bumper of the beat mini-van buckled and the glass in the reversing light smashed.

He phoned me straightaway and said that as it was intact when he had left it the day before, he did not want to be blamed for something he had not done. I interviewed Tony, of course, who denied all knowledge. I checked his pocket book and found amongst the entries a visit to the Christian Aid Centre off Writtle Green. As the gate at the end was always closed at night, I knew that one could only re-emerge by reversing out.

At the exit was a series of short wooden posts, and there, lo and behold, I found the broken glass of a reversing light and marks on the post which exactly corresponded with the height of the mini-van's bumper.

I suppose Len felt honours were now even when Tony eventually admitted the incident and I charged him with failing to report damage to a county vehicle. Not long afterwards, the two of them went their separate ways. It seems on the face of it somewhat draconian to have pursued these matters in the way I did, but even then discipline was still tight enough for any wrongdoer to expect a visit to the super when caught. Usually, I meted out summary justice for minor infringements but anything more serious than that usually resulted in a formal report from me to the guv'nor. It rarely went beyond that. It was beholden on me to maintain discipline and my own authority, for if the rot sets in, there is only one result – the sergeant goes!

These two incidents, and one other, were about the most serious I had to contend with during all my years at Ingatestone, and must show either the professionalism of those concerned, or the fact that they were adept at hiding things from me!

There were other occasions, however, when I had to remove those who were simply no good. One such was PC Vincent Mulchrone. He was the replacement for Len Frain, and within a very short while I was having to get on to him about the way he worked, or rather didn't work. A month or two after joining us, he went off sick!

The statutory three-day period came and went, and was then followed by a medical certificate from his doctor certifying that he was suffering from depression. Seven days later came another certificate, then another. After twenty-eight days of sickness, it was my job to call on the officer to determine how he was and to submit a report about his condition and likely return to work. Thus it was on a particularly fine summer afternoon, I visited Writtle where Mrs Mulchrone showed me through the house to the back garden. There I found Vincent, wearing only his swimming trunks, lying on a sun-bed blissfully strumming a guitar! He looked extremely fit, tanned and healthy to me.

Sometime later when he deigned to come back to work, he found himself on the end of a posting to Grays, not the most salubrious of places. I wondered how much more depressed that made him until I heard much later that he had left the job.

The mention of officers going off sick reminds me of an episode that occurred during the mid-1980s but which actually had its origin some years before. The women police had for many years been agitating for equality with the men. Until then, they did not work night duty, but apart from that they patrolled with us and were expected to pull their weight should anything occur. They rarely if ever patrolled alone so were never thrust into situations in which they would find themselves out of their depth, such as disturbances, fights, violent domestics, sudden deaths etc. In return for their not working nights, and for their rather restricted day duties, their pay had always been ninety per cent of ours. Not for the women's libs though – they demanded equal parity with the men. The result was that they got what they wanted but only in return for being treated exactly the same as men, full night duties and being allocated lone beats.

Having achieved this, they then demanded that their titles be altered, why should they be known as women police constables when a man was not called a male police constable? There was a certain irritating but undeniable logic about that, I suppose. In the end though they got their way and the women became known simply as police constables. It so happened that since time immemorial a WPCs' collar number (still called thus because they were once on our collars but had now been transferred to our shoulders) always began with the figure '3'. Now, this did not change when they became plain constables so they were still instantly recognisable. This was a necessary aid for supervising officers when drawing up duties requiring male officers.

Something then happened which we on rural beats had always considered impossible, and which with a certain poetic justice rebounded on the ladies. Undeterred by the fact that they were being thrust into situations which would normally have been dealt with only by men, the tentacles of feminism were to stretch even further…

I had for some time been badgering Chelmsford for a replacement for an officer posted elsewhere. Eventually, I was notified by memo that a P.C. would arrive for duty on a particular date. As I read the memo, it dawned on me that the newcomer's collar number began with a '3'! I grabbed the phone and got through to Jock Brown.

"Is this true?" I asked. "A woman, out here?"

"Aye, John, it is," he replied.

I protested, "But don't they know that all my men patrol alone? What happens if she comes unstuck in the middle of the night miles from anywhere? Who'll pick up the pieces if she gets herself injured, or worse? I'm not going round holding her hand day and night." All to no avail.

"That's the order from the top, John, you'll have to make the best of it."

My last and somewhat feeble protest was that we had only one loo!

The day dawned when WPC (sorry, PC) Sue Edmonds reported for duty. She was in her early twenties, dark wavy hair and looked very pretty in her uniform. I think she had only a couple of years' service – which even in those days of slackening standards was unusual for detached beat work. However, she did her work pretty well and it was no surprise that the younger male officers, despite their initial protests, now saw nothing daunting in walking the High Street with her. Her presence, of course, was the talk of the village, much of it I had to admit favourable.

Despite the fact that one of her first acts was to place a vase of flowers on the window-sill in our toilet, and then remark that the regulation brown curtains looked awful and how much better it would look if they were of floral chintz, the time came for her to perform her first week of nights on her own. I worried about that, I can tell you. Imagining all sorts of problems, I instructed the other officers working out of Writtle, Roxwell, Margaretting and Stock to make regular contact with her – something I would certainly not have done had she been male.

After some months, though, I began to notice that she was taking increasing periods of sick-leave. Three days' uncertificated sickness was allowable and she was always back after that but its regularity was becoming noticeable. I tackled her about this and received a predictable explanation. I then found that her punctuality was becoming a problem (she only had to travel from Chelmsford in her own car), and I was obliged to tick her off a few times. Lateness, for a police officer, was to arrive on the hour, for everyone had to report for duty fifteen minutes before the appointed time to be advised of various problems they were likely to encounter.

In addition to this, on one-man beats if someone is late then the outgoing officer has to remain behind to cover.

One day, a calamity arose for her. She was due on duty at nine a.m. and at exactly nine a.m., she telephoned and tearfully reported that she was going off sick that day. The following day, she returned and I naturally asked what had been wrong with her. Apparently, she had reversed out of her driveway the previous morning and had run over her pet rabbit which had got out of its run. Now, I had to admit that this was a pretty nasty thing to happen and I commiserated with her. The thing was though that she was still in floods of tears! After an hour or two, with little progress being made, I had to send her home.

That she was an emotional woman there can be little doubt. I particularly remember my officers telling me how upset she became at the sight of a dead hedgehog or rabbit in the road.

Not just upset but tearful! Compassion is all very well but we couldn't have a police officer becoming that emotional!

On the subject of compassion, PC Ron Taylor would not thank me for recounting the fact that on one particular night whilst driving his beat-mini through Margaretting, he thought he had run over a mouse which was scuttling across the road. Full of remorse, he got out of the car and re-traced his steps to where the little beastie was writhing in the middle of the road... it turned out to be a dead leaf!

Back to Sue. A little while later she went off sick again, this time with a cold. I had by then kept a record of her sickness and was fast losing patience with her. The following morning, I telephoned her at home and told her that she was to report for duty at two p.m. that day (her allotted shift) or I would ask for the police surgeon to visit and examine her. This was a power I possessed but had never exercised with any officer.

Bang on two p.m., she flounced into the office, banged down her bag and sat at her desk, her face white with anger. When I asked whether she was all right, she rounded on me and accused me of being cruel to her! By then, I was beginning to get rather exasperated with it all.

Things were never quite the same after that, although we had all done our best. The cohesion of the section was beginning to suffer and I could not afford to have dissension in such a small, close-knit team as ours. In the end, a vacancy arose in Headquarters Information Room and I think she gratefully accepted the opportunity to get off the streets into a more predictable and manageable environment. I bumped into her some months later. She greeted me warmly and appeared to bear no ill-will.

In recounting this, our first experience of working with the opposite sex on country beats, I may well appear to be chauvinistic. I hope I am not, and hope I have never been – at least not outrageously so. The rampant feminists would undoubtedly seize upon my remark that Sue was pretty. Would I have described a PC as handsome, they would ask. Of course not, but I can see no harm in my remark. Would she have been upset if I had called her pretty to her face? I doubt it. No, we were not chauvinists, far from it. We were used to working with women in the larger towns where WPC's (whoops, there I go again) on all shifts are commonplace. At Ingatestone, we had been handed an experiment. We had tried hard to make it work. It was an experiment directly related to the demands that all police officers should be treated equally whether they be male or female. On paper, like all grand designs it works, but in practise it has its problems.

Perhaps potentially the most serious matter I had to deal with occurred in 1979, and concerned one of my men, a PC Butcher, who was another of the two replacements at Writtle (I always bemoaned the fact that I would die with the name Writtle' engraved on my heart). He had, some months before, put in what looked like a routine prosecution file against a Mrs Joyce Gard of Writtle for (1) motor vehicle no insurance, (2) no test certificate, and (3) no vehicle excise licence.

On reading his evidence, it appeared straightforward so I marked it up for prosecution. Mrs Gard eventually appeared at Chelmsford Magistrates Court where on the advice of her solicitor, she pleaded not guilty on the grounds that the vehicle was not hers but her husband's. He was, therefore, responsible for the insurance etc. Mr Gard corroborated this and the case against her was rightly dismissed. This, of course, drew comment from the bench who had heard PC Butcher give evidence of her saying that she owned the vehicle – a point she vehemently denied in court. My boss, Chief Insp Brown, instructed me to interview all concerned and submit a report.

Within a very short time, I completed my enquiries and in my covering report stated that I believed the Gards, not PC Butcher's account of what had happened, fully aware in doing so that I was accusing one of my own men of committing perjury – an extremely serious offence for a police officer which, on conviction, normally resulted in a prison sentence. The upshot was that my recommendation for no further action to be taken against Mr Gard, despite the fact that he fully agreed that he had been responsible for the offences, was acceded to, and in light of the fact that the Gards wished to have no involvement in any action against PC Butcher, he remained at Writtle but was eventually posted away.

Suicides and Sudden Deaths
From problems with personnel to problems of a graver nature, the one subject that every policeman gets to loathe perhaps more than any other – sudden and violent death. My baptism of fire at Jutsums Lane railway bridge had stood me in good stead for the future for only a small majority of sudden deaths were more gruesome than that. It is those that I shall recount here, so if that does not appeal to you, then simply move on to the next chapter!

I can say with reasonable safety that in my thirty years, I had dealt with a wide range of sudden and violent deaths, from hangings, shootings, stabbings and bizarre suicides, to those which had occurred as a result of road accidents. Only a few still remain sharply in focus at the moment but I am sure that a gentle prod will bring others streaming back with equal clarity.

Behind every sanitised head line lies a human tragedy. For me at Ingatestone, one particular suicide is remembered for the rather grim humour shown by our excellent village G.P. Doctor Valerie Lacey. Living in a very expensive house (aren't they all in Willow Green?) was a lady who was then in her middle thirties. From all accounts, she suffered from depression and had been treated for such by Doctor Val. Her ministrations, however, were not altogether successful for this woman had tried to put an end to things by cutting her wrists.

The first indication I had that anything was wrong was when I received a telephone call from Headquarters to the effect that an 'incident' had occurred at a house in Willow Green.

Within a few minutes, I had arrived at the scene to be met by a man and a teenage boy. They told me that they had been doing some work on a neighbouring house that overlooked this lady's garden. On looking across, they were horrified to see a woman's body swinging gently from the apple tree in her garden. With commendable haste, they ran 'round, cut her down and dragged her into the kitchen.

A neighbour had called Dr Lacey and she had arrived a minute or two before me. As I walked in, she was kneeling beside the woman giving her heart massage, that is thumping up and down on the woman's chest with the heels of her hands, muttering as she did so, "Silly bitch, silly bitch!", which sounded rather unprofessional on the one hand but perfectly understandable on the other – and she was normally such a quiet, polite woman! I noticed then that both the woman's wrists were bandaged from a suicide attempt only the week before.

"She has made a good job of it this time though," said Dr Lacey.

Suddenly, there was a dull but distinct crack and she murmured, "Damn."

A few moments later, another crack and another "Damn."

"What's that?" I asked, already suspecting what it was.

"Her ribs," she replied, "there's no resistance. I'm breaking them, I'm afraid."

There came the third crack. Doctor Lacey looked up as if in answer to my unspoken question. "If it has to be her life or a few broken ribs, then it's easier to mend ribs, isn't it?"

It was another two or three minutes before she finally gave up. "It's no good," she said. "She's gone. I can do no more. What a waste of a life!"

As I started the procedure for a routine suicide, I stored those rather profound words in my mind in case at some time in the future I should be faced with the same situation.

Without a doubt, one of the most callous killings I ever came across occurred late one night at Mountnessing, opposite the Prince of Wales public house. I say 'killing' because to my mind, it was exactly that, although on paper it was classified as a road accident.

At around eleven p.m. on the night in question, a young man aged about twenty-eight years was driving his Bedford Dormobile van along the A12 Mountnessing by-pass when it developed engine trouble and came to a stop. There being no telephone within immediate reach, he walked up to the main road running through Mountnessing and telephoned the AA from the call-box opposite the Prince of Wales.

A short while later, an AA vehicle, another Dormobile-type van, turned up and parked on its offside of the road facing towards Brentwood. As the young man stood in the roadway talking to its driver through the passenger window, the AA man noticed a car coming towards them at very high speed from Brentwood. He estimated its speed to be in excess of 80 mph in a 40 mph limit. Seeing that the road was both wide and empty of traffic, he did not take much more notice of the approaching car, assuming it had plenty of room to pass on its way to Ingatestone.

Suddenly, though, there was a loud crack and then a bang as the approaching car sped past. He turned his head again to speak to the young man but found he had gone! Wondering what had happened, he called a couple of times but getting no reply, he got out of his vehicle and walked 'round into the road way. There was still no sign of the man. It was then that he noticed that his nearside wing mirror was shattered and a heavy graze mark ran along the nearside wing. Scratching his head, he walked around for a few more minutes and with no further sign of the man, he got back into his vehicle and drove off. He was to have a rude awakening the following day.

PC Alan Rowlands was the Ingatestone officer-on-duty that night. A short while later, having of course no idea of what had transpired in Mountnessing, he was called to Willow Green following a report from a local householder that a drunk was lying in the gutter. He reached the spot and immediately noticed something very peculiar. The man was lying almost as if he were in a coffin, perfectly straight with his arms close to his body. Alan examined him and quickly discovered not only a number of injuries but the fact that the man was very dead! He immediately called for a traffic unit to attend along with the CID and forensic team. I did not attend the scene immediately, I think it was my day off and was out at the time. Alan was waiting for me when I got back though and told me what had happened.

A preliminary examination of the body revealed not only the man's identity (he came from North London) but the fact that he had suffered multiple injuries similar to those found in road accident victims. But there had been no accident in Willow Green. Bleary-eyed residents disturbed from their beds confirmed this. In addition, there were no tyre marks and no dried mud or other debris one always finds at road accidents.

They were now faced with the inescapable fact that the man had died elsewhere and had been dumped here. But this sort of thing simply did not happen in sleepy old Ingatestone, least of all in affluent Willow Green!

We held a midnight meeting at Ingatestone Police Office, which included the Chelmsford Inspector, the detective inspector, scene of crime officers and traffic men. It was agreed that somewhere in Ingatestone, perhaps in the vicinity of Willow Green, there was a badly damaged car locked up in a garage.

But where? I took out a street plan of the village and divided it into sectors. At seven a.m. the next morning, a team of police officers would knock on every door in the village and ask to be shown the contents of every garden and garage. It promised to be a long and arduous job but one that had to be done.

I was in the office by six-thirty and had brewed sufficient tea for the ten officers who would be turning up. Most had arrived by a quarter to seven when suddenly we all jumped as the telephone rang on my desk. I answered it.

A guttural voice sounding very German then spoke to me. "I want to report a road accident last night," he said, "I think I ran over a fox!"

Not daring to give anything away, I raised my hand to alert the onlookers and then said very calmly, "How do you know it was a fox?"

He replied, "I can only think it was a fox, or dog, or something like that because I have blood on my car and there is some damage."

I then said, "Can I have your name and address, please?"

He replied, "It's Klein. I live at Willow Green."

I stuck my thumb up to the onlookers and said, "Just stay

where you are, Mr Klein, and I will get someone to come 'round and see you."

Minutes later, the detective inspector, two traffic officers and I were knocking on his door. He was a man in his early forties, smartly dressed and spoke good English. He told us he was an executive at Fords of Dagenham and drove a company car, a new Ford Granada, which was in the garage now. We trooped through the kitchen and into the garage. There stood a sight I shall never forget. A blue Granada with the front smashed in, half of the windscreen on the passenger side torn inwards and almost touching the passenger seat. Not only was the bonnet and windscreen covered in blood but the interior of the car bore heavy blood splashes too.

I turned to Klein and said, "And a fox did that?"

He shrugged his shoulders resignedly. We walked back indoors leaving the traffic men to examine the car and call up the police photographer.

Within minutes, he was telling us the sorry tale of having been out the night before with a friend, whom I knew lived in Norton Road. Both were very drunk and he thought they had a nice empty road to get home safely. Suddenly, there was a bang and the windscreen shattered. He carried on regardless. He then heard his friend shouting and realised there was a body sticking through the windscreen showering blood everywhere. Telling his friend that the main road was too dangerous to stop and unload the body, he continued to drive towards Ingatestone. They reached the High Street, travelled along much of its length before turning left into Fryerning Lane and then right into Willow Green – a distance of nearly a mile with a body sticking out of his wind screen! Once in Willow Green, they found a dark spot where they stopped, hauled the body out, having to bend the windscreen further in to do so, and laid it out neatly in the gutter. By that time apparently his passenger was in a state of almost total panic, which is not surprising really when you consider he had travelled all that way with a corpse in his lap dripping blood all over him!

Thinking themselves now in the clear, they continued on to Klein's house where they spent the rest of the night drinking brandy and discussing what to do.

Minutes after our conversation, I was knocking on the door of his friend in Norton Road and telling him to get dressed.

There was no reaction from him when I told him it was to do with a road accident the night before. Now, most people would have protested, "You can't be arrested for a road accident," but that he knew what it was all about became evident a few moments later when he went upstairs to dress and I heard him say to his wife, "It's that road accident. He's dead."

I had made no mention of any death! By the time he came downstairs, he was already a bundle of nerves.

Not so Klein, however; he was made of sterner stuff. With typical German arrogance, he remained indifferent to the whole affair, at one time shrugging his shoulders and calling it 'no big deal'. I had the job of interviewing his friend from Norton Road, who being English and in an extremely apprehensive state was much easier to deal with. By the time I had finished talking to him, he was trembling from head to foot and asking me to take down a written statement about the affair. Klein's cold-bloodedness shone through with every word!

In the end, we could only really press charges against Klein, for he had been the driver after all and the main mover behind what happened afterwards. His erstwhile friend, however, leapt at the chance to give evidence against him in return for immunity from prosecution for perverting the course of justice. Klein subsequently appeared before Chelmsford Crown Court and despite being represented by very expensive barristers (no doubt paid for by Fords) he was sentenced to three years' imprisonment. Knowing the way Ford look after their executives, I doubt whether that conviction and sentence made a lot of difference to Klein's career.

Another incident that sticks in my mind occurred in Park Drive, just a hundred yards from Ingatestone Police Office. The bedside telephone rang at four a.m. one morning. It was Brentwood. On answering it, I was told that as the Ingatestone car had gone off duty at one a.m. their area car had been sent to an address in Park Drive following a 999 call from a resident who had heard the sound of breaking glass. The crew of the car had looked around but had found nothing. I thanked them for the call. An hour later, that is five a.m., the telephone rang again. It was Brentwood reporting that they had received a second call and had despatched the same car. This time they had found the house in question, had noted that the front door glass was broken but had been unable to rouse the occupier. Could we check it out in the morning? I confirmed that we would. Now, with hindsight, warning bells should have started ringing in my head, but they didn't. I suppose I was still not fully enough awake.

Soon after six a.m. the telephone rang again. This time it was Ian Pigney, my early-turn officer. It seemed that Brentwood had left a message with Information Room to advise him about Park Drive when he came on duty. A few minutes later, he was at the house telephoning me – could I come 'round straightaway, we've got a problem!

Within ten minutes, I was there. Walking up the garden path the first thing I saw was what that the bottom half of the glass-fronted door was smashed and there was broken glass littering the doorstep. Equally obvious too was that much of this glass was blood-stained. How could Brentwood have missed that? Ian was waiting in the hallway for my reaction. I did not have to look around for any clue, the place looked like a slaughter-house. If someone had taken a bucket of blood and simply splashed it everywhere, they could not have done a better job than this. It was all over the hallway carpet, all the way up the stairs and all over the walls. Even the ceiling was spattered with it. I then saw two distinct trails of blood; one leading into the kitchen and the other back again into the front room. Ian pushed open the door.

More blood stains on the carpet, but there lying full-stretch on a settee beneath the front window was the body of a man, his head resting on a cushion which was saturated in blood. A glance told me that he was dead, the death-pallor was obvious. I stared in disbelief wondering what on earth we had walked into. This was almost certainly a murder and therefore out of our league, but how had Brentwood missed all this? Darkness was the only possible, if feeble, answer.

My first reaction was to ask Ian what he had done since tele-phoning me.

"I have phoned Doctor Skeoch to come and certify death, and have notified Chelmsford."

I looked around again, much more carefully this time. and then again at the body. As I looked, I could have sworn I saw a slight flicker of his eye-lids! I looked even more closely. Another flicker!

"Good God! He's still alive!" I exclaimed.

After all I had seen, he could not have had much blood left in his body, and yet here he was still living.

Thankfully, within a few moments, Doctor Skeoch and an

ambulance arrived and the still-unconscious man was taken away. About an hour later, I was surprised to see someone as senior as the Chelmsford Superintendent, George Tame, arrive and ask to be put into the picture. I told him everything I knew and he appeared quite satisfied, apart from asking me to contact the original informant and get a written statement from him. He would do the rest, he said. I did not give much thought to those words until much later.

About a month afterwards, I was summoned to Chelmsford by Wilf Partis, our chief superintendent and an absolute gentleman. He had Superintendent Tame's file in front of him.

"Right, now Sergeant," he said, "tell me everything about it."

I told him that the man was now recovering in Harold Wood Hospital and that he had told us exactly what had happened. It seemed he suffered from some disorder which, if he did not take medication regularly, resulted in blackouts. He had woken in the middle of the night and gone downstairs for a drink. There, he had felt an attack coming on and had walked out of the front room to find his tablets. In the hallway, though, he had collapsed, falling backwards against the glass of the front door, smashing it in doing so. Not all the glass, however, had broken, about six inches remained intact in the bottom of the door. He had fallen on to this which had had the effect of a guillotine in reverse – instead of the blade coming down on him, he had come down on the blade, which had sliced into the back of his head from ear to ear. Amazingly, he remembered getting up and going in search of his tablets, oblivious to how seriously injured he was. Moving from the hallway to the bedroom, then from the kitchen to the front room, spraying blood everywhere in the process, he felt himself losing consciousness and decided to lay down on the settee! There he lost consciousness altogether and would almost certainly have died.

The chief accepted all this and was relieved that the man was making a full recovery. Disciplinary action was being taken against the Brentwood car-crew for neglect of duty in failing to pursue the matter in the first place.

"But, as for you, Sergeant," he said, "I shall recommend to the chief constable that no further action be taken against you."

I stood there completely shocked. "Action, sir?" I said. "What action?"

Wilf looked back at me. "Neglect of duty, didn't you know?"

He could tell I was now floundering. "What neglect of duty, sir? This is the first I have heard of it."

The chief looked down at the file again. "Weren't you told you were facing a charge of neglect?|" he asked.

"No, I wasn't," I replied rather hotly. "Were you cautioned?| he asked.

"No, I certainly wasn't," I said.

He looked again at the file. "It seems that the 'neglect' arose when you failed to attend the scene after receiving the first 'phone call at four a.m., and again at five a.m. I can sympathise with how you felt at that time of the morning, particularly after being told that the two visits had found nothing. There seems to be a misunderstanding somewhere. Rest assured though that you are not facing charges. That is all I want to say about the matter.". He closed the file.

I walked out wondering how George Tame had managed to reach such rank if the best he could do was to put someone on a charge without telling them! It was contrary to all police regulations. Again, how little things stick in your mind – I always remember George Tame for walking around with a white handkerchief stuffed inside the cuff of his jacket, both uniform and civilian, with just enough showing to make it obvious. I thought it rather foppish and wondered how many he lost that way.

It was about this time too, around the middle 1980s, that I dealt with another somewhat memorable death. This occurred one summer Sunday afternoon in Transport Meadow, now re-named Seymour Field, immediately opposite the police office. Set up in the meadow was the annual fair along with the usual caravans owned by the fair people – some of whom were gipsy-types.

PC Dave Sawford was on duty with me and we were both sitting in the office looking out onto the meadow when the door burst open and a gipsy-woman entered.

"Can you get over right away?" she exclaimed in her strong gipsy accent. "My father's fallen over and I think he's dead."

Now, Dave was a bit of a first aid buff so I felt confident that we could do something.

Hurrying over with the woman, she told us that her father was about seventy, had suffered with heart trouble for years and had just keeled over.

As we entered the caravan, we saw the old man lying on his back on the floor. His eyes were half-closed in death and his mouth gaped open. My stomach turned over as I looked at him. He was filthy! He stank! His face was covered in a week's growth of stubble and all his teeth were black and rotten.

It had only been a few months since we had passed our three-yearly first aid which had incorporated mouth-to-mouth resuscitation, so we knew what was needed and how to do it. However, the plastic doll we had used was nothing like this! I looked at Dave and he looked at me.

"No way," I whispered. I would have been physically sick if I had put my mouth over that, it was bad enough just looking at and smelling him.

"Righto! Dave," I said, exuding confidence, "heart massage."

He knelt down and started the procedure with the heels of his hands exactly as we had been taught, while I felt for a pulse. We both knew though that the old man was dead. A few minutes later, Dave paused and suggested I go back to the office to 'phone for a doctor. This I did, and a short while later Dr Skeoch attended and pronounced the man dead.

The family, obviously impressed by our efforts, thanked us warmly, which made a change really for we were usually moving them on from grass verge to grass verge amid loud cursings. They were not to know that had he been Marilyn Monroe or Sophia Lauren, then we might, just might, have made a greater effort... but they don't mention this in first aid, do they?

Death at Peacocks

Now, this was not a nice experience, especially for one of my colleagues, PC Alan Brown, for it involved death from a shotgun blast and shotguns do very nasty things to a person's body.

The incident occurred in October 1974, and involved a man named Duce who had worked for twenty-eight years as gardener-cum-handyman for Lord and Lady Chelmer at their beautiful house 'Peacocks' at Margaretting. He was sixty-nine years old, an age at which most people have decided to retire, but he was still active and loved his work. He actually lived at Hawkwell but had fallen out with his wife some months previously and had received permission from the Chelmers to bed down in one of the out-houses. I believe he was under pressure from his family to return home and this had depressed him.

I was out on routine motor patrol with Alan Brown when we received a radio message to go to Peacocks. The operator was good enough to warn us that it was a suicide involving a shotgun. At this news, Alan groaned. He had not been with us very long at the time; in fact, I think he had only two or three years' service before coming out on the Section, so I asked him whether he had ever dealt with a shotgun death. He replied that he had never dealt with any form of death, least of all one involving a shotgun! Shades of me and Jutsums Lane again. I could see he was getting a bit worked up as we got nearer to Peacocks, so tried to reassure him. In all fairness to what he was likely to encounter, though, I warned him that such a death could go two ways; a nice clean entry wound (as I had recently experienced when dealing with Tom Pryor's death at Woodbarns Farm, Fryerning, when he had put his shotgun just below his ribs and fired upwards, and had died in my arms), or a head wound which could be really messy.

On arriving at Peacocks, we were met by Lady Chelmer who explained that she and her other gardener-cum-handyman, John Weston, had been drinking their morning coffee in the kitchen when they heard the sound of a shotgun blast coming from the large garden at the back of the house. There was only one person out there at the time and that was Stan Duce.

After a moment or two of total silence, John Weston said he would go out and investigate. With considerable courage, for they both had a premonition as to what had happened, Lady Chelmer followed him.

"Well, we found him," she said, "I'll take you." With that, we walked around the house and made our way up the garden. To our right, we saw a large greenhouse. "I won't go any further, if you don't mind," she said, "it's really too upsetting. You'll find him at the far end of the greenhouse."

As we walked up the path, I glanced up to the roof of the greenhouse at its far end. It was covered in red. Poor Alan was by now getting rather nervous. Reaching the end, we turned the corner and immediately came upon the body. One glance was enough to place this death very firmly in the 'messy' category.

Duce was lying face-down on the path with a double-barrelled shotgun lying beside him. When I say 'face-down', this is only figuratively speaking for he had placed the shotgun between his eyes and then pulled both triggers (I checked the spent cartridges). This double blast had had the effect of blowing most of his head off from the tip of his nose upwards – hence the blood and debris splattered over the roof of the greenhouse.

I recounted to Alan almost word-for-word what I had been told on the Romford railway line. It did not seem to have much effect though for he simply stared down as if mesmerised by the sheer bloodiness of it all. My next and most anxious thought was for an explanation, and the first thing was to search his pockets and failing that his lodgings for any form of suicide note. These are commonly left behind by those who commit suicide.

Now, going through a dead person's pockets is an unpleasant but necessary chore. Going through pockets which are saturated with fresh blood though is something else, especially when you have no gloves (plastic gloves were not introduced until several years later). You have to keep repeating to yourself, "He's dead, he's not going to jump up and bite you." But it is still nasty.

I turned to Alan, more to snap him out of his reverie than anything else, and said, "Right, let's go through his pockets then." His reaction was immediate. "What? You're not expecting me to do that, are you? Look, Sarge , I don't care what you say or what you do, you can put me on a charge if you like, but I am not going to do it, and that's it!"

I turned to him, "Alan, it's got to be done, you know that as well as I do. Now, let's get on with it."

He stood his ground though, shaking his head in refusal. I had sympathy for him, of course, but we all had to accept these things if we were to do our jobs properly.

What would he have been like if he had had to deal with this alone? I relented only to a certain extent, "Well, you stand there and watch me do it then," I replied. With that, I bent down, turned the body over, and systematically worked my way through his jacket, waistcoat and trouser pockets. Nothing. Our next port of call was a search of his lodgings in the stable-block. Again nothing.

By now, a courageously calm Lady Chelmer had come out and invited us in for a cup of coffee (laced with something much stronger), and over the kitchen table we took down all the details required for a coroner's court. This was subsequently held a couple of weeks later. We all had to attend, of course, and the verdict was a predictable suicide, but I was again struck by Lady Chelmer's composure and self-discipline (she was then about sixty years old) as she re-lived for the benefit of the court the horror of that morning.

September 1977

Mentioning as I have Alan Brown's aversion to messy bodies (well, let's face it, who doesn't have such an aversion?) reminds me of an incident involving the very same Alan early one Sunday morning two years after the Peacocks incident, and serves to prove the rule that you get used to anything given time.

We had a bit of a weird fellow in the village called Brian Appleton who was in his early twenties and lived with his parents and brother Alan in Pemberton Avenue. I say 'weird' for he was certainly not all there. There was a story that when he was a toddler, he had bitten through the cable of an electric fire at home and had received such a shock that it had affected his brain. I rather doubted this for his brother Alan was much the same, and indeed spent considerable periods of time at Severalls mental hospital at Colchester, which tends to indicate that it was congenital rather than accidental. It's funny how these stories circulate and stick in the mind.

On this particular Sunday in September 1976, I walked into the office at the usual time of nine a.m. By nine fifteen a.m., Alan should have returned for his early-turn break. By nine forty-five a.m., I was beginning to wonder where he had got to when in he walked, looking more than a trifle shattered.

"What's up, Alan?" I asked.

He slumped down on a chair. "Well, I've done it," he said, "on my own this time."

He then went on to tell me that he had received a message on the car radio to go to the railway bridge in Stock Lane to meet an ambulance crew who were on their way to a body on the railway line. Now, bearing in mind his reaction to Peacocks I could well imagine what state he must have been in when he got there for railway deaths had by now become very messy indeed.

For some years, British Rail had suffered from objects being placed on railway lines by young hooligans who thought it funny to see what would happen when a train hit them. Some trains had actually been derailed as a result. British Rail had, therefore, fitted a vertical steel bar immediately in front of the leading wheels and almost touching the rails. This was intended to remove any object before the wheels struck it. However, this only proved to make our lives more difficult for instead of the wheels cutting cleanly through a body, the bar now pushed it along the track chopping it up into little pieces and scattering them over a considerable distance.

Alan had, of course, been sent to such an incident. Perhaps being on his own had helped for he had no one to fall back on now and could not show his feelings to the ambulance crew – one of whom was a woman who, according to Alan, treated the whole incident with an almost blasé attitude. They were obviously well-equipped for the job in hand and in no time at all had produced large plastic bags and handed Alan a pair of plastic gloves – a gift for which he was extremely grateful! Thus protected, they set about picking up the bits off the line.

The outcome was that the ambulance delivered the remains to the Chelmsford mortuary at the C & E Hospital where, of course, the worst part of the job still remained – identification of the victim. An hour or so later, I received a telephone call from the Chelmsford Scenes of Crime officer who asked whether Alan could meet him at the mortuary. Poor Alan could not believe it when I told him that it was for him to identify the remains for 'continuity of evidence' at the coroner's court.

On our arrival, Alan once again dug his heels in when invited to assist in sorting through the bits and stated that it had been bad enough filling the sack in the first place! For my part, I confess to being rather relieved too when the SoC officer said that it did not really matter as he was paid a special 'dirty' allowance of £4.50 to do this and did not mind getting on with it alone. All he wanted was for Alan to indentify the sack which he had labelled at the scene.

Three items subsequently came to light; a tobacco tin with tobacco inside , a cigarette lighter, a scrap of paper from Severalls Hospital, and piece of forearm bearing quite a distinctive tattoo. I was handed the first three items and a full description of the tattoo.

It was not long before a telephone call to Severalls revealed the fact that they logged all such tattoos in their records and that they had indeed found such a match which belonged to one of their patients who had been missing for a couple of days. He was Alan Appleton from Ingatestone.

Within half an hour of that phone call, I was at Alan's home where his mother identified the tobacco tin and lighter as her son's and confirmed not only the clothing he had been wearing on the night he had gone missing but the description of the tattoo as well. This informal identification took the place of a formal identification which would, of course, have been out of the question. Thus, another mystery was solved.

Murder at Writtle
After twenty-two years of varied service, I was beginning to wonder whether, during the remaining eight years left to me, I would ever be involved in dealing with a murder. It was not that I particularly relished the thought but it is after all the most gripping of all aspects of police work and a form of death that carries with it a totally different aura.

As I patrolled peacefully with PC Ian Shead of Writtle one sunny but cold January day in 1981, I was blissfully unaware that all this was to change so dramatically.

"Charlie Golf One Three, Charlie Golf One Three. Go to the reservoir in Hyland Park. Report of a drowning. Informant on the scene."

We were between Ingatestone and Writtle at the time so it was no more than a few minutes before we were walking across the field to the small reservoir on the right-hand side of the approach road to Hyland Park. We saw a solitary figure standing beside the water.

He told us he had been out for a walk when he saw the body of a man in the water, near enough to the edge of the reservoir to be pulled to the bank. We looked down and saw the body of a man, aged about thirty, dressed only in trousers and a pair of wellingtons. He was very dead. Hauling him up onto the bank, we began to go through his pockets for any sign of identification when Ian suddenly exclaimed, "Hang on, I think I know him! Yes, I do, I'm pretty certain he lives in Hunts Drive, round about number 93, I think." Now there's local knowledge for you!

We radioed headquarters to whistle up a local undertaker and while we waited for them to arrive and cart the body away, we examined the area around the reservoir but the search yielded nothing in the way of clues. We had by then been joined by Detective Sergeant Mick Haig, an old friend from my days at Ongar, who had read the message at Chelmsford and had come over to see if he could be of any help. Once the body had been taken away, we went to Hunts Drive where I knocked on the door of number 93.

A girl in her late teens and her mother were at home. I asked as gently as I could whether a man answering the description of the deceased lived there. To my surprise, they both replied 'No'. Baffled now as to where we went from there, we continued to make light conversation during which the girl and her mother almost casually mentioned the behaviour of their next-door neighbours.

Apparently, they were a Mr and Mrs Harvey whose son Malcolm still lived with them. They were in their middle to late fifties while he was thirty and still unmarried. He also had, we were told, a long history of mental illness which led to their having long and loud arguments with each other.

"Take last night," said the girl, "I sleep on the other side of the wall to the parents' and there was a terrible row again. I woke up at about three o'clock in the morning to hear them yelling at each other. Then I heard the mother shout, "God help me", and then the father shouting, "Stop! Stop!". The next thing I heard was their back door slamming and then their back gate crashing. It was all quiet after that."

We looked at each other meaningfully. I slowly repeated the description of the dead man.

"Does that sound like your neighbours' son?" I asked.

She thought for a moment and said, "Yes, I think it does… why, what has he done?"

Thanking them for their trouble, I told them we would keep them in touch with whatever we found out. Little did I know how soon that would be!

Going next door to number 95, the first thing I noticed was the newspaper still in the letter-box and milk on the doorstep (by now it was about midday).The curtains too were still drawn. Getting no reply to our knocking, we walked 'round to the back door. Again, there was no reply. I tried the door and it opened.

We walked into the kitchen calling out as we did so but the only response came from a small dog which ran around barking. Walking into the living room, we again called out. There was total silence in the house. It was then that I smelled it, and I say this in all seriousness for death carries with it an unmistakeable odour, a sweet musty smell I had encountered too many times to have any doubts about.

We walked through the living room in to the hallway and then into the front room. All were empty. In the silence, I pointed my finger up the stairs. Both Ian Shead and Mick Haig stood stock still!

"You go," said Mick.

I slowly climbed the stairs knowing full well that I was going to find something awful!

The atmosphere was heavy and brooding, and it might have been my imagination but I had an overwhelming feeling that there were spirits all around waiting to be released – and I am not a Spiritualist! The smell of death got stronger with every step I took, until halfway up the stairs I stopped as I saw something lying on the landing at the top. Another couple of steps and I could see it was the body of an elderly woman still in her nightdress and curled up in what is called the foetal position. She was covered in blood and obviously dead. The walls around her were covered in blood splashes while on the carpet beside her lay a blood-stained commando dagger.

I stepped over her, my mind already registering the fact that I must not disturb anything but having no idea what else I was going to find. It occurred to me also that the killer could still be up there waiting for me!

At the first door on the landing, I quietly turned the handle, stood back and pushed it open with my foot. It was the bathroom and empty. I turned to the next door and pushed that in too. It was the back bedroom and again empty. I then turned to the front bedroom door and dealt with that similarly. Only half of the bedroom was visible from where I stood so I walked quietly in. There, kneeling on the floor and curled up in a defensive position, hands locked behind his head, was the body of a man. He too was dressed in pyjamas and again was covered in blood and very dead. I had found Mr and Mrs Harvey and was pretty sure now that I knew where their son was.

Going to the top of the stairs, I called the other two up and for some moments we studied first the bodies and then the rooms, registering in our minds everything we saw for the inevitable questions which we knew would be asked at the inquest. Only the front bedroom and hallway bore blood splashes so that was obviously where the murders had taken place. Walking down the back garden, we saw that the gate opened out onto a field and across that field in a straight line from the house was the reservoir.

We then set about a train a of events which was to lead to the solving of a double murder and suicide. While other officers attended the scene, I took a statement from the shocked girl and her mother next door, and later from the family doctor, Doctor Graves, who confirmed a long history of schizophrenia in thirty-year-old Malcolm Harvey. It appeared, from all accounts, that he had finally 'flipped his lid' that night, and in his frenzy stabbed his parents over seventy times before running from the house and ending it all by leaping into the reservoir.

In the meantime, I realised that at long last I had completed my quest and had actually dealt with a murder – and a double murder at that!

Before closing this chapter I shall, as promised, say a little about Lord and Lady Chelmer. I met them both at their beautiful home at the top of Margaretting Hill very soon after my arrival at Ingatestone. They were really charming people, he an international company lawyer with a thriving practice in the City, although soon after meeting him he was running down towards retirement and spending more time at home. She was very much a force within the village and surrounding area, interesting herself in all matters to do with Margaretting and its people.

They had only one child, a boy named (I think) Roger, who through accident or birth suffered from some form of disorder which affected his speech and reactions. This was not sufficient to incapacitate him for he married a young woman who bore him a pretty little daughter. They lived away from Peacocks, thus Lord and Lady Chelmer had the huge house all to themselves.

Both were extremely welcoming, even on unheralded visits, and before long we were all three of us on Christian name terms. Whenever I rang her up for a visit, she would simply say, "Of course, my dear, just come along and let yourself in." I would therefore drive 'round to the back of the house, open the back door, climb the short flight of stairs to their large kitchen and call out.

She had one small though very convivial failing, she did rather like the bottle. For some years, it had been gin and tonic until the doctor advised her to lay off it. She did so but went onto martinis instead. It was only after my first visit that she got to know my weakness. "Ah! yes, don't tell me, malt whisky with a splash of water." The only difference was that the whisky was always very large and the glass held for only a second under a leaking tap! It was only when I got to know her better that I accused her of being an excellent hostess but an awful barmaid. I never worked out whether it was I who kept pace with her or vice-versa, but the end result was always the same, memorable afternoon discussions in her comfortable kitchen and wobbly legs as I made my departure. A peculiar feature of our friendship involved her husband Eric, for his favourite tipple was fine Bordeaux (in fact, another of my weaknesses!) and whenever he was at home, he would insist on opening a bottle for us while Enid stayed on the martini.

There were times, I am ashamed to say, when I would most definitely have failed the breath-test. On one or two other occasions when I knew I had been too generously treated, I would whistle up one of my colleagues from Ingatestone to take me home. This was not taken too amiss by them for the Chelmers treated them all exactly the same whenever they called on them! In fact, it got to the point when, on receiving a phone call asking me to pop up for some little problem or other, I would suggest calling during the afternoon, for we all knew that such a visit could only be followed by a journey home. The stock reply to my announcement that I was calling on the Chelmers was always "Right, Skipper, see you tomorrow!"

In short, they were two wonderful people, generous to a fault, lively, entertaining and without a trace of 'side'. We talked about everything under the sun and our families were often the topic of our conversation. I soon found myself being asked for detailed reports on our children, and before long it was, "Joan really must come down and see us, we would love to meet her". And that's what she did.

'Peacocks', Margaretting
Home of Lord and Lady Chelmer

Just a few miles south of Margaretting lies the pretty little village of Stock. Its only drawback in modern terms is that the main Chelmsford to Billericay road runs through its centre shaking and rattling the centuries' old houses which stand alongside it. Because of this the more affluent of our society who seek the peace of village life tend to build their houses in the lanes running out into the country rather than in the village centre.

It was to such a lane, called White's Hill, that I was called one sunny weekend day in July 1971 when I received a report that a man had indecently exposed himself to two young girls aged about twelve who were out go-karting in the lane. On speaking to them, I learned that this had occurred only twenty minutes before and as it had taken me over ten minutes to get there, somebody had been quick off the mark. They explained that the man, driving a blue Ford Cortina, had passed them twice in the lane before pulling up on the grass verge. He then stood by the car and waited until they were no more than six feet away before dropping his trousers and performing an obscene act. They not unnaturally ran off in tears. A few moments later, a passing motorist, on finding he could not get through because of the abandoned go-kart, got out of his car to move it. He then saw the girls who told him what had happened. A local householder came out and on being told what had happened telephoned the police. In the meantime, the motorist went off in the direction indicated by the girls and found the culprit's car. With no sign of the driver, he set about temporarily disabling it by letting down one of the tyres. There's citizenship for you.

While the girls were giving me a description of the man, I was joined by the householder who had telephoned the police. He lived in a particularly expensive-looking bungalow nearby. On hearing me telling the girls to stay where they were while I searched for the man, he volunteered to accompany me. He was in his late forties, very pleasant and courteous, and spoke with an accent straight out of Eton and Oxford. Within two or three minutes we had found the blue Cortina parked at the side of the road but there was no sign of its owner. A few minutes later, I saw ahead of me the figure of a man standing behind a hedgerow and as I stopped alongside him, he stepped out into the lane. He not only fitted the description but actually appeared to be waiting for us!

Making no bones about getting into my car (I was authorised to use it on duty), I started to question him. As soon as I was satisfied that he was the man we were after, I cautioned him and then for some inexplicable reason, for it was not common practice then to take what is now called 'contemporaneous notes', I took out my pocket-book and wrote down everything he said. It was a confession which actually started with the words, "It's a fair cop, I'll tell you everything."

Even I was surprised at his use of this hackneyed phrase which one normally hears only on films or television but rarely in real life. Nevertheless, I wrote it down thinking that no magistrate would ever believe it. When I had finished, I got him to sign the entry in my book. He then agreed to accompany me to Ingatestone for a full interview and a statement under caution. He had, he said, a lot to get off his chest!

While matey-boy got out to change the wheel on his car, my still-unknown passenger who had been sitting there listening to what was going on was now shaking his head as if in disbelief.

"What's the matter?" I asked.

Holding out his hand, he said, "I would like to sign your pocket-book too if you don't mind."

Now this took me back a bit, particularly as I didn't even know his name or what he did.

"Oh yes, I am sorry," he said, "my name is Sparrow and I live at Croyde Lodge, (the expensive bungalow). I am a Queen's Counsel!"

As I more than willingly handed him my book, he explained, "In all my years at the Bar, I have always tended to dismiss such evidence as 'it's a fair cop' so theatrical. Today, though, I have actually heard it with my own ears! This is something I can really crow about on Monday!"

As I drove back home, I thought of the pathetic creature who had seemed so pleased to have been caught. If he was to suddenly change his mind in court and accuse me of doing horrible things to him, I had an unimpeachable witness! As it turned out, though, it wasn't necessary for he pleaded guilty and asked for about twenty others to be taken into consideration for which he had not been caught. He was fined £50 and ordered to undergo psychiatric treatment.

Chapter Twelve

Where the subject of promotion is forever the by-word, there will always be some who regard it as the be-all and end-all of their lives; to reach the top no matter what the cost or who is hurt in the process. For them, their family is a secondary consideration and happiness and contentment simply another word for sloth and lack of ambition. The police are no exception, indeed I believe they are one of the worst offenders.

In the early 1960s, a scheme was introduced which was really a re-hash of a failed 1930s experiment to create an elite among the ranks. Young men with educational talent and barely out of their probationary periods (two years) were sent off to university with all expenses paid to emerge four years later with a degree – it did not seem to matter what! With this under their belt they were assured of promotion. That they possessed only a basic knowledge of practical police-work was of little consequence for they were destined to become administrators not policemen.

Now to us ordinary mortals who simply loved the job and regarded it as a vocation, it was obvious from day-one that this scheme had two serious drawbacks. Firstly, it was divisive and bred scorn for an elite who had served precious little time on the streets where all practical policing is learnt and where decisions are made based on sound experience and common-sense. Secondly, it imbued these fledglings with even greater ambition for improvement while spending only the minimum time in each department as would qualify them for the next rung on the ladder. But how good was a university degree when dealing with a serious punch-up in a pub, or confronting a bunch of hooligans on a street corner? Where was that man when the rest were out there battling away? In the nick co-ordinating things!

If I sound bitter, it is because I am, for I have seen too many with inverse-ratios of intelligence to common-sense make high rank. There was one saving grace in all this though, it kept them out of our way most of the time!

One of those that I encountered to my cost was a Chief Inspector Roger Phillips, a university graduate with a law degree. In 1982, divisional boundary changes had resulted in the Brentwood Division being relegated to a sub-division under Grays of all places, a crazy decision made more bizarre by the fact that it now comes under Harlow! The same scheme also split the Ingatestone Section in two (one of the few, if not the only Sections to have remained intact since 1840) with half of it now going to Brentwood and the other half to Chelmsford.

Ingatestone itself now came under Brentwood while Writtle, Roxwell and Stock remained with Chelmsford. To compensate for this loss (Margaretting had already closed), I was given Blackmore, Mountnessing, Kelvedon Hatch and Pilgrims Hatch.

In charge of my new sub-division was Chief Inspector Terry Roberts whom I had known for many years and with whom I had always got on well. He was a bit of a rough diamond of the old-school with a propensity to fire from the hip and ask questions afterwards. During his short stay with us, he made one or two bad decisions but was always man enough to reverse them and apologise to us. He was replaced by Roger Phillips. The two were like chalk and cheese, for Terry would march up Brentwood High

Street and take the place apart, to the delight of the residents and the discomfort of the hooligans, while Roger preferred to discuss the matter in committee.

Brentwood Police Station

It was in the fateful year of 1985 that my book on the Essex Police was published, and along with all the hype and press-releases came the revelation that after sixteen years in the village I was by far the longest-serving sergeant Ingatestone had had in its history. I was not to know that this simple fact would rile my new chief inspector and give him the opportunity to flex his new-found muscles.

That summer, we went away on holiday and returned refreshed and ready-to-go. I had not been back more than a day when one of my lads innocently mentioned my posting to Brentwood!

Posting? What posting? Whoops, sorry! I quickly enquired around and discovered that during my absence, Roger Phillips had decided that I should be replaced – just like that. My successor would be Harry Ruston, the Brentwood Custody Sergeant, a nice enough chap but with no experience of rural policing. One of my phone calls brought Harry hot-foot over to me. He was, he said, embarrassed by it all but had been approached by Roger Phillips and offered my Section. As if to compound the felony, he had then been sworn to secrecy. What could be so secret that would not eventually appear on Force Orders?

I decided not to fly off the handle but to sit tight and see what happened. Someone, sometime, would doubtless call me in for interview and break the news. A week went by during which I called in at Brentwood several times on routine matters, on each occasion passing the time of day with Roger Phillips but nothing was said. Could it be a wind-up? Not if Harry Ruston was to be believed.

Eventually, I decided to take the bull by the horns and request an interview with Roger Phillips. This was immediately granted and I went in that same day. He greeted me so warmly that I wondered if I was about to make an idiot of myself. However, behind the facade of a smiling, smooth-talking diplomat, I could see that he was distinctly uncomfortable. It still came as something of a shock though when he confirmed everything I had heard on the grapevine. I must confess I let rip a little and then went on to ask why, with just three years remaining of my thirty-year service, he had seen fit to remove me for no other reason than to swop me for a custody-sergeant with no rural experience. Surely, this gained him nothing in terms of manpower so why was he doing it?

Roger simply replied, "I think you have been at Ingatestone long enough."

I asked whether he had any complaint about the way I did my job and he confirmed that he had not, but went on, "Just because you have been at Ingatestone all this time does not give you the right to remain there in perpetuity. We have to move with the times."

"Move with the times?" I asked. "How does that come into it?" A straight swop is no move at all unless it is on a disciplinary basis, and he had already assured me this was not so. He would not move, however, and I walked out of his office closing the door a little harder than I should. It had dawned on me that this was nothing more than an academic exercise designed not for my benefit or Harry's but his own. It was to show the guv'nor at Grays that he had a vibrant chief inspector who was not afraid of making unpopular decisions. It was as plain and simple as that. I was to become custody sergeant at Brentwood (on full shifts again) and there was nothing I could do about it. Or was there?

For twenty-seven years, I had been a disciplined officer who had accepted most decisions without argument, but this one stank! Getting back to Ingatestone, I sat down at my type-writer and reeled off a report (of which I still have a copy) outlining the facts as I knew them and not forgetting to include the dubious secrecy involved. I felt compelled to ask that 'I may be posted out of the Grays Division altogether and allowed to finish my remaining service within the Chelmsford Division in which I had served harmoniously as Town and Rural Sergeant from 1967 to 1982'. I asked that my report be forwarded to the chief constable knowing full well that Roger Phillips would not dare 'lose' it but must pass it on to the chief superintendent at Grays who in turn must forward it to the chief constable. That was my right.

disbelief. He too smiled in disbelief.

"Skipper," said Fred, "there's a car outside waiting for you. I want you to come with me."

I looked over his shoulder and through the frosted glass of the door. Sure enough, there was the outline of the Ingatestone beat vehicle waiting just outside.

"What's going on?" I asked, already smelling a rat. "OK, let me just finish this drink and I'll be with you."

A few moments later, we were outside, much to the amusement of the Star's regulars, and Fred opened the rear door of the police car for me. "Not your usual seat, I know, Skip, but I'm observer today." With that, he got in and Alan Rowlands drove off down the village High Street.

"Am I allowed to ask where we are going?" I asked.

"No," they replied in unison.

"You know that half the village thinks I've been arrested, don't you?"

They simply laughed.

At the end of the village, we turned left onto the slip-road and then left again into the car-park of the Heybridge Moat-house, a very posh restaurant boasting very posh prices.

"Thought we'd buy you a farewell drink, Skip," said Fred.

"Well, I'm all for that," I said. "But why the kidnapping? I would have come without all this."

Alan said, "We just wanted to make sure you did."

As he said this, we walked into the Heybridge bar – and there standing with big grins over their faces were all my men from the Section. I couldn't believe it!

"Right. What'll you have then, John, it's on us," they said.

Getting over my surprise, I was told that I had been the subject of great consternation only half-an-hour previously when

I had suddenly declared that I was going out for a walk. Alan realised that if I disappeared, all their carefully laid plans would be in tatters.

Where had I gone? I thought he knew me and my habits well enough to have known what 'going out for a walk' meant! Fred Mussard arrived a few minutes later to be told that I had disappeared. Panic began to set in. Alan said that he would take the car if he, Fred, could check all the shops in the High Street. A short while later, Fred looked through the window of the Star and saw me. Panic over.

We were less than halfway through our first drink when the head-waiter glided in and said, "Your table is ready, gentlemen."

With that he turned and we followed him. I thought, *This is a funny drink.* We were led not to one of the areas normally given over to customers but upstairs to a private Executive Suite. There, in this intimate room, a beautiful mahogany table was laid out with dazzlingly white tablecloth, candlesticks, variously sized crystal wine glasses at each place setting, heavy silver cutlery, and to finish it off a selection of very fine red and white wines were strategically placed around the table. As we sat down on a matching set of red-plush high-backed mahogany chairs three things flashed through my mind; one, who was going to pay for all this? Two, was this how real executives live? And three, what a motley collection we looked with most of us still in uniform shirt and trousers with only a civvy jacket as any form of disguise.

As champagne was brought to the table I realised we were in for a lengthy and heavy session – and we only got forty-five-minute lunch-breaks! Alan reassured me though that it had all been taken care of, Brentwood would cover any calls for the Section. Thank goodness for that, the entire Section was here!

The meal that followed was one I shall never forget; for its excellent cuisine, fine wines and first-class service. As I looked around at my lovely lads, the thought crossed my mind, *If only Roger Phillips could see this.* At that moment, the door opened and in walked a reporter and photographer from the Brentwood Recorder. He WOULD get to see it!

I was called upon, of course, to make a speech which I did with alcohol-aided eloquence, thanking them for all their support over the years, how truly sorry I was to be leaving them and what a send-off this had turned out to be. As I finished, the door opened again and in walked a waiter pushing a trolley upon which lay a most a beautiful iced cake in the shape of a police helmet and perfect in every detail. That in itself was a masterpiece. I learned afterwards that it had been made by our good friends Valerie and Ron Lacey, our High Street bakers. Behind the waiter came Errnis Kyprianou himself, the Greek Cypriot proprietor of the Heybridge, whom I had known ever since my arrival in 1969. With a beaming smile, he shook hands and wished me all the best for the future. I in turn thanked him for a superb afternoon. He then looked at his watch (it was nearly four o'clock!) and suggested that if we wished to retire to the downstairs bar, the staff would be happy to serve us.

We did not need to spend too long there after such a tour de force. Let it just be said that by the time we left, I was in no fit state to drive. One of the lads took me home in the police car while another followed behind in my car. I managed to get myself upstairs to bed at a quarter-to-five and that is where Joan found me when she got home from work. Far from being annoyed, as many wives would, she saw the funny side of it, bless her cotton socks. I remembered little after that.

The following day, I called in at the nick to pay my share of the costs (dreading the thought of how much it would be) and to thank the lads again for what they had done. Dave Sawford was on duty when I arrived.

"You are not paying anything," he said. "None of us are. When we went to settle the bill, Kyp turned us down and said it was his contribution to your farewell."

Half an hour later, I was in Kyp's office thanking him again.

A few days later, I got my own back on the lads when I invited them all, with their wives, plus my own family and friends to a last farewell at the Ingatestone Community Club. There, the cake was displayed (we being too full-up to touch it at the Heybridge) for all to see, and our old Trinidadian mate Gus regaled us with calypsos on his guitar.

Before we leave Ingatestone, let me tell you a little story about Joan. In front of the police office was an open-plan garden, mostly lawn, and a small lay-by for visitors. On the lawn at the kerb edge was a blue police lamp. It was fairly large and sat on top of a single post about twelve-feet high.

Whenever the bulb went, it was always me that had the job of balancing a ladder against the post and climbing up. This has absolutely nothing to do with the story but I often wondered what would have happened if I had fallen and broken my neck.

I could hardly call Chelmsford and ask them to send someone out to change the bulb, could I? This has always been the famous grey area in police work, for if you do your job and arrest a villain after a chase across a roof-top, you are a hero. If you fall and kill yourself, you are definitely exceeding your duty and are uninsured!

One fine day, Joan and I were out for a driving lesson. She was doing very well but was still a trifle tentative and lacking in the natural confidence she shows now. Normally, at the end of a lesson, she would drive the car into the lay-by and leave it to me to reverse back into our driveway. This time, though, as we approached home I thought she should try turning into the driveway, a fairly straightforward manoeuvre with the open lawn forming an escape-route if things went wrong. But they couldn't go wrong, could they…?

Much against her better judgement, she accepted the challenge, slowed down to the right speed and commenced her turn. She was, however, a trifle early and I realised that she was going to hit the hedge that divided our house from next-door. Quickly telling her to cancel the move she instead swung the wheel to the right and drove straight across the lawn in an attempt to bounce down onto the lay-by. She almost made it. With a resounding crack, the front of our beautiful Vauxhall hit the lamppost! In the seconds it took for PC Pigney's head to pop up in the office window to see what had disturbed his rest, Joan, poor girl, had leapt out of the car and fled indoors! I was left ruefully examining minor damage to the front of the car and a lamppost which now tilted drunkenly at a twenty-five-degree angle pointing down the High Street. My first thought after I had returned the car to its rightful place on the driveway was, *How do I get 'round this?* The thought of all the paperwork, not least of which was determining whether it was a road accident under the Act, filled me with misgiving. I could just imagine the faces of my guv'nors at Chelmsford when they read about it. I decided to sleep on it for a day or so.

It just so happened that only a day or so later, a husband and wife, whom I knew quite well for they lived only a couple of hundred yards down the road, decided they would try out their car's handling capabilities with a new caravan they had just bought. As they drove up the High Street towards our house, an awful thing happened. The caravan detached itself from the car and careered across the road towards our garden. They stared in mounting horror as it entered the lay-by before crashing ignominiously into our lamppost!

Leaping out of their car, they ran across to survey the damage and offer their apologies. In a trice, though, I saw that my problem was now solved for the leaning-lamppost-of-Ingatestone was no more; it was standing proudly vertical again! All I had to do was stamp in the loose earth about its base. They thought they were facing charges of dangerous driving or insecure load, or whatever other agony I could come up with, and they fell over themselves when I calmly informed them that it was 'just one of those things', and to 'forget about it'.

For us, it provided a good subject at dinner parties for a long time afterwards.

Chapter Thirteen

My return to Chelmsford was, in some ways, a return to my original roots. As Sergeant of 'D' Shift, coincidentally the very same shift I had supervised back in 1967 but with a host of different faces, of course, I paraded about ten or a dozen constables. Now, as then, two sergeants were allocated to each shift, one to act as station/custody sergeant responsible for the internal running of the station, and especially that of the charging, care and custody of the prisoners in the cells which the recently introduced police and Criminal Evidence Act had foisted upon us. The other was responsible for everything outside the station, i.e. patrolling with the lads, attending incidents etc. The duties of custody sergeant were onerous, tightly bound by the many new provisions of the Act.

This created pressure, which on Friday and Saturday nights could be considerable as violent prisoners gave vent to their anger at being banged up for silly little things like getting drunk and beating up people or smashing shop windows. The pressures were such that the duties of the two sergeants were swapped around every month. To be able to get out onto the streets again after four weeks in the station and cell-block was bliss indeed. Nevertheless, it was back to good old basics again and I quite enjoyed it all. What I found particularly rewarding was taking over new arrivals from the Police Training College and teaching them the ropes.

I remember particularly well one night in question which, because of its circumstances dates it to October 1985. I was on night duty, and as it was beholden on the sergeant always to be the first to arrive, I duly walked into the parade room at about nine forty p.m. No one was about. Five minutes went by, then ten, then fifteen! Still no one. Where were they? It took a good ten minutes or more to read out the messages and informations, allocate their beats and deal with any problems. But there was no sign of them. I went into the sergeant's office and spoke to the late-turn skipper. He had no idea where they were. On my way back, I glanced in to the rest-room which was next-door to the parade room and there found my entire shift huddled round a radio listening to BBC Essex. They all looked up as I entered and one or two actually *ssshh'd* me into silence. They were listening to the author of *The Essex Police* being interviewed on his recent book! There was not a lot I could say really, especially as I knew that it was being broadcast from nine thirty p.m. to ten p.m. and that they must all have made the effort to get in early to listen to it! Who told them about it I don't know, except that it wasn't me.

I think I spent about six months on shift when sergeant 'Nobby' Clarke came up for retirement. He worked independently of the shift sergeants, being in charge of the TPU the Town Police Unit. This was an experimental scheme comprising six officers whose sole responsibility was the town centre. It was here where all the big stores and dozens of lesser shops were located, and where ninety-five per cent of shop lifting took place. Their job was to patrol the area from eight a.m. to eight p.m. and reduce crime in the area. All the store detectives were known to them, many persistent shoplifters were also known to them and stores warned of their presence. A scheme was also introduced whereby the stores themselves immediately notified the others whenever shop lifters were recognised.

Co-operation between the stores and the police was excellent and the concentration of foot patrols kept deliberately high-profile. The result was an ever-mounting tally of shop-lifting convictions – upwards of a dozen a day on Fridays and Saturdays and probably half that during the week. Not every operation was high-profile though for it was by no means uncommon for two or three of the team to turn up in civilian dress for a particular job of surveillance where a uniform would have killed it stone dead. The TPU Sergeant worked permanent 'days' patrolling with his officers or processing their paperwork in the office. It was an intimate little unit well worth the effort, and a good example of a bright idea actually working, proving the theory that a particular problem can be more easily overcome by isolating it and concentrating your resources upon it. In this case, a sergeant and six men had been 'written off' to tackle town centre theft – and had proved how successful it could be.

Shortly before Nobby retired, I was offered his job and spent a very happy six months or so working with these town-beat officers, all of whom had volunteered for the work or had been hand-picked. For me, it was yet another facet of police work with which I had had no experience until then.

South Woodham Ferrers. A view of the surrounding countryside from the Maldon road.

After about a year at Chelmsford, I was called into the superintendent's office and told that a vacancy would soon arise for a rural sergeant at South Woodham Ferrers, a fast-growing new town some fifteen miles away in the south of the division. Much larger than Ingatestone, I think the population then was in the region of twenty-five thousand, the section comprised sixteen constables including two detective constables (luxury indeed and a sure sign of how busy the place was) along with three detached beats at East Hanningfield, Rettendon (one officer each) and Danbury (three officers), all supervised by two uniform sergeants who worked days and half nights about, nine a.m. to five p.m. and five p.m. to one a.m. With my experience at Ingatestone, he said, I was the obvious choice to replace the outgoing sergeant who was moving on promotion. If I were interested, I could move in a couple of weeks. Interested!

South Woodham Ferrers
South Woodham Ferrers, although only about twelve miles from Chelmsford, was a part of the county I had never seen before, all my service thus-far having been spent in the west of the county

rather than the south. I knew that it had always been a rural section under Chelmsford and that it was a growing new town, but believing it to be something on the style of Harold Hill or Harlow (for which I bore no great affection) I had never bothered to explore what lay beyond those quiet fields to the south of the A130 Chelmsford-to-Southend Road. It was something of an eye-opener, therefore, when I drove down to see what my new territory looked like.

The village of Woodham Ferrers is a centuries-old community with its medieval church, High Street and pubs. Well established at the time of the Domesday Book, indeed the Romans had built large salt-pans in the area fed by the tidal River Crouch, it had been granted by William the Conqueror to one of his knights, William de Ferrers, who had fought with him at Hastings. It had then gone into decline and slumbered peacefully through the centuries until the bulldozers of the 1960s disturbed its rustic dreams. Even then the village had opened only one eye to take a look at what was happening before turning over again and going back to sleep. It was several years later that it opened its other eye to see that a much larger community had appeared and in doing so had usurped its name to that of South Woodham Ferrers.

True to police tradition, but more especially county-planning, no great thought had been given to providing the town with a police station. As the first few thousand of its population settled in, it was realised that the local village Bobby, who for years had little else to cope with but the old Woodham village (which was still asleep) and who still lived in his old red-brick, two-up-two-down house, was now sorely in need of help. Hey Presto! Two sergeants and a dozen constables found themselves members of a newly created section. But where to put them? A new police station would take years to plan, approve, re-plan, re-approve and then build, by which time South Woodham might have grown as large as Southend! That old English panacea for all ills then came to their aid, it was called panic.

On the edge of the fine and aesthetically pleasing town centre stood the new community centre. Surely they could rustle up something, a couple of rooms perhaps? But what about that most essential requirement of all busy police stations – cells? Out of the question. Drunken, violent prisoners could always be taken to Chelmsford, couldn't they? Let's get our priorities right.

The upshot was that two rooms (plus a toilet and small kitchen) were made available on the ground floor of the community centre. The larger of the two was to be the parade room / report-writing room / interview room and detention room, while the smaller became the sergeant's office. Trust him to get the luxury item. This then was the set-up I found on my arrival at South Woodham.

South Woodham Ferrers Police Stations old and new (above and below). The window to the left of the green door, above, was the general office, to the right was the sergeant's office.

New Police Station c. 1994 A vast improvement on the temporary offices but catering for the same number of constables

Dennis Hicks was the other sergeant-in-charge. He was in his early to middle thirties, married with a couple of young children and very easy to get along with. There was, however, one fly in the ointment; he had passed his promotion exam and PAB (Promotion Advisory Board) and was now anxiously searching each morning's post to see when and where he was to be sent. In the meantime, he warned me, Chelmsford was claiming him as an acting inspector on a pretty regular basis so I could well find myself running South Woodham on my own. This is exactly how it turned out to be.

My fears that Woodham would turn out to be like another Harold Hill were unjustified. In fact, while the 'Hill' comprised ninety-nine per cent council houses, Woodham boasted the exact opposite and was very much smaller. Indeed, there was no shortage of public speakers with, I suspect, more than a trickle of socialist blood in their veins, who demanded to know why there was such a dearth of subsidised housing to sit alongside the already-established and often elegant estates of South Woodham.

The residents had a quick answer to this. "Nuts, we're quite happy with the way things are, thank you," and successfully warded off all plans to turn the town into another London overspill. The result is a pleasant series of estates, many with tree-lined thorough-fares, and houses which alternate regularly in design. The countryside a mile or two in land from the Crouch undulates gently rather than spectacularly, while that bordering the river is flat, indicative of an area which only a few years before had been tidal marshland. Acknowledging that one cannot entirely defeat nature, only ward her off, earthwork barriers now well grassed over were built along the Crouch estuary and the more low-lying areas protected by underground pumping stations which, in theory at least, will pump out any water that gets through the artificial barriers. As if in recognition of its close proximity to the river and the sea, a marina was built on the Crouch at the edge of town. There, anyone with a yacht, dinghy or power-craft could while away the weekend hours tacking and scudding before a pleasant breeze. On a sunny summer's day, it was a very pleasant place to be as dozens of sails strived to turn the little town into another Cowes regatta. Essex, for all its close proximity to London, still manages to trumpet its independence to the world.

So far as we, the police, were concerned, there was still little enough for youngsters to do of an evening. Apart from a couple of youth clubs, there were only local pubs and wine bars in which to while away their time. Youth clubs are all very well but you have to be a special type of person to appreciate them, and most youngsters preferred to spend their time wandering around in groups or going into Chelmsford for their discos and other kicks. What kicks they found there was none of our concern.

On the whole, though, they caused us very little trouble, and much of this was due to the fact that we still policed the town in rural fashion with police officers of long-standing who were well aware of the trouble-makers and who made sure they knew we knew them. Recognition is an age-old and very effective form of deterrent. It is not always the case though that local youngsters cause the trouble. In an age of easy travel, it is a well-known fact that much of the hooliganism stems from lads who live well outside a particular area and are attracted in by successful discos etc. Such was certainly the case in Chelmsford where the night-clubs and discos attracted (and still attracts) youngsters from as far away as London, Kent and Suffolk.

At South Woodham, we had two very successful pubs in the town centre, the Oaklands and the Town Crier. From almost the first day, each of these pubs attracted a well-defined clientele.

The Oaklands was very much the higher class of the two and catered for the more mature customer. It boasted a fine restaurant and was quiet, comfortable and civilised. On the rare occasions it ran a disco, it was always 'ticket only' and had dinner-jacketted personnel at the doors to deter all who were not properly dressed or had no ticket. There was consequently never any trouble either inside or out. The Town Crier, on the other hand, whilst still a very pleasant pub during the day was more noisy and brash at night. Its loud booming music attracted youngsters from miles around, and if there was any trouble in the town, it was always with teenagers who had spent the evening there. On Friday and Saturday nights, we always employed two or three special constables to augment our strength and posted uniforms at both the front and back of the pub at closing time. The streets around would also be heavily patrolled to deter misbehaviour and fights.

I arrived at South Woodham in about September 1986, and soon settled down to a well-ordered and pleasant existence. Life was relatively busy but not hectic and time could be taken out to cruise around the lovely old villages like Stowe Maries, the Hanningfields, Danbury and Woodham Mortimer. My lads, as I have already mentioned, were first-class police officers, the majority having at least ten to twenty years' experience and most having spent a good number of those years on their respective patches. With only the odd one or two that needed an eye kept on them, I counted myself as fortunate as when I had served at Ingatestone.

Principal among those who needed an eye kept on him was Pete Tanner, the Rettendon officer. He had previously served for about ten years with the Metropolitan Police before deciding to come out to Essex, and had been at Rettendon for three years before my arrival. I never really found out what there was on his beat to keep him occupied. It had no shops, only a few pubs, and ninety-five per cent of his area was peaceful agricultural land. With the growth of South Woodham, Rettendon had become nothing more than a suburb of the new town, so it came as no surprise to me when in April 1987, his beat was closed down and amalgamated with East Hanningfield. Tanner himself moved in with us and took up shift duties again.

I always found him to be an agreeable sort during my weekly visits to Rettendon, and had little to complain about so far as his paper-work was concerned. It was patently obvious that he had little to do but that was hardly his fault. Whether his three years of virtual inactivity had affected him or whether he was a naturally lazy person, I do not know, but soon after he joined us at Woodham, I was confronted for the first time in my career with a deputation from the rest of the lads asking for his removal! Now, as I have already shown, it was not unusual for me to ask for a man's removal but to have it requested by his own colleagues was unheard of. I listened very carefully therefore to what they had to say.

In a nutshell, he was bone idle, unreliable and lacking the enthusiasm the rest had for the job. On night duty, as soon as the sergeant disappeared off home, he would invent excuses such as report-writing to sit for hours in the nick while the rest were out there doing what they were paid to do. Then came the really serious allegation. It was alleged that he was actively 'moonlighting' – engaged in paid business outside the police service, a serious offence which normally results in dismissal. Not only was he engaged thus but was boasting about how much he earned. It seemed he had teamed up with a second-hand car-dealer at Rettendon and accompanied him to a major Ford sales plant to buy cars. He boasted that he then went on to sell these cars and earned £200 for every one sold!

I made a few discreet enquiries locally only to learn that what I had been told was true. I had no option but to submit a confidential report outlining what I had learned. That was May 1987. My report was acknowledged by telephone, and then everything went quiet. Over the ensuing weeks whenever I raised the subject with Chelmsford, I was told that the matter was in hand. I could do nothing more than to advise my lads similarly.

The bombshell came some weeks later when I was asked to instruct PC Tanner to report to Chelmsford forthwith. An hour or two later, I received another telephone call to the effect that he had been suspended from duty but would continue to live in his police house at Rettendon. Strict instructions were given that we were not to approach him or engage in any form of conversation with him. This was really serious stuff!

Some months later, I received a visit from Detective Chief Inspector 'Jock' Gamble, Headquarters Complaints and Discipline, who, incidentally, had been my uniform PC at Writtle ten or fifteen years previously, so he had done well. Once seated in my office, he took out a huge roll of computer print-out which I saw was liberally embellished with red under linings. He asked me if I kept a record of the occasions when I had telephoned Headquarters Information Room for registered owners of vehicles we checked on an almost daily basis. Very fortunately, I had. On each occasion, I had made a note in my pocket book to show that it was official and not for any other purpose – a serious offence under the Data Protection Act. We checked the records and established that my name and collar number had been used about fifteen times over the past year without my knowledge or sanction, three times while I was away on holiday in Scotland! Similar enquiries with all my lads revealed that they too had had their names and numbers quoted for calls they had never made. Who had done this? PC Tanner! But why? He was as entitled to use the PNC (Police National Computer) as the rest of us so long as it was legitimate. When Jock showed me the computer print-out, I saw literally dozens of entries for South Woodham officers, only a fraction of which turned out to be genuine. It was then that Jock told me that Pete Tanner was working not only for the local car-dealer, and using the PNC to check the bonafides of each car purchased, but was also tied up with a Chelmsford private detective who paid him for obtaining this strictly confidential information. He had realised, of course, that the frequency with which his name appeared on headquarters records would soon show up so had used everyone else's – including his sergeant!

The upshot was that he remained on suspension for a full year during which time he appeared before Chelmsford Magistrates Court to be remanded to the Crown Court. There, he eventually pleaded guilty to a number of specimen charges and asked for numerous others to be taken into consideration. He was not fined, as we all thought he would be, but jailed for twelve months. No doubt this heavy sentence reflected the judge's feelings about the manner in which PC Tanner had abused the position of trust we all enjoyed. Certainly, that sentence served as a salutary lesson for the rest of us. We had all, over the years, been approached at one time or another to do a PNC check as a favour for someone. Now we knew how expensive such a favour could be.

I later learned that my report had gone in at the very moment that Headquarters were getting suspicious of the number of calls from South Woodham asking for PNC checks. My mention of his dealings with a Rettendon car salesman had clinched it and a full investigation was ordered.

Like most other places, Christmas was always quiet enough to warrant only a skeleton police-strength while New Year was a lot busier, of course. So far, there had been no problems. At the end of that first year, with fingers crossed, I took New Year's Eve off and to my relief everything went well. Murphy's Law dictates that whenever anything big erupts, it will be when I am off and I have to explain why I wasn't there to deal with it!

Christmas 1987 also came and went very quietly. With New Year approaching, though, and with Dennis Hicks again absent, which meant that my duties reverted to discretionar, I had to determine whether or not I would work the New Year's Eve. We all have families and the temptation to take a chance and spend it with them is strong, especially when it is left to you whether to work it or not. This year though, despite an invitation for Joan and I to spend the evening with my daughter Diane and her husband Lance, I decided not to take the chance but work a half-night (six p.m. to two a.m.) to support the lads who had to work. As it turned out, it was a good job I did.

The run-up to New Year always entailed pin-pointing those licensed premises that were running New Year discos and dances, evaluating each as to how much trouble was likely. So far as the Oaklands was concerned, they advised us that it was to be another 'tickets only' affair and entry restricted to just two hundred. We did not anticipate any problems there. The Town Crier though was throwing open its doors at six p.m. and remaining open until one a.m. with no control over the numbers and no checks at the door. God help us! That's where we would get trouble if it was to occur at all.

Long beforehand, I had detailed duties and issued a form of

Operational Order to cater for whatever might be thrown at us. On the night in question, I paraded six men comprising four of my own officers and a couple of specials. Two of my own men were working half-nights with me and the other two came on at ten o'clock for a full night. As a precautionary measure, we borrowed one of Chelmsford's crew-buses and parked it outside the police office – just in case.

During the course of the evening, everything remained quiet and well-behaved. I had instructed my constables to keep a high profile, not to wander too far from the town centre, and to make half-hourly visits to the Town Crier. I had been out on foot patrol for an hour or two with one of them when we passed a house which I knew belonged to friends of mine, Detective Sergeant Mason of Chelmsford and his wife who was a clerk in our prosecutions department. Their house was just across the square from the Town Crier. We naturally could not pass by without a seasonal greeting and within minutes we had joined their party. It was then about eleven-thirty.

In no time at all, it was midnight and we were all noisily celebrating the coming of the New Year when my radio suddenly burst into life – "All personnel get to the Town Crier immediately, serious fight in progress!" Within seconds, my colleague and I were out of the house and legging it across the square. On arrival at the Town Crier, I told him to take the front entrance while I took the back – both were equally favoured by the customers so it did not really matter which we took. When I reached the back, I could hear the pandemonium going on inside but the place was so solidly packed that I could not get in. At that moment, one of my men, PC West managed to struggle out of the melee and make a dash for his police car parked nearby. There I heard him make a 10/9 call to head-quarters. This is a rarely used but ultimate emergency call for a police officer who is in trouble and needing immediate assistance. Once that is broadcast by Information

Room, every- one drops everything and gets to the scene double-quick. The only snag was that Woodham's fairly isolated position meant that any help was going to take at least a quarter of an hour of hard driving to get there.

I went straight back 'round to the front door where customers were spilling out onto the pavement. Most were young girls who were in various stages of hysteria. One of them cried out to me, "Get in there quick, it's terrible." Using brute force now, I barged my way through the crowd and into the pub. It was a raving mad house with fights going on everywhere. At the far end, I saw two of my officers, PC West and PC Franklin fighting a group with drawn truncheons. That was something I had never been reduced to in nearly thirty years. They, of course, were my first priority so I pushed and punched my way through to where they were. My build, uniform and chevrons were enough to assure me a fairly trouble-free passage amongst youngsters who were no more than middle to late teenagers. Within a few moments, I had reached my colleagues who had apparently each made an arrest and were now fighting to retain a hold on them while their mates tried equally hard to release them. My arrival ensured that the officers could get their prisoners out while I dealt with whoever got in our way.

The crew-bus stood only a hundred yards away and once we had handcuffed the two prisoners we proceeded to march them over to the van. I took over one of them while the arresting officer ran over to open up the van. At this moment, a friend of the youth I had hold of approached and started yelling at me to release him as he had done nothing wrong (except to hit PC West over the head with his own truncheon!). I told him to shut-up and clear off. Drink was talking now and providing the bravado.

"Let him go! Let him go!" he yelled. He then, foolish youth, decided to intervene physically to release his friend. Within a few moments, I had two prisoners being marched to the van.

Once thrown into the vehicle, they all went very quiet. I think it was beginning to dawn on them that they were going to spend their New Year locked up in police cells. It was only then that I recognised one of my off-duty men, PC Reed, assisting with the prisoners. He had been walking home from a nearby party when he came across us and promptly got stuck in himself. I would have expected nothing less, in fact, but his presence was much appreciated. Back we went for more.

South Woodham Ferrers The Oakland Hotel

The Town Crier

By now though with the four of us having shown that we were willing to take anyone on things started to quieten down. It was obvious too that we had removed the ringleaders.

Eventually, we managed to persuade the three hundred or more of them to leave the premises quietly. As they did so, they milled around outside, and at that moment the Seventh Cavalry arrived in force. There was the Force Support Unit (thirteen men), area cars, panda cars and two dog units from as far afield as Burnham-on-Crouch, Southminster and Chelmsford, all responding to the 10/9 call. For the next half an hour, the streets around the Town Crier were swamped with police ensuring that the revellers broke up into small groups and left the town centre in peace.

Sometime in the early hours, I got home to Writtle and within minutes of my arrival Joan turned up, having been driven home by Diane.

"Hallo," they said, "we've had a lovely evening. Has it been all quiet with you?"

The following day, my guv'nor, Superintendent Terry Roberts (ex-chief inspector at Brentwood whom I mentioned previously) came over and we visited the Town Crier. There, in the cold light of day, we found the licensee surveying a wrecked pub. The very least of his troubles, he said, were three hundred smashed glasses! Needless to say, I had briefed Terry before our visit so it came as no surprise when he proceeded to give the licensee a dressing-down par-excellence, telling him that his licence was now on the line and that in future he must seek and heed the advice of the local police.

"In addition," he said, "the Licensing Justices will require a report from the sergeant about last night's disturbances before deciding what is to be done about your licence." It wasn't actually his licence, poor chap, he was only the manager. I wondered what his brewery would think when they heard that their pub could not open for business that day.

We held our own enquiry as to the cause and discovered that on the night in question, everything had gone surprisingly well until about midnight. Then some silly joker with too much drink inside him decided to dance on a table-top. He over-balanced, of course, and fell onto a group of similarly drunken revellers, one of whom thumped him for his trouble. That led his mates to retaliate and within seconds the place had become a war-zone.

We got half-a-dozen prisoners out of it, all of whom went down at Chelmsford Magistrates court a few months later. During the proceedings, the seventeen-year old youth I had arrested for trying to release my prisoner had for some reason decided to plead not guilty and be represented by counsel. Now, had he known it this was an extremely foolish thing to do. With a guilty plea, only the bare facts would have been given to the court. As a result of his obduracy, or who knows, perhaps his counsel's advice, I was now obliged to attend and give full evidence of what had happened that night. This I did and in the process the court was treated to a far more descriptive account of that evening than it would otherwise have received. I could see from the way the three magistrates were looking at the defendants that they were far from impressed with them. Those expressions had not been lost on the defending counsel either. When I had finished giving my evidence, the youth's solicitor stood up to cross-examine me.

After a few minor questions, during which he quickly realised that my replies were only rubbing salt into his client's wounds, he suddenly paused and said, "I have no doubt that on the evening in question, you presented a very formidable obstacle. I wonder what made my client think he could take you on."

The bench could have answered that for him. He then turned to the youth, had a few whispered words in his ear, the youth nodded and he then re-addressed the court, "Your worships, my client has expressed the wish to change his plea to guilty!"

I cannot remember now the exact penalties imposed but they were all hefty fines. What I appreciated more than anything though was receiving a letter from Superintendent Roberts, written just three days after the event, in which he sent his *"congratulations to all officers concerned for subduing what may have been an horrendous public disturbance* (may have been?). *I consider that their courage and dedication to the job in hand was within the best traditions of the British Police Service, and without doubt their actions gained much credit for the service in South Woodham Ferrers".* Such a quiet little old place, South Woodham!

My stay at South Woodham lasted some fifteen months or more, and all of it a continual pleasure. Some little while before the Town Crier incident, Dennis Hicks had got his promotion and had left for Southend as inspector. After yet another period on my own, I was joined by Ian Smith, a newly promoted sergeant from headquarters. Once again, we got on very well together.

It was some little while after Ian joined us, I suppose the middle of 1988, that I received a telephone call from Supt Terry Roberts, asking me if I was free for a chat. I told him that I was just about to leave for a routine visit to Danbury, would he like to meet me there? He agreed.

He walked into Danbury nick where I had just finished doing the books. After a bit of banter over a cup of tea, he came to the point. "How is Ian getting on at Woodham?"

I was a trifle surprised but answered, "Fine, he's settled down well. He'll make a good rural sergeant. Why?"

Terry then went on, "Do you think he can cope on his own for a bit?" I replied that he was quite capable, but again, why?

"Well, we've got a problem at Chelmsford and need an experienced station sergeant. We'd like you for the job, would you be interested?"

Now, at Chelmsford at any rate, this was a position of some importance for in addition to his usual duties involving station discipline, control room, public / prisoner reception and press-liaison, it also included responsibility for the running and safety of the property store which housed not only found property but, much more important, all exhibits for criminal trials. The accurate recording and safety of up to five hundred items was therefore essential.

Did I need this aggravation? Not really. I was quite happy at Woodham, was my own boss and accountable only to my guv'nor in far-away Chelmsford. There was also nice countryside around and a fine team of men. Terry though pressed hard.

My mind was already running along the lines that Chelmsford was only a couple of miles from Writtle while Woodham was fifteen. Permanent days was also worth considering, no more tipping out at all hours for a thirty-odd-mile round trip to check early and night duty men. No more Town Criers! I told him that there was no comparison between the peace of the Crouch estuary and the constant upheavals at Chelmsford. He persisted though and in the end it was the day duty and the travelling that finally decided the issue. As it turned out, I did well out of it, thank you!

Thus, with little more than fifteen months to go before I retired, I returned to Chelmsford. I must say I quite enjoyed the work but had no idea (and I am sure Terry didn't either) that it would be so short-lived. Within three or four months, I was 'approached' yet again. Chief Inspector Armson, who was in charge of administration, was going off sick more and more with leg trouble (he was to finish up on two sticks) and Inspector Brian Boon, who was in charge of prosecutions, was increasingly taking over his duties. Whenever that happened, Brian's own work suffered. They needed a permanent sergeant on prosecutions who could also stand in as inspector when Brian was called upstairs. My mind immediately flitted to retirement, for my pension would be assessed on my average earnings over the last three years of my service. If I spent most of my final year drawing inspector's pay, then this would 'up' my pension – and a pension was for life. It did not take long for me to agree to move offices.

A recent check (1996) on the strength of police in present-day South Woodham revealed the following: 1 inspector,

4 sergeants, 1 detective sergeant, 3 detective constables, 12 uniform constables and 3 part-timers (not specials but literally part-timers, which I had never heard of until then!). Bearing in mind our strength only seven years before (2 sergeants, 10 constables and 2 detective constables), it is interesting to reflect on the huge increase of chiefs over Indians.

At a time when most policemen look forward to slowing down a bit as they approach the last year of their service, I now entered what was perhaps one of the most interesting and unremittingly busy periods of my career. I was very thankful for the experience I had gained over the years in having to read officers' files to determine (a) whether the circumstances revealed an offence in the first place, and (b) whether there was sufficient evidence to secure a conviction.

The prosecutions unit comprised, in addition to the inspector and sergeant, a team of about eight 'girls', most of them in fact married and of mature age but they were still 'the girls', whose often mundane but nevertheless extremely responsible job was to prepare summonses, informations, court papers and witness warnings.

My job started at nine a.m. with a cup of coffee taken at my desk while I surveyed an in-tray piled about a foot high with paperwork. I knew that much of it would be fairly routine; accident reports to study for possible careless driving, speeding cards, most of which I could mark up for proceedings knowing that the officer would have verbally warned any motorist who was just near the mark, and other miscellaneous files. It was the thicker of these files that would command more attention for they contained multi-charges and numerous witness statements which would need extra time spent on them. One tiny omission could make all the difference between success or failure at court.

In addition to the office-work, I would be required to prosecute at court at least once a week, generally at the Thursday traffic court. I was no stranger to this for all through my years as a sergeant I was regularly called in, often at the last minute and before I had had a chance even to look at the papers beforehand. The only difference now was that it was a part of my job and that I would be prosecuting the cases I had myself checked and marked up for proceedings. I would thus meet face-to-face the defendants who had hitherto only been a name on a file. Most of the serious or complicated cases would be decided on in consultation with the CPS (County Prosecuting Solicitor) who then went on to prosecute them as well.

Most of my prosecution work at court involved 'guilty pleas' which meant that as the defendant had admitted the offence, there was no necessity for him to turn up at court. The magistrates, of course, had to be informed of what had taken place and to do this the prosecutor read out a brief statement of facts – a resume of what had occurred. As the defendant was not present, it was only right and proper that the statement should not be embellished in its telling. However, they had been composed and typed by one of my 'girls' and I rarely had a chance to read them until I was handed the prosecution files on the morning of the court. There were odd occasions when I felt that the office-girl had not expanded sufficiently on the facts, facts which I thought the justices would appreciate knowing. I would thus, quite illegally I admit, slip in the odd word or two to emphasize the true nature of the facts. Whenever this happened, I would immediately receive a pointed glare from Fiona, the young red-haired clerk to the magistrates, who would indicate with her finger that she too was reading her copy of the same statement. "The facts, stick to the facts!" she would hiss. I would apologise and use my innocent look and she would say, "One of these days, I'm going to shop you," but she never did. In fact, she helped me out on a number of occasions when I suddenly found to my embarrassment that the 'girls' had cocked up something in the prosecution file. We finished up such good friends that when I retired a year later, I took her out for an excellent lunch at the Saracens Head. Over the table, she handed me an appropriate retirement card and an outrageous pair of black slippers with huge white 'Playboy' bunnies on the toes. I keep them to this day and have never dared wear them. She was a lovely girl and must by now be a practising solicitor.

My job was made easier by the fact that I dealt only with traffic and non-criminal matters. To this end, I had sitting opposite me Det Fred Nichols who dealt with crime files, and as his in-tray was always as full as mine, I was glad for that division of labour.

In the course of a day, I would probably send back to the originating officers, through their sergeants, a handful of files with various comments as to the admissibility of evidence, correct procedures, additional statements etc. After the first week or two of scanning files, I was able to identify those officers who took a pride in what they did against those whose work needed extra scrutiny. There was little personal confrontation unless, of course, an officer disagreed with what I had written and wished to argue the matter. In this respect, I was once again instrumental in having an officer dismissed from the force, and all without clapping eyes on him. I had received a road accident report from a PC Peters of Maldon who was apparently a young probationer. It was a straightforward case of careless driving so I marked it up for prosecution and forwarded it to the CPS for their approval. They agreed, and eventually the case appeared before Maldon

Magistrates Court where the defendant pleaded not guilty. Had he pleaded guilty, the case would have been dealt with there and then but now witnesses had to be contacted and statements obtained. This, of course, was PC Peters' job.

Over the next month or six weeks, I sent him three reminders to submit his file but with no reply. I telephoned his sergeant at Maldon and he told me that both he and his colleagues were fed-up with Peters' antics and that he could not be trusted with anything. Since Peters had just started a two-week Probationer Course at Headquarters, perhaps I could pursue him there?

I 'phoned Headquarters and had him dragged out of the classroom. He told me that he had called on all four witnesses, but they had refused to make statements! Now, this was very odd.

No fewer than four people had volunteered their names but had then wanted nothing further to do with it? I told Peters that I wanted a written report confirming this – immediately. This arrived a couple of days later and I sent it off with my own report to his Chief Inspector Brian Ladd asking for an enquiry to be made with the witnesses. This was conducted by Maldon's Inspector Giddings who visited the witnesses and discovered that PC Peters had never called on them after the accident and that they had certainly not refused to make statements! This was now becoming serious for I had both verbal and written lies from him.

The upshot was that the inspector took the required statements and forwarded them to me for inclusion in the forthcoming prosecution. PC Peters found himself charged with 'falsehood and prevarication', which are extremely serious offences for a police officer and triable only before the chief constable. Peters had shown a very laissez-faire attitude to the truth and no doubt his previous poor record was also taken into account when the chief dismissed him from the force.

Whenever Brian Boon was called upstairs, which happened with increasing frequency as Chief Inspector Armson's condition worsened, or was absent for any other reason such as annual leave, I took over his duties and was required to swap my epaulettes bearing the sergeant's chevrons for those with inspectors pips. Then, as now, constables and sergeants wore blue shirts while inspectors and above wore white, and as the swapping of my epaulettes did not involve swapping shirts, it was often quite amusing to see the confusion on the faces of newly arrived recruits as we passed in the corridor. It was usually, "Morning, sarge – sir – sarge – damn it!", as their eyes flicked from shirt to epaulettes and back again. Older hands took not the slightest notice, of course.

Thus employed I remained in this comfortable job as the weeks and the months sped by. In April 1989, the fateful day arrived when I walked into Admin and asked for a resignation form – we faithful work-horses were never honourably put out to grass but had to resign first. One part of the form included 'length of service' which was always counted in years and days, never in weeks or months. I was accustomed to seeing this on Force Orders when it was announced that "PC Smith retires after 30 years and 256 days" etc. While completing this form, I fulfilled a long-standing ambition not to give the county so much as one more day of my life than was absolutely necessary. It was with something of a flourish, therefore, that I requested that my retirement should take effect from 17 June 1989, "on completion of thirty years and zero days' service". You can't get more minimum than that!

I was in many ways not sorry to leave. On reflection, my early years from 1959 to 1967 had mirrored almost exactly the job which thousands of policemen had performed for a century and a half before me. In fact, until the mid-1960s, the only aids that we enjoyed over them was the bicycle, the car and the telephone. In every other respect, we performed exactly the same duties, endured the same nit-picking discipline and walked over exactly the same ground as our forebears had done all that time ago. Now, personal radios had done away with 'points' and the ever-accusing, "Where were you at your ten o'clock?" Likewise, there was no ducking out of the way for a cup of tea, safe in the knowledge that no one could find you for another hour. Panda cars (1967) had brought about swift response but at the same time had destroyed both the pride and the intimate knowledge one gains off one's beat. Computers now ruled, Station Control Rooms had become centralised and sanitised, civilian staff manned the public counters and typing-pools of girls churned out our reports on state-of-the-art VDUs, doing away with our five-shillings-a-month typewriter allowance, while plastic security-tags dangled from every lapel.

It is precisely because of these modern innovations that I take my hat off to the bobby of today. He has much greater pressures to contend with, or if not then a different kind of pressure, than we ever did. Despite it all, and however modern, complicated and expensive the equipment becomes, the job still remains the same, for people do not change – and that is what policing is all about, dealing with people.

I, therefore, count myself extremely lucky to be able to say, "I had the best of it but above all…

I had FUN!"

Brian Boon on left and Brian Palmer on right. My farewell party at Chelmsford Police Station. June 1989. Note inspector's pips on both blue and white shirts

Presentation of my Service Certificate by Chief Constable, Mr John Burrow, at Police Headquarters. June 1989

With PC Alan Brown at Margaretting witnessing the recovery of a Hurricane which crashed in 1939 and the recovery of the pilot's remains. Site is in a field opposite the Red Lion public house. September 1977